CW01583151

Comments

Bill's first book, Home Truths

(under the *nom de plume* **Bill Murphy)**

"New travel book sparks outrage."

The Times

"This is the kind of book I really like to read!"

Johnny Vaughan, Big Breakfast Channel 4

"Hilarious and depressing by turns."

The Guardian

"Man from Bath does the dirty."

Stoke Sentinel

"Women hit out at sea-monster jibe."

The Gazette

"[He] should be hand-bagged by half-a-dozen women on Lord Street."

Phil King

"This is the man who calls the Welsh ugly . . . he's no oil painting himself is he?"

Welsh Daily Mirror

THE RELUCTANT TRAVELLER

Bill Lumley

PROSPERA
PUBLISHING

Acknowledgements

In no particular order, I would like to thank all the people who have worked hard on the edits, including Tony Hickey - not least for his help with correcting difficult Ethiopian place names.

To all those I met via Hot Rock, I appreciate you putting up with me. To my long-suffering friend Gar, I owe you a pint (maybe two) for the cover photo and a once-in-a-lifetime, never-to-be-repeated experience. Thanks also to the cycling marvel Alastair Humphreys, from Hope and Homes for Children (www.hopeandhomes.org).

And finally to Mike - sorry about the jacket!

For Liz

Axum
Yeha
Mount Wehni
Lake Tana
Gondar
Bahir Dar
Addis Ababa
Airport
ETHIOPIA
CLIMBING KILLS

Prologue

I WAS BORN a coward.

The dark, the tube, cars, water, the dark. Endless is the list of things I am afraid of.

On the few occasions I've been forced to go camping, I took with me an unbreachable code of conduct. I would not, under any circumstances, leave the tent after sunset (no matter how strong the call of nature), for fear of snakes or scorpions. In north Gloucestershire.

As I grew up – slowly for my age – I devoted myself tirelessly to creating subplots that could get me out of not having to do anything that worried me by its potential consequences.

In the early 1970s, I was well ahead of my time in terms of health and safety. A row of tall trees stood between me and the school bus stop on the other side of the A46. I'd be late for school on what I considered to be fiercely windy days – generally when only a gentle breeze was blowing – because I was waiting for the gusts to die down long enough for me to sprint the 30 metres past the menacing wooden brutes.

Then quite suddenly in 1974, at the age of eight, I put myself into a coma when I accidentally ran into a van at a moment when both I and the van were travelling at our top speeds. Residual brain damage and physical uncoordination were thereafter going to rule out all threat of ever having to go on any more dangerous a mission than hitching a ride home from a public house.

I remained comatose for some weeks, to the point where I was not expected by anyone except my mother to make a recovery. Those who'd by now operated on my brain half a dozen times harboured a certainty that if I did regain consciousness I would be so severely brain-damaged that I'd be spending the rest of my life in a wheelchair.

This reasoning prevailed until one day, several weeks into the coma, my mother paid one of her daily visits to the intensive care unit at the hospital in Bristol. She sat between me and the ventilator and began to talk to me as she had done every day that I had been there.

A staff nurse passed the bed.

'I wouldn't waste your time talking to him, dear. His brain's quite dead,' she said, indicating the monitor beside the bed.

Mother expelled the worst expletive known to plumbers, and I laughed, the brain monitor flickering to life.

I spent the next few weeks drifting between semi-conscious and conscious, my left side still paralysed, my fractured right leg healing. A pair of educational psychologists eventually visited my bed with a pile of books. First they showed me a Dr Seuss book containing a few simple words, notably cat, hat, sat and mat. Still unable to speak I frowned and brushed it away. Then they produced another illustrated book that comprised unusual alliteration with words such as big, brown, bear, blowing, bubbles, biking and backwards. I was mildly absorbed. My full attention was finally gained, however, when I was presented (accidentally), with a rather risqué paperback. Assured that I could still read, the psychologists left, mildly disgusted, their job done.

Unfortunately I did have to learn to walk, talk and write again, something most people have to do just the once.

There was one massive positive, however: my condition meant that I was able to get out of every kind of school sports. I even managed to procure a laminated note from my mother excusing me from any such activity. It was to become the single most valuable document in my possession. I still use it today.

But I became increasingly frustrated by denials – from everyone in the world except me – that I had an excuse for my clumsiness, poor handwriting and generally uncoordinated demeanour. Six months of physiotherapy, followed by years of learning to walk evenly, meant I didn't *look* particularly brain-damaged and occasionally I even had moments of clear thought and speech.

Some 14 years after the accident, to put my mind at the same level of ease as the rest of me, I booked myself in to see a clinical psychiatrist and a psychologist. I wanted to establish just how much of my self-perception was wishful-thinking.

A fortnight later I received a letter confirming that the two of them agreed with me – there were indeed areas of residual brain damage and so many years after the accident, there was very little that could be done. I framed the letter and hung it on my bedroom wall.

I was to have a lifelong, cast iron excuse for not performing very well at anything. My existence would thenceforth be a breeze compared to everyone else I'd meet and I would never be called upon to exert myself. Moreover if conscription was to be reintroduced or war declared then I should not be called upon to do anything about it.

So quite how I ended up as a prospective snake feast in the wild, bandit-ridden mountains of Ethiopia is still beyond me.

Oh, by the way, the *Gloucestershire Echo*'s headline on 15 March, 1974 simply read: 'Accident boy, 9, 'critical''. All they got wrong was my age. The local free-sheet, however, was ahead of its time when (in what I presume was a spirit of editorial independence), it went a bit further than it feasibility ought to have done, referring to me as 'Brave Bill'.

As if you need proof you really can't trust what you read.

Chapter One

Not drinking anymore. Or less

'What about it? Fancy a trip to the top of a lost mountain in Ethiopia?'

My answer to this question should have been obvious. In my case it'd be largely rhetorical. By nature I am unadventurous, unutterably idle, usually inactive and in the pub whenever possible.

Asking said question was my old friend Gar. The location, unsurprisingly, was my local den of insobriety, The Birdcage, on Columbia Road in London's salubrious Bethnal Green.

Quite the opposite of me, Gar loved the great outdoors. A professional photographer and rock climber, he'd disappear for weeks on end to places like India, Mongolia or Uzbekistan, to climb mountains, take pictures and then get kidnapped or at least mugged.

The question hit me unawares because I was more pissed than usual. And to those who know me, that is worthy of remark.

We ended up at The Birdcage that day thanks to payment I had received for a 4000 word magazine feature on the London insurance market. With a little under two grand in my pocket I was feeling flush, so had waylaid Gar (en route to more important things) and ordered us a couple of pints.

The most adventurous I get is when I am jostling for a seat in the pub. Spying an elderly man balanced between two walking sticks, tottering towards the only free seat in the place, I lurched into action and sprinted towards the booth, sliding onto the aging vinyl like an illegal oil slick swept by the tide onto a beach.

Gar arrived a few moments later, as did the old man. I shrugged apologetically, acknowledging yet another pact with Lucifer, and the old man shuffled away, balancing his sticks and a pint to give us both the finger.

'So, how are things?' asked Gar. Strange, given that he had asked me the same thing earlier, whilst I was considering a clay egg timer in the window of a Columbia Road store.

Gar's behaviour was unusual that evening – dark, even – and I felt unsettled.

He leaned towards me over his pint. 'So, how are things?' he began again, as if we hadn't been in each others' company for the past few minutes.

Not one to pass up an opportunity to whinge, I began to mutter about the shortage of work when he began gesticulating wildly, hands clawing at the air.

It started off innocently enough. 'I'm sick to death of photographing crappy little stories about bloody Christmas window displays and supermarkets at Canary Wharf,' he moaned. 'I remember when I was on the Mosquito Coast.'

He paused briefly at my blank stare.

'It's in Honduras.'

Still nothing.

'Central America.'

Dressing down for dinner with drug lords and poisonous insects – got it.

'I was up this river. I'd been staying with gold miners, sleeping in a hammock, eating plantains and beans from the forest. Lost for days trying to hike over the watershed into Nicaragua . . .'

He took a swig of Guinness then looked ahead, smugly. 'Great story. Sold it to a travel mag for a few pence, but that's not the point. It was fun.'

I felt my blank stare become more inscrutable than ever. I was accustomed to Gar harping endlessly back to his travels, but *fun*? The man was clearly a dribbling imbecile. Maybe that's why, against all the odds, we got on.

He started again. 'And then there was this time in Kalimantan . . .'

I made a quick conversational shimmy in an attempt to steer things onto a more promising path, like which politicians should be the first up against the wall when the revolution comes. But it came out wrong. 'Sounds interesting. So, have you got anything new lined up?'

Gar fixed his steely eye on me for a second before rising determinedly to his feet to buy yet another round. This willingness to buy the drinks brought a certain element of drama to the situation as I scaled new heights of relaxation.

A minute later he returned and planted two more pints on the table. 'Ethiopia,' he stated boldly.

I drank and continued to half listen, pondering the chances of Gar paying for beer all night.

'You remember I was out in the Alps last summer with Des? Of course the weather was terrible, but we still managed to do a bit . . .'

Des was Gar without an MoT. Like Gar, his friend was a keen mountaineer but there was something dramatically more worrying about Des. Des is the sort of person that would have your grandmother in fatigues climbing an ice-clad vertical mountain.

Gar was off again, boring for England. I lost him somewhere among the crevasses and crampons. I looked tired. I yawned. It didn't elicit the desired effect so I queried him.

I strained my eyes as they approached the pint. 'Let's see, that's in Uganda, right?'

He sighed, giving me a strained look; half anger, half pity. 'France', he said before returning to the point. 'Des bumped into this guy he knew. A fellow called Dave.'

Unprompted and certainly uninvited – but hey, he'd bought the beers – he proceeded to tell me of the next expedition he had planned for the following month, this time in Ethiopia. It made as much sense to me as hearing someone reading out a football match report. In French. As far as I could work out, he was planning to meet up with a group of mountaineers who were on a three-year trip around the world climbing remote, unusual and unclimbed peaks, hoping to gain their place in the Guinness Book of Records for driving a convertible truck the entire length of six continents. Their mission for the Ethiopia leg would be to find and climb a mountain, Mount Wehni, in a remote part of the Gondar region, supposedly northeast of Lake Tana.

'Mount What-i?'

'Of course, no one knows where it is!' Gar said enthusiastically. He had the most irritating tendency to present life's shortcomings in a positive light and to discard even the strongest hint anyone he knew might not get as excited as him about, for example, suicide.

'Cosmic. So you don't even know where you're going then?'

'That makes the trip all the more exciting!'

I frowned at him, trying to focus.

'It means nobody else has climbed it,' he continued. 'And it's known as the lost mountain!'

'This has got to be worth a pint,' I said, perking up unconvincingly and stepping up to the bar. I had failed geography and history outright at school but put it down to the way they were taught. That and the fact that I was never a fan of geography or history.

The forest of empty glasses of various shapes and sizes continued to grow before us on the table. I heard that Milton and Johnson – and more recently Thomas Pakenham – had written about this lost mountain, how some had tried to find it but returned home disappointed, how others had reached but failed to climb the rock, how an ancient royal prison stood on its summit, and about the mountaineering expedition itself, but of such details I only have a blurred recollection.

A couple more hours passed before I finally added another round to my tab.

Gar chose his moment perfectly. 'You should come along and write a book about it.'

Yeah. Right after I join the Royal Marines. I nodded, mainly to put my face in contact with my beer.

'We'll go down in history if we make it – the first Westerners to climb it while touring with the first round the world expedition in a convertible truck.'

More likely go down in history for being the world's greatest imbeciles. Mental note to look that up in the *Guinness World Records*.

'Great idea,' I said to Gar, sarcastically.

The following morning I awoke with a world class hangover and I couldn't immediately remember where I'd been nor why my head felt as if I had used it to hammer in nails. This wasn't unusual so I didn't worry about it until Gar called a few days later.

'Have you started getting fit?' he asked.

Hilarious. 'Well, considering my idea of getting fit is lifting an extra pint, I think not.'

'Well, we're both going to have to,' said Gar with an odd keenness that made me question his sanity. I am to fitness what Darwin may have been to clubbing.

Suddenly, Gar realised I actually had no idea what he was talking about. 'You don't remember, do you?'

'No.' I usually don't after my first 10 pints.

'Great. Thanks a lot. I've already told Chris Hart he's not in.'

We had a mutual friend, Christopher Hart, also an author, who would not have missed the chance to go on the Ethiopian mission. His first book, *The Harvest,* was a study of rural decay. Although his sense of adventure wasn't as insane as Gar's, he had holidayed once in Kabul. Considering that when it came to just about anything outside business journalism my sole speciality was fear, Chris (or anyone else on the planet for that matter) would clearly be the better person for the job.

Gar started to tell me about a lost mountain in Ethiopia. With a feeling akin to the shock of finding myself in a car with its handbrake off rolling downhill towards the edge of a cliff, I slowly but surely remembered what he'd been going on about in the pub.

I now had just one single mission in life: get out of any trip to Ethiopia with Gar.

A week later things were looking promising. I had not heard anything from the agency that was arranging my next freelance assignment and I was confident that I would have to stay in London ready for the job as and when it kicked off. Any day now I would be able to make my excuses to Gar, still leaving him plenty of time to enlist Dr Hart.

My real intentions however did not prevent me from talking – well, boasting, I suppose – of the trip to anyone who knew me. I was drawn by the comedy of the very idea of my participation in something as strenuous and potentially dangerous as finding a lost mountain in Ethiopia, the whereabouts of which no living person could pinpoint.

I told Gar that if I could get out of my very important work commitments, I would go, but said he shouldn't get his hopes up.

I was certain it would never happen; that I would have sufficient commitments to keep me in London.

I was later to read author Thomas Pakenham's account of his own trip to the mountain in 1956: *'Eventually, more with an eye to impress my friends than with any serious hope or intention of making the journey, I put out the news that I was off to Ethiopia.'*

That Friday night, Gar's wife forced him to invite me and my wife Liz to a party at their flat in a converted warehouse.

In the firm belief that I wouldn't, in fact, be going to Africa, I stood with Gar and his guests whilst they excitedly evaluated the pros and cons of visas and immunisation jabs, donkeys, climbing mountains and trekking 400 kilometres from Addis Ababa to a mountain of whose whereabouts no cartographer was apparently quite sure.

30 minutes later, I was doing my best to avoid Gar's questioning of my intentions by taste-testing the impending meal while Gar's wife wasn't looking. Then my mobile rang, and she slapped my hand from a saucepan full of gravy, muttering something in French about people who couldn't be helped.

'Ouch!'

My wrist smarting, I put the phone to my ear and heard: 'There is no problem. We've found someone else for the job. You can go.'

My one and only client.

'Go where?'

'Mountain climbing in Ethiopia. Your friend Gar called and told us all about it.'

'I beg your pardon?' I suddenly needed the loo.

'Gar told us how you felt you couldn't break your commitment to us, but no need to worry, we have already replaced you. Lucky you! And good luck on the trip!'

My mouth was wide open with shock. So they'd replaced me in the job that was my only source of income? Shit. Liz had got quite fond of an uninterrupted heat and electricity supply.

'Thanks,' I lied, and as I rang off my head began to spin.

I was surrounded by around fifteen people, all of whom had heard both of my alleged plans and my phone conversation.

Just at that moment the CD that had been playing suddenly ended, and in the brief moment of peace, all heads turned to me.

I sat at the table, trembling. I took a swig of wine and considered my position.

'You said you'd do it.' Gar's steely blues pierced my alcohol-addled skull. 'Now there's no reason not to.'

Indeed.

*

Apparently, in order to visit a country and engage in an activity that will almost certainly kill you, it is essential to be inoculated against diseases that might just kill you.

I set off for the doctor at Liz's insistence, and in the vain hope that the laminated note from my mother would cause any sane clinician to gape in horror at the thought of someone as physically and mentally incapacitated as I visiting somewhere as dangerous to my health as Ethiopia.

My local east London health centre was a squat 70s monstrosity, its interior walls decorated with ominous dos and don'ts – like don't even think of troubling reception if you haven't already booked an appointment and do use your mobile phone if you wish it to be smashed into oblivion.

I have always hated going to the doctor as much for fear of contracting something even worse than my ailment of the day from the other sick bastards in the waiting room.

I looked around me at the vast collection of malady-ridden Londoners. To my left the guy with facial warts sneezed and as he did so his colostomy bag burst and I realised the tragedy of the situation: I was putting myself in danger by just being there.

I began to wonder just why I was voluntarily preparing for this unnecessary trip in which the likelihood of being killed or maimed seemed by all accounts, and in the words of Dick Francis, a dead cert.

I put that to the nurse, a young woman of Far Eastern origin, as she eventually led me through to her surgery. She wasn't listening. I sat down and explained what I wanted, with as little emphasis as I could manage on the word 'want'.

'Are you alright? There's no need to be frightened,' she said as though she was addressing a four-year-old. I wasn't aware my fear was that obvious.

I explained where I was going and that I believed I didn't need the rabies vaccine. 'Well, you do,' she said, as she thumbed her way through what I assumed to be a medical directory of incurable Ethiopian diseases.

Gar had told me helpfully that there was little point in having the rabies jabs because they simply bought time. When bitten I would be so far from a hospital that I'd be dead on arrival anyway, he assured me. He suggested I save myself about sixteen quid. Besides, he'd argued, if I were bitten how would I know the dog was rabid? Well, Ethiopia's not known for its miniature toy poodles, is it? The very thought of a half-wolf-like beast digging its teeth into my leg left me cold. The remedy, if I lived to witness it, was supposedly a massive injection straight into the stomach. I courageously opted for the vaccine.

The nurse sat down and began to list all the other vaccines I would need, before pausing to tell me I would need to order the rabies dose from a chemist and that I would have to come back the following day to have the injections all at once. So I was to face another 24 hours in which I could change my mind about going to Ethiopia. Or get bitten by a feral dog.

My wife and I were both freelance. No work meant no money and no money meant our flat would sooner or later be repossessed, something that had hitherto featured as my greatest worry. Now it was overshadowed by the spectre of a cursed journey across Ethiopia to be concluded with certain death.

Liz's chief concern was that with me out of the country for an indefinite period of time, she would be shouldering the household costs with sparse work for herself and no contribution from me.

'Please do something,' she instructed less harshly than she could have.

'I will,' I promised, wondering if I had enough money to escape to a small Scottish island and lie low in a cosy boozer until both Liz and Gar forgot all about me.

I was wearing myself out with worry and using every remaining drop of energy plotting my escape from the whole Ethiopia venture. But that wasn't enough for Liz, who was familiar with my tendency towards failure. She wanted, pragmatically, to secure me in work and if I strained I could follow her logic. For me, getting out of Operation Certain Death was all about lining up a sequence of dramatic excuses. I'd have a migraine perhaps followed by a fall. But Liz's idea seemed a bit easier. A job it would have to be.

No sooner had I accepted this as the lesser evil than Liz shoved in front of me an advert for a six-week project working for a government agency. It was perfect. It would start in a week and last until well after Gar and his bloody mountain gear were off these shores.

She packed me off to the interview, for which she assured me I was more than qualified. I headed off down the road, turning to wave goodbye to Liz, who was standing by the gated entrance to our flat. Just around the bend ahead of me I saw the turnoff that led to The Birdcage. No, I told myself sternly. I needed to win the contract to pay the mortgage – and get a swift exit from the Ethiopia nightmare.

However, I *was* in plenty of time for the interview, so I decided on taking a detour for a quick pint.

Approaching the pub, I gave Gar a bell on the mobile in the hope that he might pay. He wasn't far away and 20 minutes later Gar came through the door and approached me warmly, his arm outstretched in greeting. He smiled broadly, placed his laptop and camera on the bar and without a word bought a round.

I felt a worrying sense of déjà vu.

My split loyalties became very confused. I was on a mission to get a job I didn't really want, I reasoned. Surely that deserved a drink?

'You're going to need some sturdy walking shoes,' he announced. He was firing out these staccato military instructions with increasing frequency but they never failed to hit their target. My loyalties were getting more and more tangled the more beer I poured down me. A few more pints and I staggered off to a 99p store to buy the shoes, interview and mortgage forgotten. When I returned, Gar was still there working on his laptop. 'Let's see,' he said eagerly. His camera wasn't required for his face to be a picture. 'You f*cking idiot,' he said with a 'these won't even get you back home from here' expression.

With the designated interview time long gone, I crept back into the flat to find Liz had gone out in search of work herself. Relieved, I checked my emails. News of my alleged plans had spread and most messages were asking whether I could incorporate people in my will before I left and could they have my record collection. Or in some cases my flat. Liz would have something to say about that.

I sat late into the night reading through various library books, working on research and generally working myself into a state of psychotic fear. And I still didn't really believe I would be going to Ethiopia. Promised myself there was still time to get out of it.

After all, I never did things I didn't fancy.

In the background was a TV documentary on Africa, the sound of which I was trying hard to screen out. But at one point the presenter said the two evil words, 'venomous' and 'snake'. That was the rest of the night spoiled. The first thing I did was to type 'poisonous snakes in Ethiopia' into an Internet search engine. Up came around nine hundred thousand sites. Some of the world's most aggressive snakes appeared to inhabit the area through which we were planning to hike. Most of these were nocturnal – and we were planning to camp out at night. So *that* was why it seemed nobody had ever produced a guidebook of that particular region: wild animals must have killed anyone who had tried.

I'd been hiking just once before, when I was 15 and living in Melbourne. Part of the annual school curriculum for each Year Ten class was to walk cross country a few miles through the Victorian bush to Lake Eppalock.

I was to see just one snake then, a harmless-looking brown thing sunning itself on a rock on the other side of a small pond in which I was bathing my sore feet. The Australian brown snake, I subsequently learned, which was one of most venomous in the world.

These Ethiopian snake websites contained hugely helpful hints such as, 'Instant haemorrhaging with the slightest bite. Best to leave this one alone.'

Ethiopia evidently had many varieties of venomous snake, a number of which were said to live in the very trees under which we would be passing. A significant proportion of them apparently tend to feed by swinging down and attacking the jugular of passing mammals.

I lay motionless and staring at the ceiling until a cruel dawn uncomfortably nudged me out of bed.

It was with disbelief that I answered the doorbell moments later. Gar walked in, unprompted, carrying a large white envelope.

'The girl at the travel agency asked me whether I wanted BA or Ethiopian Airlines. I said I don't know,' he announced excitedly. 'She recommended we try Ethiopian Airlines as nobody ever flies Ethiopian, apparently. So I booked with them. It would have seemed such a cop-out to fly to Africa on a British airline, especially if you're writing a book.'

Gar's smarming was unpalatable.

'You haven't actually *paid* for the tickets, have you?' I asked.

Immediately I pictured planes taking off in the desert; the pilot starting up by spinning the propeller. Gar's suggestion was worse than an outlandish joke. I'd winced in the past at harsh and unkind jokes about Ethiopian restaurants being very cheap to run, with no need to hire a chef, but this joke was even less funny.

It certainly wasn't a joke to him. He frowned, reached inside the envelope and passed me my return ticket to Addis Ababa. I was horrified, but realising I didn't have a ready excuse to call on, I reluctantly wrote him a cheque for just over five hundred quid.

Slamming the door with a loud bang as he left, I imagined our Ethiopian Airlines plane might make a similar sound – as it landed with one wing and a missing pilot.

The next few weeks were to give the concept of danger an entirely new perspective.

My only sense of relief since accidentally committing myself to this ludicrous venture came when I reflected on the fact that I had no intention of even attempting to climb the mountain if we ever found it, and I was not going to let anyone make me. I would rest, drink and avoid snakes.

I was duly stripped of this sense of relief when I saw a few sites that ranked countries by safety levels in four categories: Usually Safe; Generally Non-violent Thieving; Sometimes Violent Thieving; and Don't Even Consider.

Guess which one Ethiopia is.

I had found a dozen maps of Ethiopia, most of them at a glance noticeably different from each other. The only person I found to have visited the mountain, author Thomas Pakenham, drew his own of the areas he visited and I was of the impression everyone else had based his or her own creative works on that one.

While nobody was quite sure of the exact whereabouts of the mountain we were aiming to reach, Gar was confident that it would be, at most, three days hiking. However when I studied various maps, depending on which one was telling the truth we were looking at a hike of anything up to 200 kilometres.

Research moved on from geography to nature. There was the Ethiopian wolf and the leopard. And innumerable varieties of aggressive birds of prey. And, of course, a very high risk of earthquakes.

A few days before we were due to fly, I was up at 8:00 am to go and get the visas. I turned up at the Ethiopian embassy to find no queue.

News of the World shocker: Ethiopia didn't have many visitors from the UK. On the wall was a large painting of the elusive Wehni Mountain itself. I began to wonder how many others were heading off to find it.

And how many had never made it back.

Chapter Two

Researching my own death

Now that I had a non-refundable air ticket on the Death Star, Liz suggested it might be time to start researching the wretched book I was supposed to be writing. She had decided that in the face of unemployment and huge travel expenses, the only way to recoup some losses was actually producing a worthwhile tome of my adventures.

Idly stroking my laminated note, I felt a strong determination to get out of Gar's suicide mission, but to appease Liz I schlepped along to the local library and dusted off some books on my alleged destination.

The target was the summit of the lost mountain known as Mount Wehni. The rock was known by some as 'Wachni', James Bruce wrote it as 'Wechne', while the Royal Chronicles of Abyssinia had it as 'Wahni'. Each form translates into the Amharic word wehni, or prison.

Both Milton and Coleridge, meanwhile, refer to

it as Mount Amara. Don't ask me why. None of these writers had been to it of course – and all credit to them.

One of the first things I read was Thomas Pakenham's quest to find Wehni.

'I had an uneasy suspicion that if I ever reached Gondar I should find an embarrassingly large number of mountains to choose from.'

Brilliant. Just how many bloody hills was that lunatic Gar planning to climb?

Apparently this volcanic plug – a dark and miserable protuberance of death surrounded at every point by 300 metre vertical drops (in what looked like the Valley of Despair from the few pictures I'd seen) – had captured the imagination of Europeans for over one thousand years.

God knows why, given Europe's own fairly engaging wars, political and industrial revolutions, not to mention plagues.

Located close to the Simien Mountains in northern Ethiopia (so-called cradle of civilisation), the summit of Mount Wehni was once used as a prison for potential contenders for the throne, the princes. The history books tell of emperors wanting to ensure all their offspring were kept out of view until it was time to assume the throne.

I would be quite happy to see such a procedure applied in England. It'd provide the House of Windsor with a refreshing kick up the backside and stop the blighters from frittering away public money in trendy nightclubs.

Instead of letting One's offspring and grandchildren loose to roam the globe by yacht or Learjet with their aristocratic cousins One could simply incarcerate them atop some miserable peak in Wales until One pops her clogs.

The top of Mount Wehni, accessible through a manned gatehouse up a winding staircase built hundreds of years ago, apparently had a church within its walls. No mention of nightclubs.

In Search of Sheba by Barbara Toy, the explorer who landed on Wehni in the early 60s by jumping from a helicopter piloted by a braver man than Pakenham's, refers to three ambas – vertical rocks or volcanic plugs – known to have prisons at their summits. *'These sheer-sided mountains made escape impossible,'* she wrote about Debra Damo where, in the 10th century, Judith the Falasha queen attacked the amba, massacring all the princes but one. The amba prison then fell out of use for a few hundred years, when Amba Geshen in Lasta Province became a prison before being attacked by Muslims who wiped out its regal population.

One hundred or so years after that, in the 17th century, the final mountain prison, Wehni Amba, was established in the reign of King Fasilidas of Gondar (1632-1667). It was still a prison in the mid-18th century (according to James Bruce, on return from his visit to the country).

It fell out of use at the end of the Gondar period in 1769, if you are to believe the Amharic version of Tekle Tsadik Mekuria's intriguing tome,

History of Ethiopia from Emperor Lebna Dingel to Emperor Tewodros.

According to Dr Richard Pankhurst at Addis Ababa University, the Ethiopian tradition of detaining members of the ruling house in fact goes back as far as Axumite times, perhaps as early as the 5th century BC. It is believed to have been abandoned in the 10th century, owing to a massacre of the princes imprisoned there by Gudit, the pagan Queen of the Agaws. Then, late in the period of the Zagwes reign (1150-1270), the custom of detaining royals was revived in order to put an end to the problems of royal succession of the time.

According to Fransisco Alvarez, chaplain of the first Portuguese mission to Ethiopia in 1520, King Lalibela's predecessor in the 12th century – King Yimrha-Kirstos the Zagwe king – had first instituted the royal prison by divine inspiration.

Another massacre in the 16th century led to a further lapse in the custom of royal imprisonment, until King Fasiladas once again revived it, this time choosing Mount Wehni.

Or, as I called it, the destination of death.

The stairway on Wehni (presumably built to carry up the stones to build the church) had collapsed many decades ago. I'd have sabotaged it myself if there'd been any danger I might have had to climb the bloody thing. The absence of access only seemed to excite Gar more.

Perversely, Wehni had exercised the minds of writers for hundreds of years. Milton wrote of it, James Bruce travelled to try and find it and Samuel Johnson, who had written about Rasselas, later disputed its existence as anything more than mythical. After all, no one who'd written about it had ever actually seen it, located as it was, deep in the Belesa Mountains southeast of Gondar: Ethiopia's capital city between the 17th and 19th centuries.

So although many knew about the prison mountain, nobody from Europe had actually found the wretched thing.

But then in 1956. the young Oxford graduate named Thomas Pakenham set out on the 1950s' equivalent of his gap year to find the mountain. He was fit, keen and, as the son of Lord Longford, titled. This latter quality enabled him at least to travel first class wherever such a facility was available. It would gain him a high level of useful assistance from certain political figures in Ethiopia, whose co-operation would simplify his journey.

At the time he was classed as a true adventurer. (Right. Like Gar.) The result was the book: *The Mountains of Rasselas.*

As Pakenham was to discover, even with help finding the mountain was not an easy task. He enlisted the help of the Governor-General of Gondar; a guide in the form of the governor's nephew; and the native Colonel Shifferaw, an expert on the area's topography, to help locate and climb the mountain. They achieved their first goal and found the mountain, but were defeated in their attempt to reach the summit.

I met Gar for a drink to submit yet more cast-iron excuses for not going. Leprosy (not mine), insanity (mine), alcoholism (also mine). Nothing worked until I lied and said Liz was pregnant.

'No problem. You've kissed away £500,' he said, raising a pint of Guinness to his mouth.

I couldn't believe it. I had been willing to sell my soul to raise that sum, in order to extract myself from dire situation I was facing, when all that was required was a fake pregnancy.

He put his glass back on the beer mat. 'But you know, I have found Wehni is just a short walk from a new car park.'

I was baffled (and quite drunk). On the one hand I would do anything not to have to step foot in Ethiopia, let alone join a truck load of dedicated mountaineers on a six week hike. On the other, if what he was saying was true, I would be able to coast it.

I found myself declining a golden opportunity to escape.

'Okay, I'll go,' I said, admitting that there was, in fact, no pregnancy.

'Didn't think so,' replied Gar.

The next morning, nursing a sore head and neglecting the wrap-up work I was supposed to be doing for the Department of Trade, I picked up Thomas Pakenham's book and discovered Gar's new car park story was dubious to say the least.

According to Pakenham, Mount Wehni was about three days' journey by mule into the mountains of

Belesa – apparently an area never penetrated by the Italians during their occupation from 1936 to 1941, so Pakenham felt secure in the belief that he would be the first European to lay eyes on it. Accompanied by a small army of gun-toting guards and a pack of mules, he trekked through the mountainous terrain southeast of the ancient city of Gondar and, sure enough, found it.

He was the first recorded European ever to have located it. But the vertical face of the thumb-shaped rock was too steep to climb. Not content with this discovery, he then hiked his way on to Debra Damo, another prison mountain established in the Middle Ages.

'Spectacular as it was, the Debra Damo amba was not of the order of Wehni,' Pakenham wrote.

The more I researched, the more this fascination with Wehni seemed unhealthy and absurd.

Gar had gone to ground so I couldn't interrogate him on just how a remote three-day trek (that probably still required mules) had a car park at the end of it.

I had my first insight as to how remote and relatively uncharted much of Ethiopia was when I discovered how hard it was to find two maps of the country that were the same. Thomas Pakenham himself had on occasion to rely on the sketches drawn by James Bruce nearly two hundred years earlier.

I established that nowhere in the UK were any large scale maps available to lend help in finding this mountain. Gar tried Stanfords, reputedly *'Britain's most famous map shop'*, but to no avail. With just two days to go before our departure, I rang the British Library. After a while I was told they had some 1:50,000 maps of the region drawn by the army during the Second World War.

Perfect. After enjoying a yellow fever jab from the Hospital for Tropical Diseases, I caught the tube to St Pancras.

It was rather like a school exercise. I made it past security and safely into the reading room in a little under five hours. I explained at the desk what I was after and a mousey woman with long plaited hair proceeded to scuttle between the aisles and the table bringing the Ethiopian maps in batches of large folders. In one of these was a 1978 road atlas of Dorset and Cornwall. Naturally, the map I wanted was missing.

There were quite a few maps of Ethiopia, but none of them covered the region I was interested in. Presumably they'd been nicked, possibly by individuals concerned that foolish travellers might be tempted to try and visit the godforsaken place and get eaten by wolves or shot by bandits.

I'd tried my best. Now we'd just have to rely on the right map turning up at the Ethiopian Mapping Authority in Addis Ababa.

The thought of those words alone conjured up cruel images of a blend of khaki and chalk, featuring mad, menacing grey-haired geography teachers with the power to prescribe the most fiendish detention – cross-country running through thickets on a Saturday.

Devoid of further plausible excuses, I realised that if I really was going on this ridiculous jaunt, I would need some kit or whatever it was these outdoor freaks called it. I headed to Covent Garden for some sturdy walking shoes, but all I seemed to find were these things called Converse with skulls on them. I was never *that* young.

Liz rang and said that Gar had phoned with a list of instructions about kit, an address of a shop on the Strand, and what was this rubbish about her being pregnant?

The shop manager was an old friend of Gar's, who I also knew quite well. He evidently knew me quite well too, because when I walked into his office he was sporting an inane grin, relishing the prospect of sending someone so uncoordinated and hopeless out into the wilds. Gar had evidently already contacted him and they'd both clearly had a good chuckle over me.

His grin was punctuated by stifled bursts of laughter as the pile of kit I was to buy grew ever higher – this from a man who wore Jesus sandals with socks.

I walked out a poorer man with walking shoes weighing in at a tad under a tonne. These, I was assured, would keep my feet cool regardless of the climate, as well as ensuring a firm grip on even the steepest of surfaces. I had also acquired a plastic plate, cup and a traveller's knife, fork and spoon.

Before catching the bus home, I dropped into another store to get a carrier bag in which to hide the logo of the one containing the new goods, just in case someone I respected saw me.

Chapter Three

Bread and other weapons

We said farewell to our respective spouses and headed off to the airport, where we decided to partake of our last Western meal (and possibly any meal) for the foreseeable future. We eventually found a table in one of the charming and individual eating houses one finds in these places.

Any chance to escape was lost and I knew for sure that the following morning I would be in a terrifying land of – in no particular order – war, famine, malaria and venomous creatures.

'What're you having?' asked Gar, studying the menu.

'Kittens,' I replied.

I'd been so absorbed with the impression that I'd be confronting certain death at the hands of Ethiopian bandits; by the teeth of rabid dogs or wolves; or from the venom of snakes, that I'd momentarily overlooked the likelihood of the mortality presented by the plane that was going to take us there.

Needless to say, I was terrified of flying. I hadn't always been scared, but there was an occasion in 1982, when the door beside me on a six-seater aircraft flew open a few hundred feet above the Taupo Volcanic Zone. I'd tapped the pilot's shoulder. He shouted out instructions on how to close it again. Something like: *pull yellow lever, push down red button whilst using right elbow to hold rear handle in place whilst sliding green bolt to the left with other elbow. Grow another limb or get neighbouring passenger to press down hard on black lever and secure lock.* New Zealand technology at its best. Still, it'd have been a novel way to die I suppose: falling from a plane straight into an active volcano.

Then there was the time I flew from Malta back to Gatwick. As we began our descent, I heard a series of disconcerting bangs beneath the fuselage. If I didn't know better, I thought, that's the pilot trying unsuccessfully to get the landing gear out.

It was. We were nearly on a level with other planes on the tarmac when there was an almighty roar as, without touching down, we soared back to 10,000 feet. The air hostesses were nowhere to be seen. For two petrifying hours we went north, west and then southeast again, the deathly silence of the cabin punctuated by intermittent banging beneath the plane. Death was imminent. We would either crash, land or run out of fuel.

As we recommenced our descent to the airport

the sound of banging beneath the plane continued. Everyone braced themselves of their own accord as there was no word from the cockpit – a sure sign of doom. My eyes were clenched along with fists and arse as I prayed (mostly that I believed in an afterlife considering this one was about to end). Then, suddenly, after a couple of shocking bounces and a short skid, we realised we were going to live after all. I released my grip on the hand of the girl to my right and apologised. She scowled and said no, she wouldn't buy me a drink.

And then – get this – as we taxied past the rows of ambulances and fire engines that had been stationed at the far end of the runway, the overhead speaker came to life for the first time since take-off: 'Ladies and gentlemen, we hope you had a pleasant flight and look forward to seeing you again.'

Back on Ethiopian Airlines, as dinner was served and I had my first taste of Ethiopian-style cuisine, Gar began to talk about our movements once we arrived, starting with the problems we would encounter at Customs.

I was more worried about another sort of movement, once I saw my supper.

'It could take us days to get out of the airport,' Gar said, looking concerned.

That'd be a result. A few days of All Day Breakfast in the departure lounge would suit me.

I removed a spongy bread-like substance from my mouth. It was clearly indigestible. Maybe it was a sponge? No, according to the Ethiopian Airlines' menu it was injera bread. I wasn't going to induce a trip to an Ethiopian hospital by trying to chew it.

Ignoring his tray of food, my companion flicked intently through a sheaf of papers on his lap, muttering about the approach we would take to finding Wehni, the bloody prison mountain.

'When we meet up with the truck in Gondar we'll be driving straight up through the Simien Mountains to take us to an area of spectacular climbing peaks …' He turned the page. 'North of Axum.' He read more of the email he'd received from the truck in Sudan (the same one we would be boarding in Ethiopia), which he had printed out just before we'd left for the airport. 'That puts my mind at rest,' he said, sounding more reassured about the task of climbing Mount Wehni (if we were ever to find it). 'It's years since I've climbed such heights and I could do with the practice.'

I could do with a Valium. And a stomach pump.

'Did you say North of Axum?'

He nodded.

'That'll be the Eritrean border, then.'

He nodded again.

Shit. My travel insurance policy excluded travel in that area – and I was fairly sure my wife was going to need the life cover part. The latest war had officially ended over a year earlier, but there was still a substantial military presence there, and the border was said to be littered with landmines.

Being blown into two million pieces over a desert

wasn't exactly my idea of a fine holiday. And images of finding myself in the line of artillery fire didn't exactly help my already fragile state of mind.

Furthermore, it now dawned on me that these plans meant we would not just go to the country, establish we couldn't find his mountain and hightail it home again.

Clearly I was going to be incarcerated on a truck and driven around for weeks in a war zone: an excursion that was completely unnecessary as the area of which he was speaking was nowhere near where the bloody mountain was thought to stand.

Driven in a truck, I may add, that would be stuffed to the grime-coated backseat with eager mountaineering outdoor types.

To make things *even* worse, Gar had a seat-belt-bound audience of one and he turned it into an opportunity to provide me with a full historical picture.

'Eritrea was an Italian colony on and off from 1889 to 1941, when the Italian forces were driven out by the British,' he began, spouting some of the raw historical data he'd picked up over past few weeks. (Time I had spent unsuccessfully researching a plausible escape plan.)

I turned my eyes to his tray of food as he continued. Maybe the sponge was worth a go? After all, a hospital was better than a mountain.

'In 1952 it fell under British administration. A decade later its autonomy was revoked and it became the 14th state of Ethiopia.'

'And?' I said, as I tentatively tried to bite into my injera again.

'And, according to much of the press, the reason war broke out between Eritrea and Ethiopia in 1998 was down to landlocked Ethiopia's attempts to gain access to the Red Sea.'

Ah, the same school of press that had described me as 'Brave Bill'. In actual fact, the war started because, in May 1998, Eritrea sent three mechanised divisions of 12,000 men across the border, against a few dozen Ethiopian police and local militia.

I had nothing to look forward to, unless you included the possibility I might encounter the Blue Nile and possibly drown in it. Its existence and legendary charm held a dear place in my heart from the one or two geography lessons I'd attended at school.

Although Eritrea today claims it was always a separate country, the fact is, it was part of historic Ethiopia, and the ethnic groups found there are similar to those of its neighbours – Ethiopia, Sudan and Djibouti. And, unbelievably, that was where I was heading at around five hundred miles per hour. I pushed the recline button on my seat and fell into a trance.

We touched down at Rome airport, where the plane filled up with wealthy Italian tourists off to visit a country they never quite managed to conquer (despite the extensive use of chemical weapons and other instruments of their fascist regime in the 1930s).

The Italians are still, almost eighty years later, refusing to disclose the location of the chemical weapons left there. I pointed this out to Gar a little too loudly, and a chap with a startling resemblance to Mussolini called me a name that sounded like a foodstuff but was probably a less than flattering description of my private parts.

As we flew over Ethiopia itself, on the approach to Addis Ababa, I noticed how green and lush the countryside was. For a few moments I hoped that by some quirk of fate we were back in England and that I would be in my beloved local in time for breakfast. But then I saw some pointy mountains, the like of which I was sure did not exist in England.

Gar was craning his neck to see the view. 'Located as it is at 2,500 metres above sea level, the city stands higher than any other in the world,' he said to the Perspex window.

'That kind of altitude can't be good for my health, can it?' I muttered. My hand inched towards my laminated excuse note, and I prayed for salvation – or at least enough alcohol to get me through this so-called adventure.

Chapter Four

Gimme, gimme, gimme
(a way out of here)

'Mister! Mister! Gimme! Gimme!' I was barely five minutes off the plane but had already discovered that the predominant feature of Ethiopia and presumably other poor countries is not the sanitary arrangements but a sort of professional-style begging that made the gypsies in London look like hackneyed amateurs.

Not that I blamed the kids; arms outstretched, slightly manic looks in their eyes. I understood. It's a bit like being a journalist in the City of London. You have every intention of raising your hand to ask a probing question about the financial probity of a bank, but at the back of the conference hall are tables decked with the distraction of free booze.

'Gimme! Gimme! GIMME!'

I yelped and recoiled in horror from the clammy tentacles that had grasped my elbow, batting ineffectually at them with my other hand. I looked down. An Ethiopian urchin eyeballed me, hand outstretched, daring me to ignore him. I didn't have any currency of value, so I gave him a couple of old mints from deep in my trouser pockets. The look on his face said that I might as well have given him my CV.

'Come on,' called Gar, advancing towards another throng of people, clearly the second wave of beggar reinforcement.

I squinted in the morning sun of downtown Addis Ababa, feeling around for my sunglasses, only to find the urchin had apparently stolen them in retribution. He was sitting on a dirty mound of garbage a few feet away, and he cheerily cocked the aged lenses at me.

Nothing was going my way. I'd put my faith in Ethiopian Customs confiscating Gar's camera equipment – perfect excuse for a *volte face* to the departures gate and a return home. But not a chance, they had waved us through.

Oh, dear home. My last link to it was lost minutes later. The first thing I did once we were out of the airport was to switch on my mobile phone. Needless to say it found no network in the capital city: the only place in Ethiopia at that time to boast a mobile phone service. I turned the blasted thing off and didn't try using it again until I touched down at Heathrow.

I stepped into Addis Ababa. It reminded me of parts of Greece. There were hardly any modern structures that were neither still being built nor undergoing major repairs. Few structures in the city, or indeed the country, appeared to have brick walls, windows and a tiled roof.

We took a taxi to the city centre. For the very first time in my life, I found myself actually in the Third World. I am not particularly picky, mind you (I've holidayed in rural Australia, after all), but even I was unprepared for what I saw. Buildings, private or commercial, seemed to contain no identifiable building materials, just stones held together with mud or some other goo. Roofs, where they existed, were comprised of clumps of sticks or corrugated iron sheets. I vowed to never complain about British architecture again. Well, almost never.

There were few cars on the streets; a feature of the entire country as I was eventually to discover. Those vehicles that were mobile tended to be 1970s Datsun saloons or DAF trucks, held together with rope. The cars were filled to treble their capacity and many made use of their boots to cram in a couple more passengers. Not surprisingly, the World Health Organization says Ethiopia has the highest rate of deaths per car in the world.

I was reluctant to get into the taxi and my worst fear was confirmed (for once) as entirely rational. The driver looked as if he hadn't slept since Da Vinci was a boy. He told us his name was Solomon and he drove with one hand on the wheel and two eyes on us. I couldn't work out which side of the road the Ethiopians drove on, because Solomon was using both with equal enthusiasm.

My hand patted my seat urgently, looking for

the seat belt, but Solomon's glare told me that it was customary to face death like a man when using taxis in Ethiopia. I thought longingly of my laminated note and wondered if Solomon might accept it in return for seat belt privileges, but Gar shook his head when I suggested we stop so that I could root through my luggage.

We reached the Hotel Taitu surprisingly unscathed, which is more than I can say for the Hotel Taitu. Built in the early 21st century, it gave off all the panache of a dictator's bunker, without the reinforced walls and insulation. According to Gar, it was Ethiopia's first government-run hotel. Was this a good thing or bad? Hospitals in the UK are rather like government run hotels, and you die from MRSA in them. It wasn't hard to imagine what this particular establishment could do to me.

'Look, it's got windows!' Gar pointed excitedly at the mean little panes in the same way I would an unattended free-flowing tap at my local.

If he considered this to be a luxury, what chance was there that the rest of the place would meet my exacting standards? Okay, the hotel did possess windows, but as we discovered when we checked into our rooms, they were balanced in holes in the wall and would fall out onto the beggar contingent waiting for us in the street below if we sneezed too loudly.

We hurriedly dumped our stuff in our rooms and set off for a travel agent Gar knew. I looked longingly at my possessions, fully expecting them to have vanished through the portable windows when – or rather *if* – we returned.

As we stepped outside the hotel a boy pushed through the beggars and said: 'I am Solomon, a student. I don't want any money, I just want to improve my English.'

Another Solomon, this one with dreadlocks. He was the second of many Solomons we were to meet and presumably so-named after the ancient king.

An awful lot of young Ethiopians – most of those I was to speak to between the ages of ten and twenty in fact – seemed to be named after King Solomon. It was as though it reflected a strong desire for retribution over the assassination of the emperor Haile Selassie (said to be directly descended from the man described in the Old Testament as the wisest of all, King Solomon) by the socialist government responsible. A forlorn hope.

'I will show you the sights, the museums,' said our prospective guide eagerly. I rather hoped he might show me a pub or two as well, so I quickly agreed, much to Gar's dismay. Gar preferred us to explore places by ourselves – which usually involved getting lost for so long we became locals. I told him we only had one day in Addis Ababa and I wasn't going to spend it stuck down a dead end being advanced upon by an elite squad of beggars.

Gar made his objections clear by going off and finding the nearest dead end.

Solomon the Second and I settled into a slow pace, heading nowhere in particular. Apparently that very afternoon he had finished his last year of school – where he had learned to speak six languages – and he was now preparing to go to university by earning cash as a tourist guide. Hang on, hadn't he said he was free?

'Nice hair,' I said, looking at the dreadlocks. I admired people with hair.

'I am a Rastafarian.'

'Is that like a Hungarian?'

Solomon grimaced. 'No.' He told me the basic premise of the Rastafarian movement is that the 20th century emperor Haile Selassie, whose name was originally Ras Tafari Makonnen, was supposedly the living God of the black race as prophesied by the scriptures.

All this talk of King Solomon was not in vain. According to Gar, the Solomon line was integral to our quest for the prison mountain. He had informed me that the origin of the custom of imprisoning male members of the royal family on this particular inaccessible mountain top has variously been attributed to the Queen of Sheba and to the sons of a 13th century emperor.

I was (momentarily) drawn to the idea. During the Gondarian period (1632 to 1769), serious political offenders were imprisoned on remote mountain summits. This extraordinary custom involved the seclusion of the male line of the royal family, except the reigning king and his sons.

The genealogy of the Solomonic Dynasty of the House of Gondar records that Emperor Naod was proclaimed king in 1708 when he was aged just four. He was deposed by his great uncle and placed in confinement on Wehni before being killed on the legendary prison mountain at the age of 18. A successor of his later that century, Emperor Takla Haymanot II was himself born at Wehni in 1754, succeeded to the throne on the death of his father in 1769, before then being forced to abdicate nearly eight years later.

It was clearly no picnic being an Ethiopian prince.

Suddenly, Solomon's friend, Solomon (no kidding), appeared. Shorter than his mate, he was roughly the same age. I had the uneasy feeling that this might be the formation of a beggar battalion by stealth, but Solomon Number Three informed me that he was trying to write a historical book on the political situation in Ethiopia.

'The system here is bad. Take me, for instance. I can do want I want, speak freely, but I can't write anything down in a book.'

Not surprisingly, I felt a little ill. 'Do you mean I'm not actually allowed to write a book in Ethiopia?'

Solomon Number Three drew on his cigarette. 'Not without official application.'

I wondered if the Ethiopian government would find my laminated note persuasive. 'What will they do to me if I write without permission?'

He shrugged. 'Who knows? The political system dictates that the Amharic region has to learn in Amharic. Addis Ababa has to learn half in English.

That is not democracy,' he said again. 'Last year 160 students disappeared when they complained. Where did they go? Shot by the police perhaps.'

An alternative to being shot was to be incarcerated in one of the country's underground prisons. According to the Ethiopian Democratic Action League, the Addis Ababa regime maintained a number of disease-infested jails for dissidents, spread across the northern half of the country from Axum to Addis Ababa. Banged up in an underground lair for writing a travel book – just how one longed to spend a trip.

'Surely things aren't that bad?' I said. 'You have freedom of the press, don't you?'

Solomon Two shook his head. 'The university students objected to a police presence inside school – they wanted to print a free paper. The police put them in a jail. Then the police went into a library in the university and shot other students who had complained. These things are happening more and more. All the people protesting in the street – most of them get shot. Those that don't escape to Kenya, although some get eaten by lions or shot by soldiers there. They are my brothers and sisters. I want to get them back because they are educated. If they come back to thc country they will be able to help.'

Get back? I just wanted to get out. And what's with getting shot for being in a library? He truly seemed to be suggesting if I simply wrote this book I'd be imprisoned. On that very day (I was later to discover), the Washington Post reported that two students had been killed and four injured by Ethiopian security forces near Addis Ababa for protesting against the indifference of the government – the Ethiopian People's Revolutionary Democratic Front (EPRDF) – to the plight of many of the country's farmers.

Then Solomon Two pointed at our guidebook to Ethiopia. 'You must be very careful. It's a dangerous book. It's very wrong. Wrong prices, wrong distances, wrong history.' He shook his head, unwilling to discuss it any further. Both Solomons seemed really depressed. It was like having a conversation with a Democrat during the George W. Bush years.

Having thoroughly depressed me as well, the two boys returned me to my hotel. I had seen little of the sights, but they had managed to put me in even greater fear for my life during that brief sojourn in downtown Addis Ababa.

Gar reminded me we had to sort out how to meet up with the Hot Rock Global Challenge: the terrifying round-the-world mountaineering expedition, whose Ethiopian leg we were planning to join on the quest for the lost mountain.

I was reluctant to walk again so soon after returning from my jaunt with the Solomons, but given that Gar fully expected me to climb the legendary – and I hoped mythical – Mount Wehni, I decided that telling him I was knackered from a walk around town was probably not going to find favour.

Ahead of us, at the foot of a hill, stood one of

the city's obelisks. Dust was their most prominent feature, but the Ethiopians are justifiably proud of them. The land stretching out beyond them looked the scene of a 1970s' BBC war report: brown, dusty flak jackets on half the inhabitants. There are three obelisks in the capital: one with a star on the top to commemorate socialism; one to commemorate the patriots and their resistance to the Italian fascists; and one donated by Yugoslavia's Marshall Tito to commemorate the victims of the massacres in Addis Ababa and elsewhere by the Italians in 1937. Beats flowers, I suppose. It was finally returned after the Italians, hanging on to those imperial days, had been embarrassed repeatedly over six decades.

As if to prove that nothing good could come of walking, a dust storm sprang up out of nowhere. I wanted to run but Gar excitedly assured me we would be unable to avoid it. Unfortunately, he was right and instead of burger and fries, I ingested about 80 tonnes of sand. When I opened my eyes I noticed that Gar had taken on the complexion of a desert. He told me that I was no longer as pale as a plate in a school canteen. Later, by way of reward, I found that the sand had made its way through two zips and to the insides of all his cameras.

We finally made it to our first destination: Village Ethiopia, the Addis Ababa-based travel agency run by former guerrilla strategist Tony Hickey.

In the early 1970s, Tony had taken a ship in the from Saudi Arabia to Eritrea, where he had been working 'to earn some serious money'. He had hung around for a couple of years, driving tourists to Kenya in his Land Rover, before leaving in 1975.

'Things were becoming much more serious with the Revolution,' he told us. 'The killings had started and I decided I had to get out.'

Why was every conversation in Ethiopia peppered with death?

I mentioned I was writing a book, but stopped short of telling him I was journalist.

And lucky I did. 'British journalists, from the BBC World Service to the British national broadsheets, produce ill-researched and nonsensical reports, especially on the war between Eritrea and Ethiopia,' Tony fumed. 'Many of them incorporate significant errors in assessing the factors that led to the war in the first place.' Notably he was critical of reporters who would write stories celebrating a new-found independence among the women of Eritrea – owing to the fact that they were at last allowed to fight and die on the front line. 'Free to kill and be killed alongside men is not really an indication of liberation,' he said.

It's hard to imagine how Tony ended up choosing a travel agency as a viable business, opposed to, say, running a dissident army training camp.

Apparently Ethiopia had been every bit as popular a destination for foreign tourists as Kenya, some 75,000 visiting during 1973 alone. Both countries had coastlines, spectacular scenery and abundant wildlife, but only Ethiopia had historic sites and an identity defined by its peoples rather than by colonialism. By 1990, this figure had dwindled significantly, thanks to socialism, civil war and famine.

It revived again in the early and mid-1990s, but crashed once more with the 1998 conflict with Eritrea. The official Ethiopian tourism body optimistically reckons that the figure will rise to 700,000 a year in the next decade – the same level as Kenya, which has far fewer obvious tourist attractions but a greatly superior tourism infrastructure – and less death, you'd have thought (notwithstanding being ravaged by a marauding rhino or some such beast).

I sat meekly in Tony's office and listened as he regaled Gar with details of other fools who had tried to climb Mount Wehni and how he might be about to get us there.

For example, he had helped plan an aborted Royal Marines expedition to climb the mountain two and a half years earlier. Ethiopian Challenge, an expedition to tackle Wehni by a team of climbers from the Royal Marines, had been abandoned shortly before it was due to depart by order of the British government, in the light of the outbreak of hostilities between Eritrea and Ethiopia at the northern end of the country a year earlier.

In the hope that Gar might forget all about Mount Wehni, I asked Tony where else people went.

'We run the standard tours, such as the Historic Route – Bahir Dar, Gondar, Lalibela and Axum, trekking in the Simien Mountains, trips to the Omo Valley, bird watching and so on. But given the unique nature of Ethiopia, we also do a lot of specialist tours for people with more specific interests and with a deeper interest in history and culture or biodiversity. We handle a lot of film crews,' he said. 'The secret here is networking with Ethiopian academics and professionals, both in terms of putting together the itinerary and in getting them to accompany groups,' he added.

I began to relax. Tony's business was clearly ensuring the comfort and safety of the groups of tourists of which he was in charge. Maybe death could be taken off the itinerary?

Then Tony told us he had actually warned the Marines against pursuing their original plans for their aborted expedition to climb Mount Wehni. 'The route they originally planned was that of the Napier expedition in 1867, from Adulis on the Red Sea down to Magdela. Not a good idea, as Ethiopians identify Napier with the death of Emperor Tewodros and the looting of a large amount of ecclesiastical and national treasures.' Tony puckered his face as one does when remembering a massacre. 'Expeditions celebrating looting and pillage are not exactly recommended here.'

We explained we needed to get 800 or so kilometres north to Gondar, to meet up with the Hot Rock truck.

Gar, who often likes to use 8000 words when two will do, confused the issue by informing him unnecessarily that the plan had originally been to get to Bahir Dar.

'I think the best way would be to hire a minicab,' I ventured hopefully, as I lit a cigarette to try to quell my rumbling stomach. I hadn't eaten since the plane – although, to be fair, I was afraid to.

Tony shook his head. 'It'd be very expensive. The bus, on the other hand, will be very cheap.'

'Excellent,' said Gar.

Usually I enjoyed thrift, because it gave me more to spend at the pub, but in this case I felt that folding myself into an Ethiopian bus wasn't worth saving about £2.50. Or in my currency, one pint. I did not wish to sit for a day trapped on a decrepit vehicle at the mercy of death and disease.

Although I made my own concerns abundantly clear, I was outnumbered as both Gar and Tony insisted the bus was an experience worth writing about, and a scout was despatched to buy some tickets.

'This is the guide I recommend you use in Gondar,' said Tony as he passed across a business card. 'He can act as a facilitator, liaising with local authorities, and he will explain what to do when you reach remote communities.'

My immediate instinct would be to run.

'He'll show you around town; the historical sites. He can take you to places like the Mini Fogara, where you can see traditional music, with a man and a woman going round like minstrels, singing about the people.'

'Sounds insane,' I said. 'Those whacky Ethiopians know how to have a good time.'

Gar shot me a look that said shut up or I'll insert a camera in your gob, so I turned my attention to the pious chanting coming from the open window.

'What's that all about?' I asked.

'Lent. It means no meat or animal products for the duration,' Tony explained. 'But a lot of restaurants may still serve you meat. Spices are addictive – you build up a dependency. I am addicted to hot foods. A lot of Ethiopians will order hot sauces to accompany their food. If you're used to curries then eating here won't be a problem for you.'

I wasn't used to eating hot curries and the only things I had built up a dependency on were booze and cigarettes. But if I didn't go home with this book written my wife Liz would kill me, so at some point I would have to venture into a restaurant, so I had something food-related to write about.

Then the local scout returned and handed Tony an envelope.

Tony beamed, which I thought was slightly inappropriate given he was sending us to certain death. 'Here, your bus tickets have arrived. Sorry, Bill, but at least you've saved a lot of money on the car rental.'

Yeah. Great.

He advised us it was best to arrive at the bus station 15 minutes earlier than the bus company suggested (at 5:45 am the following day), if we wanted seats. All buses were scheduled to depart at 6:30 am, just after the sun rose.

No assigned seats then? I searched my memory

for information on Ethiopian buses, but the only thing that came to mind was cheerful, smiling throngs sitting on roofs of rounded vehicles that even Transport of London would have difficulty passing off as suitable.

'And when you get there, there will be all sorts of hustlers,' Tony continued.

Of course. Hustlers.

'No matter how desperate they seem we should not stop to give them money,' he said. 'Don't even pause to think how upsetting it is not to be able to contribute to a one-legged kid's education or you'll find thousands more descending on you.'

It was sounding better by the minute.

'And don't give them your bags or they will probably take off with them. Ask them to show you where the bus to Bahir Dar leaves from and give them a small tip – a couple of birr should do.' That was about 10 pence. A small price to pay to keep my luggage, I thought.

Gar, however, had other things on his mind. 'Bahir Dar? But we want to go to Gondar.'

I didn't want to go anywhere, but as delaying the inevitable now seemed possible, my ears pricked up like a first-time MP learning of his or her perks.

Apparently, the guide had bought the wrong tickets.

'But we're meant to be in Gondar on the evening of the 13th,' Gar moaned. 'This is a nightmare.'

Gar clearly had tame nightmares.

The prospect of an 800 kilometre journey north

through bandit country to Gondar to meet the Hot Rock truck, followed by days of hiking through uncharted, mountainous, rabid dog-infested terrain had been delayed, perhaps indefinitely.

But my hope was in vain.

'The original plan', Gar moaned, 'was to get from Addis Ababa to Gondar in the next three or so days to meet up with the truck.' What our afternoon had achieved thus far was a one-way trip, halfway to nowhere – a two-day bus ride to Bahir Dar, which was about midway to our meeting point and further from hope, help and civilisation than imaginable.

Tony realised the mistake but quickly put it in perspective. 'You couldn't get to Gondar any faster,' he assured Gar. 'One thing I'm certain of is that all the buses north will stop at Bahir Dar – that's a quarter of the way to the region where you want to start looking for that mountain.'

I put forward my own suggestion, which was simply to get a driver to take us all the way to the foot of Wehni. Better still, I thought, to get one to take us back to the airport for an immediate flight back to London.

'Don't pay a driver,' Tony insisted. 'There are buses that leave for Gondar throughout the day. They're all part of the same organisation, Northern Bus Routes, and they will all leave from the same bus station in Bahir Dar.'

The mournful religious wailing from the megaphones positioned on the street outside made me feel suicidal. I slumped back in the chair, a hand in each pocket. With one I felt the laminated note, the other thumbed my credit card.

I was still only a car ride from a flight back to home comforts. I was about to open my mouth and announce I was off when I realised I had no way of finding my way back to the airport. Plus, I would have to find a new wife and home if I arrived back without enough material to construct 80,000 or so plausible words on my travels, so I reluctantly drifted back to their argument.

It would be five hours in a bus from Bahir Dar to Gondar, three in a car. Why were they complicating things? We'd have no problem picking up a car and driver heading for Gondar. Given that it was apparently illegal to drive a passenger vehicle after dark in the country, there was little chance that we would get a connection on to Gondar the same day if we went to Bahir Dar by bus now.

In the end, it was decided go to Bahir Dar then Gondar by bus and hope the Hot Rock crew were still in Gondar when we arrived.

It was painful to hear the two of them still contemplating a bus trip on which the odds of escaping unscathed would be the same as guessing someone's telephone number. Or winning the lottery. My clothes were soaking in two types of sweat, from heat and from fear.

Deciding I may have to forgo my marriage, my plot to escape began to take a new shape. I would get a car up to Gondar, a major city by all accounts. I would then find an urgent reason to fly back to the UK. In the meantime, a 24-hour respite meant a chance to locate a pub.

Oblivious to this change of plan, Tony kindly offered to email the Hot Rock team, saying we were in his office that day and we would try and make it to Gondar by Wednesday evening, but otherwise we should definitely be there by Thursday lunchtime.

Thinking about saving myself from the evil hustlers of the bus depot by stuffing my money in my pants, I segued into a question on changing currency in Ethiopia.

'You'll have a hard time paying with travellers' cheques,' Tony warned me. 'Changing cash is in itself usually a lengthy procedure.' It appeared to be beyond the capacity of Ethiopia's banking system to enable foreign visitors to spend their money. I realised I would find it close to impossible to buy my freedom.

Deciding I couldn't cope with any more distressing news, I made it known I was eager to get out of Tony's office and do something I hadn't done in at least eight hours. Eat.

Chapter Five

The sweet taste of unease

'Where can we go for a pint or two and some good food?'

Tony suggested a nightclub.

'Well, we're not really clubbers,' Gar said, the subtext of which was: 'Bill wouldn't get in'.

'No, I mean traditional Ethiopian nightclubs with traditional Ethiopian singers.'

He was kidding, right? Luckily, Gar was ahead of me. 'Any good restaurants here in Addis Ababa?'

Apparently Castelli was supposed to be one of the world's best Italian restaurants. Tony raved about it like a shareholder. 'It does fantastic food. It's been there since the 40s and all the world-renowned people from the embassies go there to eat.'

World-renowned people from embassies? Who might they be?

But I was too busy salivating to be contrary. What was good enough for Mussolini would certainly be good enough for me.

'But,' began Tony.

God, there's always a but, isn't there?

'Monday's the night that everything is closed,' he said.

It was Monday.

Shit. My stomach was beginning to gnaw on itself.

'You can go to an Ethiopian restaurant if that appeals to you?'

I was mildly keen. After all, food was food. 'Yes!' I said, although apart from my battle with injera bread I had no idea what Ethiopian food was like.

Tony told us the restaurant favoured by locals was on the road to the airport. 'All the taxi drivers know it. It might be open Mondays.' He reached for the latest Addis Ababa edition of Time Out, a scrawny newsprint edition.

Time Out in Addis Ababa? The equivalent to a pedestrian's guide to motorway accident blackspots.

'Maybe somewhere closer?' Gar suggested.

Pity, if we were dining near the airport I could make a run for it.

'There are two ways they serve food – either hot, or alicha,' Tony told us. I jotted down the terms prominently on the cover of my notebook, 'hot' punctuated with a skull and crossbones.

'I like hot,' said Gar, quite unnecessarily.

'Ethiopian food is not curry as such, but can be called one for it is a blend of spices creating the characteristic taste,' Tony explained.

As a parting gift, he gave us a copy of a 1:100,000 map of the region east of Gondar, with a 'X' marking the spot Mount Wehni was said to be located – and where the Marines were to have headed had their trip not been cancelled. I shuddered. This gift provoked much excitement in Gar: a map that would lead us straight to the Holy Grail of Ethiopian prison mountains. Even if the British Library hadn't lost its own copy of the region, it wouldn't have had a cross indicating precisely where we'd find Wehni. He folded it up and put it safely in his camera case.

I had one last question: 'We're told that Ethiopia is riddled with mines. Is this true?'

'Nonsense,' Tony said. 'In 30 years I've never heard of a tourist being hurt by a landmine.'

It dawned on me later that he had (perhaps purposely) omitted to say how many tourists had actually been *killed* by landmines.

We walked back into the hostile terrain that Gar referred to as a street and made our way bravely to the map office, where we presented an official looking letter with bogus stamps that Tony had prepared for us.

It worked a treat. We took the map we'd bought from the Ethiopian Mapping Authority to a nearby café to study it and compare it with the map Tony had given us. It didn't quite tally with Thomas Pakenham's impression of the area and at that stage we were more convinced than ever – wrongly as it was to turn out – that Pakenham had not taken much trouble scribbling down a vague copy of the Second

World War military map. In fact, the puzzle we were to assemble as we tried to find this mountain was to become far more complicated than it seemed.

I looked up at the counter to find the source of an appalling smell that had just started wafting in my direction. It looked like a bowl of broiled sheep's brain. No closer to finding the ridiculous mountain, Gar folded up the maps and we walked on to find somewhere less unpleasant to eat. The discomfort of starvation was exacerbated by a terror of placing anything in my mouth for fear of picking up a mortal disease.

A child's grimy hand grabbed my own and as I jumped quickly away my left foot became wedged in a pothole and the rest of me fell sharply to the ground. I grazed my wrist as I landed. Thank God I'd had a tetanus jab before leaving on this insane mission.

'Mister! Mister!' the boy pleaded. He was about four years old and was offering small packs of tissues for 1 birr (about 5 pence). These were useful in the circumstances, so I bound my wound and pocketed a couple of packets. Toilet paper appeared to be an nonexistent commodity in Addis Ababa.

A girl who looked even younger then harangued Gar.

'Mister! Mister!' she said.

He steadfastly walked by. This shouldn't have surprised me. He'd ignored all my pleas for escape.

'I love you!' she cried.

Poor thing must have been blind too.

Around the corner of the street on which our hotel was situated was one of Addis Ababa's most lavish restaurants. Starving, we studied the menu at the entrance. It was expensive by local standards maybe, but cheap by any others we knew, so we walked in, only to be immediately stopped and body searched before passing a metal detector.

I hoped it wasn't because they feared people would try to smuggle in their own food.

The meal, however, was mostly uneventful. Once inside the restaurant we walked past a line of a dozen bored-looking waiters before being shown to our table. Eventually, one of them came and took Gar's order for spaghetti bolognese and promptly disappeared.

'What about my order?' I jumped up to follow him and he reluctantly took my own order for pizza, before continuing an animated conversation with a fellow waiter.

Finally a plate of spag bol and a pizza were unceremoniously dumped in front of us. We ate, paid and fled.

An hour later, we were back out at the mercy of cars, rabid dogs, snakes and the armed citizens of Addis Ababa. We cautiously made our way towards to the relative safety of the hotel. It was still early evening and Gar suggested a drink. I'd learned relatively late in the day that any suggestion Gar made should be handled like nuclear waste. On the other hand, I hadn't had a drink since leaving the restaurant. I threw caution to the wind and headed carefully down a stony, pot-hole-strewn road to a tiny bar.

My first visit to an African public house seemed to confirm the rumours I'd heard: women working in Africa's bars, if not employed to sing, were prostitutes. While Gar was in the bar, two girls in colourful clothing and too much make-up approached me on the wooden terrace and stood posing suggestively in front of me. Apart from the bloody sun it was the only other warm feeling to overcome me the whole time I was there.

'Sorry,' I told them, 'I am married.'

The comedy continued on the bar's terrace when Gar returned and the ladies switched their attention to him. Then, realising neither of us had come to Addis Ababa to pick up an incurable disease, they turned to two suited Ethiopian businessmen at the next table.

Which was when we realised it was actually a brothel, not a bar.

Girl One, clad in a tight skirt beneath a transparent, white cheesecloth sarong, giggled at them before announcing in a high voice with a wriggle of her hips: 'I'm horny!' She then left and entered the two-storey, dilapidated building by a side door. One of the two businessmen rose and walked in through the main door itself. Some 20 minutes later he returned. The girl herself came back a couple of minutes after that, cleaned up and ready to seek another victim.

Girl Two meanwhile had scuttled up the side

entrance, presumably on another date, although we didn't notice who would be joining her upstairs.

As the evening wore on, the number of such girls plying their trade began to outnumber the punters. Each time one of us returned to the bar, we were approached in a similar fashion by one or other of the young ladies, most of them with gabis – blanket-like shawls – wrapped around their shoulders. It reminded me of a Portuguese red light district: nonthreatening and slightly erotic.

It shouldn't have surprised me that, as the only white people in the crowded bar, we were the focus of attention from the, um, workers.

Gar arrived from the bar with a tray of drinks and the beer soon began to do what it was meant to. I took a drag on a coarse Nyala cigarette, sat back and looked around me. If a shag had been on my agenda – and, I suppose, if I hadn't also heard of the rife nature of AIDS in that part of the world (oh, and wasn't married) – I might even have ambled up to one or other of the attractive young ladies and enquired politely first of the weather then of the availability of latex products.

An hour or so later, Gar and I stumbled back through the dark and muddy street to the hotel, just as other neighbouring bars were opening their shutters for business.

I was about to go to bed when Gar knocked on my door. He had been studying the two maps closely to establish how many days' hike it might be before we found this mountain. Excitedly, he showed me where he had decided the mountain would be found, indicating some contour marks and a road. He showed me how we could drive along a particular route, park the truck and then hike no more than three kilometres from the roadside.

'It'll be a walk in the park,' he assured me.

Chapter Six

A drive to the death. Part One

My alarm went off seemingly five minutes after I fell asleep. 5:00 am! I hadn't woken up at 5:00 am since, well, ever, but the sun was coming up faster than a cop to free coffee.

I was battling with the feat of tying my cumbersome, vastly overpriced climbing boots, having just finished washing my hair with a rock that was supposed to be soap, when Gar knocked on my door.

Hoping for breakfast, I was disappointed to learn that the taxi was waiting for us. My eyes darted around for a buffet as I was led to the car by our driver, who looked like a young Nelson Mandela. Familiar with my skills for evasion, Gar had shrewdly settled the hotel bill the evening before, ensuring I paid up before I went to bed.

The taxi driver appeared to be drunk and had a malicious grin across his liquor-stained lips.

If he had wanted to kill us and steal our Western

belongings he could have done so easily, for the rest of the hotel was asleep.

Fortunately, he was simply there to do a job.

I stepped out into the dawn, boarded the rusting yellow Datsun and was driven off through the dusty streets to the bus station, which was located on the site of Mercato, the largest open-air market in Africa.

Gar, who had been more or less silent since first appearing that morning suddenly declared: 'Des won't be pleased.'

'About what?' I asked.

'He had a 20 pound bet with me that if you ever made it to Ethiopia you wouldn't last a day. This is day two. I win.'

His smugness did not warrant a response.

We passed through the city. The streets were packed with throngs of people, some still sleeping on the roadside, some lighting roadside fires, others heading into the market to buy and sell. Many were herding donkeys or mules. Often some of their precariously-balanced wares would fall to the road. Instinctively, I put myself into a brace position as a cloth sack of what might have been coffee beans fell onto the road at the rear of a mule, just ahead of us. Our driver, totally unconcerned – and as far as I was concerned totally insane – simply swerved to miss the animal, its owner and the four or five cloth-clad urchins running to salvage whatever they could from the mess.

A regular feature of every town and city in the

world that I'd visited outside Ethiopia was notably absent: apart from the occasional traffic light, there were absolutely no road signs, directions, stop signs or road markings.

The throngs intensified as we approached the station. As we drew up, I tried unsuccessfully to draw the 20 birr taxi fare from my money belt without attracting the attention of the thousands of hustlers outside.

We both steeled ourselves for the bracing walk through the throngs to find our bus – one of over one hundred assembled blue and white vehicles, all with the same scheduled departure time. We were jostled, but managed to steer ourselves as best we could through the excited masses.

'You! You! Guide!' rang through our ears. I kept a close eye on our luggage, while Gar disappeared to locate the bus. There was a lot of it to watch. We're not talking *Coming to America,* but certainly *Trains, Planes & Automobiles.* I found simply lugging my cumbersome rucksack around every bit as difficult as John Candy carrying that trunk.

Just as I turned to check I had gathered all our belongings, I spied Gar's hamper-sized lens case making its way off through the crowds. I didn't have a second to think. He was always going on and on at such length about the money he had to earn to buy the latest camera equipment, so I knew this was a non-negotiable life or death situation.

I (stupidly) abandoned the cluster of rucksacks and camping gear and charged hell for leather through the crowds. I was running in strides by the time I grabbed the man with the bag, pulling us both to the ground. The accused looked at me startled and not just a little angry. I was shaking with fear and surprise – it was unlike me to indulge in such aggressive action. I held up the bag and waved it in his face. He frowned at me, perplexed, and reached up to grab it. I snatched it away so sharply that I gashed my face with its sharp orange pockets in the process. Suddenly, I was struck by something else. Gar's bag wasn't orange.

It wasn't his. Shit.

'Sorry!' I said, before shrugging and running away as fast as I could back to our unaccompanied luggage. Miraculously their number had not decreased. Gar was standing beside them, hands on hips, looking pissed off. I told him I was just trying to save his precious lenses. 'I just put them on the bus,' he said. 'I didn't want to leave them with you and clearly that was the right decision.'

I took to ignoring him for the next few minutes. They were welcome to take our bags; I had my malaria pills, passport and money tied to a rope around my neck. It was a bit Heath Robinson but it did the trick.

'You', 'mister' and 'guide' were about the only English words I could hear from the mob until suddenly a calm, English-speaking Ethiopian man in his 20s pushed his way towards us.

I cowered behind the bus's rear wheels as he continued to approach, before stopping and asking where we were heading. Gar answered and the man pointed confidently to a bus some ten metres away. I handed him a small tip – more out of relief than for services, because he hadn't threatened to kill us, or run off with our bags.

'The thing we want to avoid is seats above the rear wheels,' Gar announced, half-knowledgeably, half-smugly, as we approached the vehicle. Then he procured a double seat directly above the two rear right-hand wheels. It could actually have been marginally worse, for the tyre that was later to blow was located on the opposite side.

It did not detract from my discomfort that the vehicle's front windscreen was more cracked than it was clear. I took my seat and looked down at the patchy floor beneath me and, beneath that, at the stony ground of the market.

Gar then disembarked to spend the next 45 minutes outside babysitting the rucksacks. Meanwhile the driver and a station operator overloaded the bus via a ladder at the rear of the vehicle. I watched anxiously as, one by one, a large number of ill-concealed aspiring stowaways were ordered back down the same ladder by uniformed officials.

Our luggage did not appear to have a very promising future – not with us, anyway.

Gar was now invisible in the massive crowds that filled the station. Streams of passengers were boarding the bus, which seemed to date from the mid-1950s and had been stretched into the latest decade with quick-fix rivets and nylon ropes. Many people hesitated and crossed themselves as they boarded. A few pointed to the empty seat beside me. Although I didn't know the Ethiopian for 'no', they all fortunately recognised what I meant when I shook my head – unlike the Bulgarians, for instance, for whom nodding supposedly means no and a shake of the head means yes.

A few of the passengers had brought livestock on board. A man with few teeth grinned at me as he shuffled on, wearing what was perhaps a tribal outfit – a once-white gown beneath a green shawl that draped uneasily over his shoulders. Of course, he sat directly behind me with his two honking geese, neither of which seemed any happier than I to be there that day.

Then, as he tied them to the legs of his seat (to my relief if not theirs), the volume of the honking went up a few hundred decibels. At least they couldn't bite me. The relief was short-lived. Moments later his travelling companion boarded, armed, and sat beside him. I took in my first view of what I would later learn was an AK-47 – a machine gun to you and me. I was cautious about carrying scissors around with me, conscious of the threat they posed should I stumble. The risks of a stray bullet in the back of my neck seemed many times worse.

Chapter Seven

A drive to the death. Part Two

The sun rose unnaturally quickly. As I stared out of the cramped, festering bus, the scene was more desert than city, inescapable sunshine casting dusty brown shadows over dusty brown buildings.

The bus driver played chicken with the crowds, small throngs of which met the challenge and darted to and fro in front of the moving vehicle as if they were on a suicide mission. Then I remembered – I was the one on the suicide mission.

Looking around fearfully, I noticed that neither the front nor rear door was firmly shut and both swung wildly as the bus, whose suspension was about trustworthy as an alcoholic in Oddbins, clanked along the pothole-ridden, rocky road.

Suddenly I felt some movement up my legs. 'Arghhhhhhhhhhhhhhh!' I screamed.

No one paid any attention except for Gar and one woman who looked around and seemed disappointed to see me still breathing.

I looked down as Gar asked what the problem was. 'Been bitten by a scorpion?' he asked, looking worriedly at the floor.

'No, shoelaces,' I explained, pointing at my feet. The laces of my wretched mountain boots were about 45 yards long and I had mistaken them for a snake.

I suppose the extra length was handy, should a noose be required.

Then Gar's question hit my temporal lobe. 'Did you say scorpion?' I asked. 'Are there bloody scorpions on this death trap?'

The look I got implied I should have known of the existence of lethal insects from the plethora of material on Ethiopia Gar had provided – and which I had left by my loo at home in the hope it might accidentally be flushed away.

Then, with an irony lost on everyone but me, a preacher stood up and began speaking to passengers, cap in hand, asking for contributions from everyone – well every native, that is. Each one seemed to give at least a birr. Desperate to give generously and become a believer, if only long enough for God to extract me from this place and my impending climb up Death Mountain, I scrambled for change. However the preacher ignored us – probably, I told Gar, because he thought white people's souls were beyond redemption.

Gar's theory was that I had managed to piss off everyone on the bus during the first 30 minutes of our journey: the preacher probably didn't want to encourage our presence by stopping. In any event, he passed us by.

The readiness of our fellow passengers to hand over notes to this priest was striking. Maybe it was their superstitions that caused them to part with their capital. I did rather wish I knew what he had been saying, although according to Gar, it was: 'Yes, as I told the last ten people, I will pray to have the annoying white man with the glasses spirited away to where arseholes belong.'

For the first few kilometres of the journey several larger vehicles drove with us in convoy, which meant our bus was clouded by the thick black smoke that belched out of other buses – in fact, out of nearly every vehicle on the dirt track ahead of us.

The Ethiopians have a curious preference for travel with the windows shut – a blessing since not having any air to breathe was far preferable to breathing in the sulphuric emissions from outside. I was curious though. Would anything compel the Ethiopians to open those little slats above their seats? I farted, entirely for experimental purposes, you understand. All around me, people began to murmur, presumably cursing the wasted birr they had paid the preacher to have God evict me. But still, those bus windows remained shut.

Incredible. I admired their commitment to health. This was the Ethiopian way, one clearly not favoured by the Western tourist, and I was seriously beginning to regret having lost the battle to hire a minicab. Particularly as I had underestimated my own smell. Must have been something I didn't eat.

'Christ, Bill,' Gar fanned his face frantically. 'Do you want to kill me?'

I pointed out that, in fact, about 60 Ethiopians wanted me dead at that point.

'60 of them and me,' replied Gar, holding his nose.

As we left Addis Ababa behind, I noticed small villages set away from the main road, unlinked to the rest of the world by electricity or phone lines – a bit like my aunt in Wales. However, these had even more of a shanty town look about them than Addis Ababa – or Wales for that matter. An estate agent would call the villages 'colourful'. The structures seemed to be made exclusively from broken furniture, woven grass and strips of brightly-painted corrugated iron. I think I recognised my aunt's orange vinyl-covered card table out there.

Then coughing suddenly began like 60 synchronised alarm clocks. Panic set in. I had boned up extensively on all the diseases I could possibly contract whilst away; tuberculosis being high up a very comprehensive list. Quite how many of our fellow passengers must have been suffering from tuberculosis was unclear. The World Health Organization reported 85,300 new cases in Ethiopia that year. Although I had been immunised, I wasn't convinced that the doctor knew what he was doing, and I tried to slide down in my seat so that the germs hit Gar and not me.

As if on cue, we passed Tibebu General Hospital,

whose foundations were built with rocks, which sounds quite proper until you realise they probably haven't been cemented together. Looking at the top of the place, I noticed the roof consisted of many layers of twigs. So, apart from the apparent absence of queues, it all seemed very much like your average, run-down, NHS establishment.

Then, in the hospital grounds, I saw a woman making her living attempting to sell a small collection of fruit and veg. I suspected she'd do a roaring trade if she was in London.

The surrounding buildings were much the same as the hospital, with no concrete or brickwork or, in fact, anything reminiscent of construction in the West, other than occasional tin sheets and odd pieces of wood or plastic.

In the midst of a group of these buildings was a yellow sign indicating the Embassy of the Federal Republic of Nigeria. Next to this, another sign read 'Embassy Gabonaise Residence' and pointed down to a shack standing in the thick hillside undergrowth. I thought it might be derelict until I saw a bunch of people come out of it, gesturing wildly. Maybe they had just realised their embassy was about to start sliding down the hill.

For mile after mile there was a constant stream of people, hundreds of them, walking in the same direction as the bus. It couldn't be to enjoy the delicate perfume the bus emitted: either the bus was too expensive for them, or there was something we didn't know about bus travel. I wanted to ask

Gar what they were doing but he was still pissed off about the fart, so I was left to my own musings.

Many of them could have been walking all the way to Bahir Dar – a town they had to reach by the main road since there were few if any side roads. That was like me walking from London to Edinburgh along the A1 (okay, not me – a person who *could* actually walk a given distance without requiring hospitalisation). By contrast there were only around 60 people on the bus heading from Addis Ababa to Bahir Dar. It was unclear quite how many other buses – if any – were heading the same way.

About eight kilometres out of town, near the top of a steep hill, the bus drew onto the forecourt of a Total garage to fill up with diesel, on sale at 2.62 birr per litre – a little over 20 pence per gallon – and to have its tyres checked. Ten minutes passed and we were still waiting for it to move on.

Maybe the driver had done a runner?

I peered nervously out of the grimy window and noticed four or five people staring anxiously at the wheel beneath our seat. Gar discovered that one of them had tried to make some kind of adjustment with a spanner, to apparently disastrous effect. The rest sported the same look as Liz when I tried to clean our bathroom shower and brought the whole unit down from the wall.

I saw one of the observers was smoking. You weren't supposed to smoke in a petrol station!

Oh shit.

The preacher looked around and I could swear he winked at me.

Whilst I tried to convince Gar to abandon this idiotic adventure and take a trip to, oh, England, the scenes of bewilderment at the state of the bus continued. Gar tried to ignore me, but after an hour of listening to me predict our imminent demise from either the bus exploding (thanks to the smoking), or blowing up (thanks to the dodgy mechanics), he gave in to my additional complaints of hunger and crossed the road to buy a couple of bottles of Pepsi and some bananas from a stall bearing a roof made from several polythene bags.

As he made his way back, the bus fell silent, its occupants staring at him from the windows. I immediately imagined the worst: roadside Pepsi contained arsenic, but Gar assured me that Ethiopians do not indulge in snacks. 'Which,' he noted, looking me up and down suggestively, 'is a much healthier way to live.'

'They probably can't afford snacks after having given all their birr to the preacher in an attempt to get rid of me,' I replied, snatching the tasty morsels and spilling the open Pepsi in the process.

Suddenly, the bus was fixed. Smiles broke out. Backs were slapped. The preacher grinned at everyone in the bus but me. But 15 minutes later we had still not left. A large crowd had gathered, apparently drawn by the fact that the bus was not leaving and that engineers were now working on another of its wheels.

'Christ,' I whispered to Gar, 'the bottom will fall out of the bloody thing next.'

Gar didn't answer. I think he was trying to disassociate himself from me, which annoyed me because, yes, I had spilled my Pepsi all over me, Gar and the nicely dressed woman who shared our three seater, and there was a stream of Pepsi congealing on the bus floor beneath people's aging sandals, but he was still my mate and after all, I was doing him a favour, wasn't I?

Just as we were finally about to depart, a Total man in a red uniform replaced the fuel hose and shouted 'Oggi! Oggi! Oggi!' This was most curious since 'oggi' means 'today' in Italian. I hope he didn't mean 'today you die.' When Total Man's eyes caught my face in the window, he stared back at me in horror, the way someone would on discovering her blind date was the Yorkshire Ripper. Before I had a chance to react, the engine started again. Momentarily. Before we could roll back onto the rocky surface of the main road and head north away from Addis Ababa, a bunch of salesmen and storytellers had to get on board to try to sell stuff to the passengers.

'Right, we sit here for bloody hours, and *now* they try to sell us stuff,' I grumbled. The preacher turned and gave me the hairy eyeball.

The first was a man in shorts, which wasn't surprising, since shorts and shirt was the preferred attire of most Ethiopian males.

What was surprising was that our guidebook,

enthusiastically asserting on the cover that it was our 'trustworthy travelling companion', claimed that *'shorts are looked down upon, particularly in rural areas'*. Given the solitary shack of the banana seller in the vicinity, I'd say this was pretty much the countryside, and the only reason shorts here would be looked down upon is because you can't look up them.

Every so often I'd see someone clad in attire that appeared to have come straight from an episode of Blue Peter circa 1970 – acrylic sweaters, bellbottoms and platform shoes. However, to confirm my shorts theory, the chap on the three-seater bench opposite me was wearing small (and tight) pale blue shorts, a check cotton jacket, some of my Pepsi, and, draped over his shoulders, a curtain.

Man in Shorts was selling bunches of Ethiopian national lottery tickets. Somewhere in the country one lucky winner would receive 1 million birr (about £50,000 – just about enough for a British politician to have his or her pool cleaned).

Next to board was a chap (yes, in shorts) apparently telling a hard luck story and touching his ear. He was soon jeered off the bus – though it was impossible to say whether he was a comedian or a beggar. If he was the former then he must have been rubbish – Donald N. Levine describes the Amhara in his 1965 *Wax & Gold* as *'a wry people with an apparently inexhaustible supply of humour, who prefer the clever, double-edged remark to comic actions or incongruous situations'*.

Oh, if only they could understand me, as I had an inexhaustible supply of double entendres. Even the preacher might come to like me.

Suddenly the driver revved his engine, the sellers reluctantly departed, and with half the morning gone, we headed on up the hill deeper into the Ethiopian countryside. It was 9:00 am and the sun was intense. The Pepsi on the front of my T-shirt sizzled.

I noticed a long culvert on the side of a rare stretch of metalled (tarmac) road. A culvert, just in case you aren't as intrigued by road construction as I am, is a conduit to enclose a body of flowing water. That's right, water in Ethiopia. That culvert was about the best piece of modern construction we were to see throughout our stay including the capital's airport – although to be fair a new airport has since been completed. Probably not as finely-constructed as that culvert, though. I might recreate one in my back garden, over the leaky garden tap, in the unlikely event of Liz letting me near concrete.

The brown haze faded and even I had to admit the rich colour of the trees and shrubs was pretty impressive, especially the rich blue, silver and green of the eucalyptus, which grew in abundance in the region. I had honestly expected the surroundings to be like something from a World Vision ad, which I am sure they are in some parts of the country (parts I definitely didn't want to visit, given I didn't want to visit the part I was in).

According to Gar, eucalyptus was first brought

to the country in 1906 when, a decade after the new capital Addis Ababa had been established (and again, I use that term loosely), the region found itself running short of wood and needed a fast-growing replacement.

We passed a small farm typical of those we were going to see en route to Gondar: a small number of round huts and a handful of cattle half the size of Scottish highland cattle, with horns half the length of said beast.

Stretching into the distance were acres of ox-ploughed fields of teff (an annual grass native to Ethiopia), maize, barley and sorghum, whilst further ahead lay the first range of mountains of the trip – a hazy blend of brown, green and purple. (Or so it seemed to me, but it must be said that Gloucestershire County Council deemed me to be colour blind when I was 14, so they could have been any colour, really.)

The bus slowed down to negotiate a series of potholes, which I thought considerate until it dawned on me the driver was probably doing so to prevent the engine falling out. A long convoy of sheep was making its way past a shack bearing a sign marked Hoteela. I was reminded of a scene from *Life of Brian*.

Next, I spied a concrete structure of the abandoned variety (think sink estate in Hull), which was strange because, unlike Hull, concrete was extremely rare in Ethiopia.

Nearby a man with a white towel balanced on

his head was strolling across a plain with a rifle, poised to shoot a small wild animal.

We rounded a bend and the driver slowed as he parped his horn and passed a farmer herding half a dozen cattle before swerving to the left to miss a bus whose wheel was being changed. It was like being on a ride at Alton Towers, without a safety belt.

I listened to the Amharic conversations around me. They were quick-spoken and involved, according to my guidebook, dry-witted exchanges. As the day drew on and I drifted in and out of sleep I was baffled by the number of clear, apparently English conversations that I could hear. This was nonsense, of course, but the intonation of their voices sounded distinctly English. Seriously, I swore I heard Ethiopians on the bus hold conversations that ran, for instance, like this:

'Me wife's out shopping. Over two quid for a pint these days, and every barrel empty.'

'What a naffing disgrace. Seven parties and not a grocer between them.'

'Sure they're taking the piss.'

I was so amazed that I nudged Gar out of his slumber and into a truce. 'Hear that?'

He listened intently for a few moments. I listened too, as the man with the chicken opposite us said: 'Customer car park only and his sister cannot drive a tractor.' I waited for Gar's expression to change.

It did.

'They just said: 'Shall we kill them both and nick all their stuff?''

I froze and heard: 'It's a shame no one's dealt with that English twat yet. I wasted my money on that preacher.'

As the distance slowly grew between our vehicle and the capital, I began to notice signposts. A metal road sign roughly cut to the shape of a triangle with a hand-painted red border suggested there would be two-way traffic straight ahead. Its very existence was mysterious, not least as there had been no discernible change to the road layout since we had left Addis Ababa that morning. A little further on was a sign saying: 'Bank of Abyssinia 40m', but after 40m, there was no financial institution, nor other sort of bank, to speak of. There were many more such signs and neither of us could work out what they were supposed to indicate.

We entered the next village at the crest of a hill and passed the Awash Hotel, which featured a hoarding advertising Pepsi. Gar looked at me and then meaningfully down at my Pepsi-covered trousers. I was a walking advertisement for anti-cola campaigners.

Gar had read somewhere that both the Pepsi-Cola and Coca-Cola bottling industries were privatised in Ethiopia in 1996, but throughout my time in the country I never got to see any adverts for the latter. It was the same in London restaurants, where they will only serve you one or the other.

Beside the Awash Hotel was a barbed wire fence. I guess that told me what it might be awash with.

We continued on and a black triangular wedge

on another hand-painted road sign told us of the sharp descent we would shortly be making. Shit. I wondered if I could have a cigarette in preparation for my possible demise. However, cigarettes were not particularly popular in Ethiopia, and everyone religiously adhered to the No Smoking sign on the bus, and not simply because it was Lent. I suspected it would not be in my best interests to light up. According to 'Building Support for Global Tobacco Control', those who do smoke in Ethiopia light up an average of just 90 cigarettes a year, compared to an annual average of over 2000 in the US.

Suddenly the bus seemed to go over the edge of a cliff. I clung to my seat as I realised the driver was making up time on a sharp downhill run.

An hour or two later, after we'd made it down the ravine alive, the scenery began to change yet again as the bus crawled up the side of another mountain.

According to Gar, who was now blabbing enthusiastically about everything again (fart forgotten), we were entering a region that featured the distinctly northern Abyssinian style of scenery. It resembled the Scottish highlands – wild, remote and all shades of grey. When I said this to Gar, he told me he preferred to liken it to the Rhône valley and reminded me I was colour blind.

My luck began to run out with the road surface as the potholes grew in number and the rocks in size. A few kilometres later we pulled in to the Muka Turi bus stop. Gar disembarked for a bottle of water (without, may I add, asking me if I wanted one) and half the women on the bus disembarked for a pee on the roadside beneath their long Victorian-style robes. So *that's* why they wore them. I could do with one in London. Very handy after a visit to the pub.

All the passengers who got off crossed themselves again as they reboarded, something they would continue to do throughout the trip. I hoped it didn't have anything to do with me.

I snoozed briefly and awoke to find we were on diversion. If it wasn't for the cattle, I could have sworn we were on the M25 for all the traffic. The resurfacing of the Ethiopian road we were on was apparently part of a project that was being funded by Japanese government aid. Clearly the Japanese haven't been to Hull. If there was any place in need of aid …

An old woman outside, shuffling along beside the bus, using a cattle stick to support herself, suggested aid to Ethiopia wasn't a recent phenomenon. Either that or the T-shirt she was wearing told a different story, namely that she really *had* been to see Jethro Tull during their 1974 tour.

We revved on up the mountainside, passing a large, colourful, circular stone church called Obebe Lands Monastery, which was located amid a cluster of traditional round Ethiopian huts with conical straw roofs. A priest in a pale grey robe was talking to a group of children who were all seated cross-legged – at least they were until they saw our approaching bus and ran towards the road.

Maybe they had learned of the evil, four-eyed Englishman and wanted to see me for themselves.

Some of the village's inhabitants also came running out to see the bus, waving fruit to sell. The bus slowed down and a man ran towards the window beside me calling: 'White friend!', but at this point we accelerated away – a little too fast for either my liking (someone actually wanted to know me) or that of the bus itself, which grazed itself on the low wall of a bridge at the far end of the village and narrowly avoided dropping into the ditch below.

My only friend in Ethiopia was left staring at the bus forlornly.

Chapter Eight

Breakdowns and shiftas

The bus journey continued. I was aching all over. We went over yet another pothole the depth of a Nottinghamshire coalmine. My knee hit something sharp. 'Ow!' I cried. People in the bus, clearly used to the deep trenches, scowled at me for disturbing the peace again. I caught the preacher shaking his head in disgust. A blood stream formed along an injury on my right knee and seeped into the ridiculous long laces of my boots. A baby of perhaps one year, who had been seated happily on the floor for the entire journey, suddenly burst into hysterical laughter at the sight. God knows why.

Gar glanced across at the scene and shot me his 'Don't You Dare Throttle a Baby on this Ethiopian Bus' face.

Finally, we pulled into a small town, and the bus parked directly outside the Hotel Kenya which, although decidedly lacking in splendour, looked like The Dorchester after my 14 hour bus ride.

Some passengers disembarked and quickly removed their bags from beneath the tarpaulin on the roof. I hoped they weren't removing mine as well.

'There goes our luggage,' Gar said.

'What?' I said, panicked. My hoard of booze was in there. And ten packets of cigarettes.

'Joke, Bill. Honestly, will you loosen up?'

'Not until I reach Heathrow Terminal 3,' I told him.

The town, named Plashi, seemed reasonably tidy with makeshift fences kept in good order. A few chickens scratched around. The town's beggars had gathered in conference outside the bus and looked as if they were unafraid to pick a fight. All except one. A man manacled at the ankles.

High above us, a huge and presumably hungry eagle circled threateningly. I felt like a doughnut at a weight loss meeting. I suspected its nest was located on a nearby pinnacle, which looked uncannily like the one in the photographs Pakenham had taken of Mount Wehni.

I was glad to be on the bus and not to have to smell any more of the place than came in through the cracks in the windows.

Aside from my own physical discomfort, from the gaping hole in my knee, I was acutely ill-at-ease regarding every feature of the landscape around us. What's more, I couldn't remember whether I'd taken my anti-malaria pill that morning. At three quid a tablet they were in limited supply, but forgetting to take even one was not an option, because – and I was particularly careful to research this one – over 100,000 people die each year from malaria in Ethiopia.

A couple of kilometres on we hit another town. Powder green dust was thrown up from beneath the bus as we passed what looked like a mule park. 40 or 50 of the beasts were tied up for rent.

The bus doors opened and begging villagers once again besieged the bus. A man with no hands stepped on board and a few passengers placed coins in his pocket for his efforts. I offered a single birr and he graciously bowed in appreciation.

As we set off again I remarked to Gar, before he nodded off, that it seemed as if we had been in the country one hell of a lot longer than a couple of days. In reply he suggested that somebody should develop and market a computerised Ethiopian bus simulator. 'Be a great cure for depression and stress,' he murmured. Given my level of depression and stress, I told him, I hardly thought so. He showed no sign of having heard.

The further from Addis Ababa we drove, the more unusual the native animals became. For a start there were feral flocks of birds. According to Gar, boring for Ethiopia in one of his rare moments of wakefulness, there are over 850 recorded species of birds in Ethiopia. I am convinced I saw a flying lizard and have no idea how Gar could have missed it, visible as it was through the window next to us.

'Flying lizards are extinct,' he sniffed.

As we entered the northern Ethiopian mountain ranges, someone appeared to have crossed hyenas with dogs, dogs with wolves, wolves with donkeys, donkeys with sheep and so on. Many of these were being traded at a market at the edge of which a priest was addressing a huge crowd. From a distance it looked like a Young Conservative Party Convention. Fewer wolves, of course.

We stopped at a village where I hopped off for a pee, before going to stock up with some Ethiopian cigarettes. I was asked by the chap in the booth how many I wanted.

'Just the one. No, better make it three. Actually, five would be terrific.'

The man counted out five single cigarettes and passed them over. Five cigarettes? Was there rationing? Didn't he know an addict when he saw one?

'I meant five PACKETS,' I said, in the infuriating way of foreigners who talk loudly in English instead of actually learning the native language.

His face lit up like Harrods at dusk. A packet of 20 cigarettes usually cost just 4 birr, worth 35 pence at the time. Fortunately, they bore no health warning so clearly they weren't going to do me any physical damage. I had tried to give up smoking two years earlier, but since arriving in Ethiopia I had reverted to a pack a day. Okay, two packs a day. Okay . . .

'Hey, white man! Wanna rule the world?'

Of course. I turned to see an angry-looking boy of about 15 shouting at me as I weaved between donkeys on my way back to the bus, busily smoking. 'Not especially,' I lied, although on reflection, I think the question was rhetorical.

He put his hands to his face and peered through his thumb and forefinger. I suspect it was because I was wearing glasses. You don't see many opticians in Ethiopia. Of course, it could have been the Ethiopian way of giving the finger.

The scenery was becoming tiring by its drama and my eyes began to hurt taking in the sight of such a continuously aggressive landscape.

On the horizon, a collection of joined cliffs surrounded a valley that lay a kilometre or two below them. They seemed to be approximately twice the size of that conventional unit of two-dimensional measurement – Wales. I could just make out the unmistakable Blue Nile running through the valley's rift. We were passing through an area whose surface featured a peculiar blue stone, which geologist-turned-comedian Gar assured me was basalt, adding that geological upheaval had left the basalt faulty.

I was momentarily distracted by my childhood favourite, the Blue Nile, so I was somewhat baffled to find Gar becoming as unpopular as I with our fellow passengers. As we approached the bridge over the huge canyon he had taken out his camera and was about to shoot when he was abruptly stopped by four or five alarmed passengers.

'Illegal! No picture of bridge!'

My best guess for the reason behind the

prohibition of pictures of the bridge was that the government didn't want them getting into the hands of an enemy who could cripple the region by blowing it up. It seemed a bit far-fetched, but then Ethiopia is to wars what a Frenchman is to cheese.

As well as outlawing snapshots of any bridge, the Ethiopian state still prohibits photographs of public buildings such as hospitals, departments belonging to the ruling party, army bases, army trucks, industrial premises, post offices and refugee camps.

Tony Hickey later mentioned that in 1996 more than 20 tourists from the United States, Germany, the UK and other Western countries were arrested and held for three days for taking pictures of the Blue Nile gorge. When they finally reached Addis Ababa they complained to their respective embassies. Following a high level investigation, the Commissioner of Police and Prisons, Ato Getachew Assefa, issued a tough and uncompromising circular to the police, government ministries and the Tourism Commission, pointing out that controls on tourists or Ethiopians taking photographs dated from the Derg era and had no place in a modern democratic society.

That circular remained a dead letter. Six years later, the police apparently continued to deny its existence and, when confronted with a copy, would refuse to accept its validity.

The heat was stifling and engine fumes began to seep through the closed windows as we started the climb up the other side of the gorge. The look on the driver's face told me I might soon be called upon to sacrifice my precious remaining litre of water to the engine.

When, worried, I mentioned this to Gar he said I should compare my own pathetic whims with the sturdiness of the indigenous people. He pointed outside. At this comparatively low altitude many of those working on the land were wearing hoods to protect themselves from the sun. Women and children – some of them very young indeed – seemed to be working every bit as hard as the men, although most of them took the time to wave at the bus as it passed.

As we approached a town, Dejen, the bus took off on a long stretch of plain. It quite literally jumped over ditches as the driver tried to make up time.

Needless to say, a short while later the wheel needed further attention.

As we waited for the repair to be completed, I watched swallows and house martins feeding on the wing over the ploughed field off to our right. I was alarmed. What were common English birds doing in the harsh African landscape?

Nothing English should be here. Especially me.

Still, it might provide an answer to the question the English were asking at the time, namely: 'Where have all the birds gone?'

Back on the move, and despite the constant need for repairs, the driver became even less cautious about whom or what he hit. He didn't even bother to slow down as another small flock of sheep, travelling as usual in convoy, crossed the road. He struck one but the impact was apparently not too debilitating, for the sheep slid across to the side of the road before staggering to its injured legs and limping away.

Nearing the next village, I saw a snaking line of women carrying huge clay pots, which were either balanced on their heads or strapped to their backs. Many of them also carried babies, while all their offspring of toddler age and above roamed the fields herding cattle.

This village had an unusually long terrace of mud huts, some of them doubling as business premises. In front of one sat a man with a manual sewing machine and a huge pile of clothes through which he was slowly working.

'These people are hardworking, aren't they?' said Gar, looking at me.

What was he implying? 'Not particularly,' I murmured.

Further on was a forest of evergreen fern trees. Very useful for providing roofing material – men and women were carrying bound green loads. But what were ferns doing growing so abundantly in such a climate?

As with many questions I asked, I never received a satisfactory answer.

At the next village, Yegesh, I noticed a boy cutting a man's hair on the street with a razor. Next to them, an army of clothmakers were sewing. The driver was apparently ogling the clothmakers as well –

moments later the bus wheels suddenly slipped off the road and put the vehicle into a skid. We came to a standstill leaning at 45 degrees to the road before tipping slowly upright with a massive thud three or four terrifying seconds later.

Now my other knee was bleeding, having been deeply penetrated by the rusty inch-long screw protruding from the back of the seat in front of me. I wondered out loud what the symptoms of tetanus were. Gar assured me the disease was usually fatal.

The road became a poor quality dirt track for a few kilometres before suddenly we hit a village with a newly-metalled road surface. Satellite dishes decorated the corrugated iron roofs on most of the buildings in the neighbourhood. This village was presumably the beneficiary of aid and must have been loathed by its luckless neighbours.

The bus was moving forward without bouncing up and down, providing me with a rare sensation: relief. It was sad how attached I was becoming to metalled roads.

I saw a sign denoting 30km/h, the first I'd seen. Later, I was informed that there is no national speed limit but simply a highway rule that 'safety must be observed at all times'. I think that is probably part of the Highway Code in the UK as well. Works so well, doesn't it?

Road-building, according to Pankhurst and Gar, had been pretty much unheard of in Ethiopia until the 1850s. That's when Emperor Téwodros II came to power (after overthrowing the feudal leadership in northern Ethiopia in 1855) and fulfilled his need to move troops and cannons around the country by using European labour to build an embryonic road network.

The afternoon dragged on and on and the bus accelerated and drove at breakneck speed along a crumbling ridge. However, the driver finally slowed a little after a rock smashed into the windscreen, leaving yet another crack.

Rain quickly turned into a heavy tropical downpour. Streams of water began to trickle through the windows. Meanwhile, the sun was fast descending through thin clouds of many colours high above a dark blue-grey mountain range on the horizon.

Gar then joyously declared that the bus driver was breaking Ethiopian law by driving after dark; that only one of the bus's headlights gave off any light; and that we were supposedly at the mercy of the bandits, or shiftas – said to be rife across that part of the country. Plus, he added, the chances of us finding a hotel for the night seemed slim.

I hadn't allowed for the possibility of being held up on a broken down bus in the middle of nowhere at night by bandits. Well, not since 1999 when I was mugged on a night bus on its way to Bethnal Green by a five-year-old kid wearing a hood.

The bus company, Northern Bus Routes, was part state-owned, so if a driver were to be prosecuted – as I hoped would happen on immediate receipt of my letter of complaint – then surely it would be a case of the state prosecuting the state? As I pondered the success of that action, the first vicious-looking flash of forked lightning lit up the sky ahead. There was a deafening clap of thunder, then immediately to our left and right two more forks, one hitting a hillside tree. Our route had converged with the front of a storm that now stretched behind as far as the eye could see.

'At least we can see the road now,' Gar remarked cheerfully.

On cue, there was a massive flash of light immediately to the left of the bus, accompanied by a colossal bang, and the rear end of the bus lurched downwards. Then it came to an abrupt standstill.

'Happy now? That was another bloody blowout,' I said, distinctly pissed off at being marooned in the middle of nowhere at the mercy of Ethiopian hoodies. 'This is precisely why I offered to pay for a minicab,' I added.

Gar ignored me and grabbed his camera.

'Yeah, don't miss riveting shots of wheel-changing after dark,' I called after him. The preacher shooshed me.

Wheel fixed, it was a further two hours before the bus reached the next town, where it was pursued by mobs of young people. God, I hoped they weren't the shiftas off to work.

No, they were all shouting 'Room! Room!' I looked around. Most buildings appeared to be offering accommodation of some description. This was where all buses heading north came to stop for the night. We had arrived at Debra Marcos about 10 hours late. I checked on the ticket to see if Northern Bus Routes was owned and operated by Transport for London.

The bus stopped in the courtyard of one of the town's hotels and we found ourselves surrounded on three sides by what looked like stable doors that in fact led to hotel rooms. People on and around the bus were scrambling as though they had all been simultaneously released by a very tight spring.

'Room! Room!' shouted the enthusiastic youths barricading our exit from the bus. We finally made it down the steps in a clutter of water bottles, notebooks and cameras.

Chapter Nine

Outside and inside loo

A tall, middle-aged local man forcefully pushed his way through the crowd and asked us in broken English what we were after.

'Teleportation to Bethnal Green?' I said.

Gar scowled and pointed at the roof of the bus, asking the total stranger if we should take our bags from the bus roof overnight.

'No,' came the too prompt reply.

Gar seemed happy with that. I most certainly was not. Now that I knew of the existence of shiftas, I was certain they were hiding in corners waiting to steal my battered, filthy rucksack full of drink and cheap tobacco.

'Are you sure my bag will be safe?' I asked, but 'want room?', 'yes,' and 'best hotel in town' seemed to be the sum total of his English vocabulary.

So I had no choice but to follow as Gar was led away.

We walked in silence through mercifully

diminishing crowds until we reached the grounds of a hotel a good mile from the town's centre.

The stranger took us to a dark, squalid fleapit of a room that was on offer at 10 birr (50 pence), and which he described as 'the best'. It had a dim light providing about half a watt of power and it offered the luxury upgrade of a padlock which we hired for a further 2 birr.

Too exhausted to put up any objection, I was horrified to later discover that if Gar had any sense we could have stayed in the Shebel Hotel, recommended by our erstwhile travel agent Tony. For a whole 20 pence more, I could have had my own room with a shower and loo.

Padlocking our hand luggage into our room, we headed off back into town where, not surprisingly, we were again harangued by crowds. I spied a café and dragged Gar inside. The place looked intriguing inside and ethnic enough to make Gar feel like he had come to the right place to eat like a local. Plus, the two girls behind the counter were as miserable as any I'd seen. I felt right at home.

I ordered a couple of dozen bottles of Meta beer and pointed at various items on the menu. Soon a 15-inch tin plate bearing a 16-inch pancake of the local bread arrived along with a greasy side tray of various vegetable and curry sauces.

Encyclopaedia Gar told me that the surface of the bread, known variously as injura, enjura and injera, had the appearance of pumice stone. And the texture of a foam mattress, I added, recalling my experience of dining on Ethiopian Airlines. Remembering some advice given by Tony Hickey, I ordered alicha – non-spicy – and (strangely) was not disappointed. The flavour of the sauces was more sweet than sour. However my hunger no doubt helped exaggerate the positive effect on the palate. I carefully avoided eating the tomato skins or outer skins of the onions in a bid to avoid food poisoning.

Unsuccessfully, as it turned out. Shortly afterwards I badly needed the loo. This involved crossing a courtyard in which two goats were tied up, standing head to head and fast asleep. At the far end of the courtyard I found the gents' urinal, which appeared to be a converted pig's trough. Or vice versa.

By the time I had returned to the café, Surly Girl Number One was investigating Gar's camera. He unzipped the bag and for a few moments they were all smiles until the moment the flash went off. Then it was back to scowling and finally we left to sleep.

At 5:00 am the next day and still in darkness, the street was already filled with hundreds of people, many carrying breakfast sticks of sugar cane. A few were asleep by the roadside.

A six-month-old baby that had been quietly mewing like a kitten for much of the journey on the previous day's bus ride was happily seated on the side of the road, chewing his own stick of cane. I approved. The impoverished parents of Africa appeared to know how to treat kids. My own sprout-loving compatriots had a lot to learn.

There was no sign of the bus and yet there were enough people waiting at the roadside to fill 20 buses. Suddenly I had the urge to go for another dump. Gar assured me that if our bus turned up he would hold it until I returned.

I didn't trust him. I ran 200 yards in the direction of the loo that I'd seen across the courtyard the previous night. I realised I had my backpack with me but I was desperate so had no time to run back and leave it with Gar. I made it to the loo, a square room featuring a hole in the middle of the floor. Shit was everywhere apart from a small area in the far corner of the room, so I flung the bag there before satisfyingly ejecting the remains of the previous night's curry. As I picked the bag up again, I noticed a certain moisture on the straps as I hung it across my back. I legged it back to the bus, which Gar was by now boarding.

We took the same seats as before and Gar resumed his usual state: sleep. With everyone back on board, the long-suffering vehicle gently shook into life and rolled back out of the town for the final, more peaceful stretch towards Bahir Dar.

About fifteen minutes into the journey the sun was up. I looked down and to my horror saw why my bag had felt moist. The corner patch of the loo had clearly not been so much shit-free as shit-filled. Strange we hadn't smelt it until now. Our noses were clearly on London time.

I nudged Gar. 'Wake up. Look what my bag's covered in.'

'Don't care,' he said, but then he smelled it, and sat to attention.

The extent to which I was covered in human excrement was truly incredible. It was down both sides of my back where I had worn the rucksack, down both my trouser legs from where I had put the bag after removing it from my back, and was plastered across the arms and back of the jacket I had borrowed for the trip. Gar's face was, as they say, a picture. The smell was now almost unbearable. Nobody objected when I opened the window this time. The preacher was too busy laughing.

Despite all the poverty and hardship these people had to undergo in their burdensome lives, and despite my comparatively extreme wealth, there was no question I was the most disgracefully turned-out person on the bus that day. I still have no idea how the Ethiopians managed to conduct themselves with such dignity, while keeping themselves so clean.

I whinged for a solid 30 minutes, until Gar told me to stop moaning about the shit and watch the passing scenery. He pointed at a spectacular parade of hundreds of people in bright white gowns, many of them carrying the distinctive Ethiopian flag. The sound of blaring trumpets faded as we passed on through another village.

It dawned on me that the last building I'd seen with glass windows had been the hotel in Addis Ababa.

Then I spied a man in full military uniform standing alone in an empty field. It was not apparent what he may have been guarding nor whether he would live to finish his shift since I could see what looked like a leopard stalking him one hundred metres or so behind his back. I watched until he was out of view. Still standing, as far as I could tell.

The bus braked hard and let off half the new passengers in a tiny place I can best describe as a lay-by. Just as it jolted back to life, the woman in the seat in front of me vomited onto her husband's lap. Clearly embarrassed, she had no means of wiping her hands or mouth. In a moment of rare empathy (given that I was covered in shit myself), I leaned forward and passed her the roll of toilet paper I had been using on my back, jacket, trousers and bag. Her expression changed from one of despair to extreme gratitude and she bowed a traditional Ethiopian thanks. It was slightly heart warming to see that the preacher managed to look at me without grimacing. It was also curiously relieving to notice that the pungent smell of her vomit had begun to overcome the smell I'd brought on board with me.

As we approached a little village named Cinjibara we passed a sign reading: 'Bank of Abyssinia 452km.' That piece of slope must be hot stuff to be advertised so far in advance. Apart from that one, nearly all the signs that we saw now appeared in Amharic rather than English.

The next town was named Bethlehem if the signpost was to be believed. I knew there was at least one town of that name since it had been marked on one of Pakenham's routes in the 1950s, but that had been about 150 kilometres east of where we were at that stage.

I was beginning to understand the scale of the difficulties confronting cartographers in Ethiopia – distance, pigsties full of poo, and shiftas – which is probably why they seemed to make most of it up.

Incidentally, there is also a town called Nazareth a hundred or so kilometres south of Addis Ababa.

We stopped and two more people disembarked. We kept our eyes fixed on the ladder at the rear of the vehicle to check that nobody was trying to remove our rucksacks, which were astonishingly still on board despite my prophecies of doom. Excitement built up on the street and people were shouting at the windows. More boarded to stand for the remaining few hours to Bahir Dar.

Nearing the northern-most Ethiopian province of Tigray there was a noticeable build-up of military vehicles. An operational army training camp came into view with huge mounds of ammunition and men parading in khaki.

Not that they were needed. This was only my first visit to Africa and I was pleased to notice the crowded bus held no delinquent youths, no rebellious children and no sulking adults (apart from me).

There are said to be over 80 distinct tribes in Ethiopia. We soon entered the domain of one whose uniform was a knee-length green cloak and a cattle stick.

Everything on the bus that was not nailed down,

meanwhile, was migrating northwards fractionally faster than the vehicle itself.

We came to another bus stop and once again I was baffled by the Amharic tongue. As the rear door opened, I am sure I heard one of the two young tribal Ethiopian men sitting directly behind us on the bus stand up and announce to his partner in a crisp Home Counties accent: 'I'm going to take a breather,' before disembarking. Gar's face dropped. He'd heard the same thing. We can't both have been hallucinating. We both began to laugh at the seemingly ridiculous coincidence of the two languages, then abruptly ceased when we noticed the looks of grave disquiet on the faces of our fellow passengers.

Judging by the looks on the faces of our fellow passengers, the men must have said: 'We must go quickly, our mother has just died.'

'Sorry,' I said, addressing the couple across the aisle. They bowled a scowl in return.

The bus banged on a few more kilometres before a new feature emerged – the abandoned tank. One, then moments later a second, then a third. Before long they were the defining characteristics of the countryside.

As if the journey hadn't been exciting enough, we then passed through a series of dust storms during the second of which the bus left the road when visibility became nonexistent. The open window meant a thick layer of dust built up over my shit-covered clothes.

Our driver managed to avert a head-on collision with an oncoming bus by putting his own vehicle into a skid. I could see the other bus's luggage was falling off piece by piece. It was being pursued on foot by an angry-looking man wearing a bicycle saddle strapped to his head with a piece of elastic, shaking his fist. I felt a certain kinship.

Next stop a conductor boarded to collect fares from the stragglers we had picked up that day. This caused pandemonium, but only by my own standards. It was not enough to cause the baby playing on the floor with his elder sister to do anything more than burst into laughter again.

As I waited for the conductor to do his business, I popped outside to do mine.

The town appeared to have a vibrant market with livestock, grain and other farm produce all up for sale. Small bonfires were burning in every spare space between each of the 30 or 40 fruit and vegetable stalls. Weren't these people hot enough?

And I swear to God I saw two zebras pulling along a gharry, which is Amharic for cart.

Finally, 320 kilometres from Addis Ababa, the bus rolled onto tarmac for only the second time on the journey. I was inconsolable with relief.

Chapter Ten

Half-star luxury and Insurance

To my great joy, Bahir Dar seemed less of a shanty town than the capital. A significant number of buildings had glass windows, and quite a few premises were built of real brick rather than stone cast-offs.

People seemed to be getting around on high quality, modern pushbikes. How they could afford them was unclear as there were no outward signs of wealth-creating industries. Other than the beggars, of course, who exceeded tourists by a ratio of about 100,000 to one. I assumed the bikes must have been part of an aid consignment.

The bus pulled into the station. Gar climbed back onto its roof and a group of youths working together surrounded us as he lowered each bag, all of which miraculously appeared present and correct.

'You need a guide,' came the predictable cry.

I turned my head sharply. 'No way,' I snapped. 'I'm going to the hotel down the road to wash and get some sleep.'

'You must have guide. We are students.'

Logic clearly had no place here. 'I don't care who you are. I must have shower and bed.'

'No, it is the law. We must take you to see the temple.'

Give me a break. 'What law says that?'

They ignored the question. 'You have to take a guide.'

When they wouldn't give up, Gar told them they could follow if they liked but were not getting any money.

'Why?' I snarled, trudging after them. 'Why?'

'This is the experience of a lifetime, Bill. Try to remember that, will you?'

This was nothing more than a means to an end, I told him. Without this trip, there was no book, and no book meant no job. And no more marriage, in all probability.

There was a ringleader. Lingren was his name; cajoling handouts from the unwary traveller his game. I kept insisting that he would get no money from us and he agreed, adding apparently spuriously that as this was a Wednesday, students provided their guide service for free.

'Free Wednesday. Is that the law too?' I asked, but Lingren just glared.

So we saw the temple (I managed to contain my excitement) and then we told Lingren to take us to our hotel (as chosen for us by Tony), but I noticed he was leading us in the opposite direction, according to my map. No way was I going to be stuck in some hut-like disaster when a palace was around the corner for the same price.

'We want the Dib Anbessa,' I said. 'Nowhere else.' To prove my point I stopped walking, and wouldn't move until Lingren demonstrated that the map of Bahir Dar in our guidebook was in fact drawn back-to-front.

True to his word, he delivered us to the door a few moments later. The hotel was one of those built in the late 1980s and early 1990s, when there had been a rapid growth in the construction sector. It wasn't bad, if you enjoy tasteless slab-on-slab architecture.

There was a vague smell of sewage everywhere in the hotel, or maybe it was just me. Gar went to check in while Lingren pointed out the bar in the hotel and led me towards it.

In Amharic he ordered two bottles of Pepsi and told the barman to put them on my account. The damage would be no more than a few pence so I shrugged and ordered a beer as well.

Lingren was only one of many who would con me into buying them a drink. He sat and told me he was spending the next year working in order to pay for his education.

This seemed to be a common theme. I had to wonder whether the education was worth having, given he had to spend time with gits like me.

The Pepsi was as refreshing as it could be when you are covered in shit. So refreshing in fact, that it took me ten minutes to realise Gar had left me at the mercy of the students and pegged it upstairs.

'Well, I've got to go. I stink,' I explained, standing up to leave.

Lingren nodded in agreement. It must be said that Ethiopians are polite to a fault. 'That will be 20 birr.'

'I thought we had an agreement?'

'That's okay,' said Lingren. 'I can wait down here until you come back, then I can show you some more things until you are satisfied.'

Blackmail? Was I being blackmailed into sightseeing? The thought filled me with horror, mostly because I knew Gar would insist upon it, so I dug deep and gave him a handful of birr and he left.

I went up to the room. Gar was emerging from the shower, looking refreshed. Bastard.

'You didn't end up giving him money did you?'

I didn't answer, just pushed him out of the way and headed into the bathroom, pulling my reeking clothes off as I went. As soon as I turned on the taps the floor flooded with cold water. Another quality Ethiopian construction.

When I told Gar he said that was nothing; when he'd touched the shower-head he had received an electric shock.

'Nice of you to tell me *after* my shower,' I said, although I suspect he might just have been exercising his sadistic tendency to alarm me.

Gar told that although I no longer smelled of sewage, we still had lots to do.

'Yes, sleep. Lots,' I said.

But apparently, sleep was not on the cards. According to Gar, we were working against the clock. Gar needed to find somewhere to check his emails in order to establish whether the Hot Rock truck had arrived in town from Sudan. We had to try out the walkie-talkies we'd brought with us, plus buy some scrubbing brushes and Omo to wash my shit-encrusted stuff, as the hotel's laundry was closed (or nonexistent).

'What about sleep?' I whined.

Gar, having been mostly asleep since we'd left Heathrow, didn't have any such requirement.

'It's just a coincidence that the washing powder in question shares its name with the Omo National Park, said to be one of the most beautiful parts of Ethiopia,' Gar told me, ignoring my need for sleep as he dragged me off to the shops. 'The original 1908 OMO powder was branded with the face of Old Mother Owl.'

A wealth of things better left unsaid is Gar.

There were no prices on the stuff in the boxy little establishment that stood a few feet from our hotel, so the boy serving us made up some price that was presumably extravagant by Bahir Dar standards. His face lit up when we didn't bother to haggle. Around 40p for two scrubbing brushes and a box of washing powder didn't seem excessive to us.

I returned to the hotel and dutifully began scrubbing away, in contravention of the house rules spelled out in about eighteen languages on the back of my bedroom door.

Meanwhile, Gar went off to find an Internet café from which to send his wife a message (which would also be passed on to Liz) – that we were alive and well and I was back at the hotel.

'Tell her I send my love,' I told him.

'He's covered in shit,' I discovered was what he actually wrote. 'It's not his own.'

I didn't know if that made it better or worse.

Gar returned to the hotel as I was rinsing the last of my washing. It was hard to see what I was doing – that half-watt lighting again, and the fact that I had no idea how to wash clothes.

The bedside lamp had no switch and it would be a brave man who tried to turn it on (which ruled me out). Two bald wires were sticking out of the top beside the bulb itself – très Parisien. Certainly an effective way of discouraging tourists from wasting that most scarce of commodities, electricity. Ethiopians complain that they pay more for electricity than anywhere else in Africa.

My travelling companion was in an unusually fetid mood. It had taken him an hour to receive one email and another half hour to send one. Furthermore Gar had received no word from the expedition. For all we knew they may have been over 100 kilometres north of Bahir Dar in Gondar, planning to set off to find Wehni the next morning, with us stuck Christ knows how many miles away.

I prayed to God that this was the case. If there was no word, surely we couldn't go anywhere? That meant precious sleep-filled hours for me.

But when I said this, Gar, ever the optimist, told me he hoped they were delayed in Sudan, perhaps due to waiting for a new vehicle part, so that we'd have a greater chance of meeting up with them.

Brilliant.

In an idle moment thinking of home I noticed that on my ticket was a note pointing out that Ethiopian Airlines required 72 hours advance confirmation of any return flight. This was puzzling: if you were on a long weekend trip presumably you'd need to reconfirm your return journey while airborne on your way out there. It was also going to complicate any escape plan.

I might, for instance, be back in Gondar, book myself onto a flight and then miss it thanks to a bus driver with a strange fixation for potholes. On the other hand, if I left the job of reserving my seat until I was back in Addis Ababa, I might have left it too late to travel before Gar caught up with and lynched me.

To my delight, Gar suggested that we skip sightseeing in Bahir Dar. My joy was short-lived, however, when he suggested we find the hotel where, if the truck had made it to town, the expedition would be camping. At least I would know for sure if I could justifiably slink off back to Addis Ababa and fly home.

'Just an hour of sleep,' I begged, but Gar was locking up the hotel rooms. He handed in our keys and I followed reluctantly as he strode off to find the riverside hotel.

About 50 would-be guides latched onto us.

We ignored them, so they sent in the big guns. A boy of 14 came up to us and said: 'Where are you gentlemen heading?'

I looked at him warily.

He continued: 'I don't want any money. Where are you from?'

'We live here,' I said, trying to put him off the tourist scent.

'I think not,' he said.

'No really, we live and work here.'

'I think not!' he said again.

We carried on walking. 'What do you do for a living then?' he asked.

'I'm a graphic artist and he's an archaeologist,' I said, picking up speed.

'You're a something artist', murmured Gar.

'I love archaeology, geography and history,' our would-be guide said perkily. 'I receive National Geographic magazine every month.'

'The English edition?' I asked pedantically.

'Of course. I met a man who works for it a while ago and he arranged me a subscription.' His English was impressive and he claimed to speak five other foreign languages. I suspected his greatest skill might lie in, well, lies.

Without taking a breath he told us of his plans to embark on a university course the following year, two years ahead of the normal age for doing so. He was the first student I was to meet who didn't stress the financial restrictions to such plans, and when I asked if this was something that he could afford, he dismissively replied that his father was a priest. I hoped to God he wasn't that preacher from the bus.

We couldn't outrun him so when we reached the edge of the local body of water – Lake Tana, about the only lake in the country – he was still in tow. We discovered his name was Insurance, because, he said, his elder brother had died at birth.

Before I had a chance to comment fully on the ridiculous nature of our small friend's name, some official, whose job appeared to be to prevent anyone from taking any pictures or having any fun whatsoever, approached Gar shaking a fist. Insurance intervened and explained that in order to take pictures Gar had to pay 4 birr (20p), which reluctantly he did.

'That's a bloody rip-off,' I told him. 'If he's an official then I am a qualified breast inspector.'

Insurance laughed out loud, probably at the likelihood of me having seen breasts of any sort. Gar insisted that once I'd spent more than a few days in Africa I would be displaying the same attitude. Only if it concerned obtaining copious amounts of alcohol, I retorted.

Clearly forgetting his mission to find the guys with whom we were supposed to go mountain climbing, Gar took photos of albatross-like birds that hung on the air above the lake and a hippopotamus standing a few feet offshore, its head and back protruding from the water. In the background a convoy of flying geese skimmed the lake.

Contrary to what I'd been taught at school, the Blue Nile River's source is apparently in fact some distance to the West of Lake Tana, through which it passes before resuming its journey south then northwest, or so Insurance told us. He said legend had it that the Nile, when it was first formed, asked permission to pass through the lake, and that the lake had refused on the grounds that the river would steal the lake's water.

'No I won't, I promise,' the river had assured the lake. 'Okay,' the lake had replied, 'on you go.'

'And sure enough it lived up to its promise,' said Insurance. 'In the rainy season you can actually see the blue colour of the Nile pass through the brown water of Lake Tana, and,' he added, 'the people of Addis Ababa travel up from time to time to take pepper pot-sized samples of the water in the belief that it is holy. We all laugh at them for doing this.'

Yeah, it must fill those long, TV-less nights.

'Do you have a guidebook?' asked Insurance, suddenly changing subjects.

I reached in my bag and his face dropped when he saw the one we had brought with us.

He pointed at the cover. 'I met this woman. She spent three days here and didn't write anything that I told her,' he said sadly. 'The book has many mistakes,' he said. He added that much of the historical detail in the book had been copied directly from a book published over a century earlier.

Well, that gave me a few ideas. Maybe I could write the rest of this book from the comfort of my

Bethnal Green sofa with missing springs and close proximity to a reliable boozer.

Insurance's revelations backed up our own experience of the guidebook. We'd tried to follow one of its maps, only to discover it had been drawn back to front.

It made Gar nervous. So nervous, in fact, that every time he consulted it he fretted. Should we trust the guidebook when it claimed the Internet wasn't available to tourists outside Addis Ababa and spend our remaining time in the capital catching up with correspondence? Or should we take a gamble on the basis that so much alleged information was proving to be inaccurate and look for a connection?

Obviously, I couldn't care less. 'Why should we believe this precocious 14-year-old upstart?'

Insurance told me the one book most Christian Ethiopians read is the Bible, every word of which they are taught to believe implicitly.

'So, the idea of having your attention drawn to something that may be inaccurate must vex you lot considerably,' I said. He just stared at me blankly.

In the event Gar need not have worried. I read on my return that despite its rave reviews, the guidebook appeared to be universally panned by anyone who had actually been to Ethiopia.

So much for the sofa/boozer idea.

Anyway, some of the information in the guidebook was, in fact, useful – for instance, the alleged rule that long distance buses must stop for the night by 6:00 pm.

'Yes, that law is always enforced,' said Insurance. 'Recently a lorry driver had converted his truck to carry passengers and arrived one evening in Addis Ababa at 9:00 pm. When people were seen climbing out he was arrested and sent to prison.'

I wanted to know if he was arrested for breaking the 6:00 pm rule, or for people trafficking, but Gar groaned so loudly at this suggestion that I didn't pursue it.

'It's because of the bandits,' Insurance explained soberly. 'They are active throughout the country. Not long ago a South African was driving his own car with his wife and two young children. He was shot because he didn't stop. They fired one bullet and killed him.'

Instinctively, I reached into my left jacket pocket to check my return ticket was there and the right one to reassuringly stroke my laminated note.

Insurance led us to a café to eat and even I have to admit this place was far superior to our most recent culinary experiences. I can quite honestly say that it consisted of far and away the best egg sandwich I had ever eaten. There were a few chips – or rather fried potato slices – a mild curry sauce, beetroot and mashed omelette in an absolutely delicious roll. You wouldn't think it from the foul-textured injera but the Ethiopians make superb bread. One quid covered two of these, two beers and a Pepsi for Insurance. Bargain. First decent bit of nosh I'd had in days. Despite my lack of sleep, I cheered up considerably.

We paid the bill and bade farewell to Insurance, who promised to help us catch a bus to Gondar if we were to turn up at the station the next morning. The hard-working lad's day consisted of waking at 5:00 am, running five kilometres to the bus station where he worked as a passenger assistant, running back at the end of his first shift to church, running back yet again to the station for another hour's work and then running on to school by midday.

'It keeps me fit,' he told us.

I did wonder if the bit about running was true since I never saw any other Ethiopians displaying a passion to make haste unless they were on an athletics field at the Olympics, but Gar told me I couldn't comprehend anyone doing any sort of exercise, which was true.

Finally remembering our original mission, we took a minicab up to the hotel where Gar assumed the expedition members would be staying if indeed they were in town.

Compared with the locals, we were living in luxury, taking a chauffeur-driven service (a Datsun Sunny) from one international hotel to another.

But on arrival, we couldn't find the Hot Rock guys. I made my way to the bar, ignoring Gar's protestations. As I relaxed at last on the terrace of the grand, dismally-run, depressing, over-priced and soulless Tana State Hotel, I watched a cavalcade of perhaps a dozen limousines (not Datsuns) sweep up the long driveway, accompanied by a police escort at least twice its length. From the limos emerged a delegation of Chinese diplomats who for the next couple of hours were treated to traditional Ethiopian singing and dancing by artists wearing the region's costume.

It seemed pretty tiresome but most of the delegates appeared quite content – hence my assumption that they were diplomats. Gar deemed it to be a picture worth shooting – the singers, the applauding diminutive delegates and the lake in the background – but on approaching the Amharic dancers, camera in hand, he was surrounded by three uniformed Ethiopian officials who calmly but firmly herded him back to his seat on the terrace.

'They didn't believe I was a tourist with all this gear,' Gar said, heaving several kilos of expensive-looking camera back onto the table.

'You should have told them you were the press,' I said. 'They'd have loved it.'

'They'd have locked me up,' retorted Gar.

Which I would have loved.

We concluded that Hot Rock was not going to turn up at the Tana Hotel that day. As we began to make our way back to our own hovel we had great difficulty negotiating our way forwards along the street.

Large groups of beggars with missing limbs or who were blind, deaf or simply hungry blocked our path. I felt conscious of the need to hold on tightly to my bag. However, as I was to discover, most Ethiopians are not thieves but are simply entranced by the sight of affluence, which they ask you to share with them. Why they were so entranced by me was difficult to identify. I am to affluence what a nun is to porn. Speaking of nuns, the Ethiopians were such God-fearing people that they would not dare to delve into another's pocket without permission.

Not if there was anybody watching, anyway.

By contrast, the warnings we'd read in our trusty guidebook were very much like descriptions one sees on ancient maps: 'Here there be monsters.' In the case of Bahir Dar: 'Here there be pickpockets.'

After my spending spree at the Tana Hotel bar, we had to get hold of some more money – our birr were fast running out and we would soon be left only with dollars. But there was still no such thing as a cash point machine in Ethiopia, and tellers in some of the country's largest banks claimed never to have heard of Visa, let alone a debit card. In keeping with what Tony Hickey had told us in Addis Ababa, I found hardly anywhere (apart from the airline) that would accept dollars for goods or services – not apparently the experience of the author of our guide book, it should be noted.

Finally, returning to our hotel, Gar let me sleep for a couple of precious hours, after which he brutally awoke me for dinner.

Insurance had recommended a restaurant that was apparently cheap, provided traditional Ethiopian food and could rustle up reliable ferangi (or foreign) dishes. The kid must have been getting a kickback, because here I was treated to some truly inedible food.

I ordered lamb. Gar said I should have known, having seen the kind of scraggy, skeletal sheep that bordered the roadside on our approach to the town, that a lamb dish would not be particularly palatable. Or, in fact, contain lamb. The dish arrived; pure gristle and rubber in a dark grey but very hot curry sauce. And I'd specifically ordered alicha – non-spicy. The function of the curry was presumably to prevent the meat from rotting any further.

As I gave up on my octogenarian mutton and Gar battled with his vegetable kebab, we discussed our options. Gar decided that if, as seemed increasingly likely, the truck was not in Gondar when we arrived the following day, then we would spend a night there before recruiting our own car and driver to take us to roughly where we believed the mountain to be. At that stage he was convinced its location was more or less due east of Gondar, rather than, as Pakenham's map suggested, southeast.

I suggested the option of returning home, which was met with a dark look.

Deciding that if I was forced to continue the literally shitty journey it would be in some semblance of comfort, I told Gar I would order a car and driver the following day to take us up to Gondar.

'Don't be ridiculous. It'd be a terrible waste of money,' he snapped. 'Besides, a bus gives you more to write about.'

'Oh, I've got plenty to write about, thanks. And anyway, it's my money and I shall waste it however I like,' I replied firmly.

He followed me to the hotel reception where I asked the woman on duty if she knew where I could get hold of a four-wheel drive car and a driver and, if she did, how much it would be. She made a brief phone call then hung up and told me it would be 75 dollars, a sum I conveniently had on me. Thankfully, this was one of the few places that accepted US dollars.

I asked to see what I'd be getting for my money.

'You have to haggle,' Gar insisted.

'The price seems perfectly fair to me,' I hissed. 'You can take the bus if you want, I'm going in this.'

'You're a fool,' he said and on seeing the vehicle, I was almost tempted to agree with him.

Gar pointed out three bald tyres but I did a deal at 75 dollars, the driver promising new tyres and to be ready by dawn the next day.

After packing, pretending to study maps and planning our strategy for meeting up with the Hot Rock truck – which by now was promising to be a most unlikely eventuality – I retired to the bar. The very idea that we wouldn't be meeting up with the expedition had cheered me immensely. Our plane tickets were open and, apart from giving 72 hours notice, I could fly back home in less than a week.

The stressful prospect of having to climb a mountain was starting to seem less likely by the minute.

Chapter Eleven

Wish I wasn't here

As it was the anniversary of the road accident that had, until then, given me licence to get out of doing things I didn't much fancy, I insisted we toast the occasion with a couple of dozen Meta beers. Shortly after, I was ready to retire.

I offered to pay the bill but Gar reached for his wallet and even left a tip. I worried for his health. In return the barman gave him a traditional mark of Ethiopian gratitude, holding back his sleeve to his elbow while holding out the palm of his hand. An incurable show-off, Gar claimed only ever to have seen this before in Mongolia. I told him I'd had something similar done to me in a British supermarket, although as I was queue jumping at the time, I suspected my version had nothing to do with gratitude.

Strangely, he didn't immediately tell me I was a twat.

I soon discovered why. He had decided to join

me in the jeep. I was gutted. I had been planning to head back in the direction from which we had come. In other words, to make a break for it.

'Are you certain you can forgo the experience of travelling by bus to Gondar?' I asked, desperately trying to sound casual.

'It's for your benefit. The bandits will have a field day with you.'

I objected vehemently on the grounds that I suspected a bandit and I would be on the same wavelength – doing anything it takes to get out of here.

Gar insisted we leave at dawn (even though I said the driver would wait for a week on the promise of 75 dollars), so we set out punctually from Bar Hadir at 5:00 am on the seemingly endless mission to find the bloody Hot Rock truck.

As we climbed into the car, its tyres still as bald as a blackboard, Gar confided in me: 'I feel shit.'

I looked down at the residue on my trousers and hands that the cold water had been unable to penetrate. 'Well, I look it,' I assured him.

As we began the drive through the city's calm – a place much cleaner than the capital, with noticeably fewer sleeping forms on the streets – religious chanting began playing through hidden loudspeakers. This was amazing: it suggested that somewhere nearby there was a power supply that actually worked.

Gar perked up, even though it was still ridiculously early, and began chatting to the driver, who displayed no reaction. Then my friend turned around and said: 'This is miles better than going by bus.' I glowered at him from the back seat. His prevarication had apparently freed him from any obligation to contribute towards the fare. It wasn't long before Gar had predictably nodded off.

After the ordeal of those long, sultry and terrifying hours of the previous two days, riding in the jeep felt like travelling first class – albeit in a Lancaster bomber. However, it was still almost impossible to take notes, despite the bumps being far less dramatic than on the bus. Owing to the fact that I had obstinately continued to be left-handed once my left side eventually recovered from childhood paralysis, my uncoordinated scrawl was illegible. In fact it was pretty illegible when penned sitting comfortably at a desk. Some things I could legitimately blame on my 1974 accident.

The hotel proprietor's son, David, was at the wheel. He was in his early twenties but was reassuringly keen to preserve the condition of his father's jeep.

'No, no,' he snapped, wagging his finger, when I attempted to light up one of my delightful Ethiopian cigarettes.

Unlike the bus, the car was equipped with suspension, so David was able to drive at up to 60 kilometres per hour rather than the steady 20 kilometres per hour of the bus. That meant I didn't have to wait so long to feed my various addictions.

Even at the greater speed, Gar's sleep was

comparatively uninterrupted. Despite the amount I was shelling out for this excursion, I didn't hesitate to wear a seat belt – once I'd found it. It felt crisp and new. My guess was that I was the first person to have used it.

After five minutes or so we reached the outskirts of Bahir Dar and the pothole-ridden tarmac turned to a rock-strewn dusty road surface. As we passed a side road, a man in a short pink skirt bowed low over his pushbike and crossed himself before mounting it and setting off in the same direction as us. It occurred to me that perhaps I should have done the same before embarking on this leg of the journey – crossed myself, that is, not dressed as a transvestite.

As we overtook more devout cyclists a bus was having its tyre changed and was surrounded by druid shapes in cloaks – a Tolkien convention, perhaps? We were then stuck behind a military truck that was struggling up a hill at no more than ten kilometres per hour.

'Come on, floor it David,' I called, feeling less concerned for my safety now that I had a seat belt tucked around my not-so-svelte waist.

Despite his concern for the condition of the car, David obliged.

What I couldn't see from the passenger seat was that thick dust eliminated the view of anything that may have been heading towards us in the opposite direction. As David began overtaking, the door against which Gar was sleeping swung wildly outwards. In the fraction of a second, as he passed from being sound asleep to wide awake, he performed a dramatic aerobatic manoeuvre and tried hoisting himself back into the vehicle.

'He insisted,' explained David, as he scrambled to avoid a collision with an oncoming car whilst Gar tried desperately to remain in the vehicle.

David slowed right down. 'Bill, you bloody f*ckwit,' said Gar, as he clung on to the car door, most of him outside the body of the car.

With both of them now not speaking to me, I wound my opaque window back down to admire the landscape, which curved around us like one of Gar's unfeasibly wide-angled shots. Grooved hills staggered into the far horizon. We passed a gleaming white UN four-wheel-drive Toyota having one of its wheels changed. Beside it were two young children who waved at us. Every UN vehicle we were to encounter throughout the trip was as white and clean as that one. They must have used a great deal of the precious water supplies of Ethiopia to keep their fleets so clean.

I wondered who it was the UN thought they were helping: Ethiopia or themselves. In Afghanistan, the 75,000 Toyota Landcruisers are locally referred to as 'the Toyota Taliban,' according to *Private Eye*'s correspondent in Kabul.

Every half mile or so men or women stood by the roadside with fruit for sale in each hand. They displayed no sign of pleading; just simply poised and looking bored out of their minds.

I felt for them, having had jobs like that myself, most notably an archaeological dig.

An hour into the journey we had passed perhaps a dozen vehicles, many parked by the roadside having their wheels changed. Whether this phenomenon was due to the quality of the roads or tyres I wasn't sure.

Most of the time drivers determinedly stuck to the left side of the road, only shifting back to the right at the very last moment, as if they hoped the obstruction might miraculously vanish before they got to it.

I knew Ethiopians were a suspicious bunch but the conviction that the road was always smoother on the other side seemed a little far-fetched.

During our journey we noticed many people carrying produce or herding cattle between towns and villages. Many of them walked unthinkably long distances and a fair number of those we passed must have set out from Bahir Dar hours before we did.

Gar suggested we might offer one of them a lift, but David misunderstood and said, 'No goats in car. No, no.'

I was glad to hear it. Having paid good money for this relative luxury, I had no desire to recreate my bus journey hell.

David turned on the car radio. A dulcet Ethiopian song was followed by someone called Kylie's latest song and after this came a radio phone-in. 'Hello – how are you?' began the announcer, before the conversation turned back to Amharic. I was fascinated by the pick-and-mix English. As a journalist, some pick-and-mix Amharic might come in handy. I asked David how to translate 'Now you big tosser, what have you got to say?' but he ignored me, pointing instead at the radio with a broad smile on his face.

'Aster Aweke!' he exclaimed.

I didn't understand. He repeated it then waved at the small town we were passing through. 'This singer!' He was gesturing vigorously at the dashboard. 'She was born in this town.' The town in question was Begemdr.

'Who is she?' I asked.

David glanced across at me in a way that suggested I was a complete idiot, before repeating her name again with an almost indiscernible shake of his head, indicating that was as far as the conversation would be going. I wondered if it would help pointing out that I knew nothing about modern British pop artists either.

'All pop singers are worthless to me,' I told him.

Gar opened one eye to say, 'Shut it, Bill.'

Later I discovered that the jazz singer is in fact extremely prolific and successful, and the daughter of a wealthy government official. Gondar is her official place of birth, but as the Gondar province covers an area of over 30,000 square kilometres (more than a fifth the size of the United Kingdom), David could well have been right.

We approached another town, Warrata or

Woreta, depending on which sign you chose to believe. David ploughed through a small group of wood pigeons, then a few yards on braked heavily to allow three hens to strut across the road. My head almost hit the windscreen.

'Why not just run them down too?' I asked, but David just shook his head again and focused on the road. Later I discovered that this attitude to animals was fairly consistent among all the drivers in the country. If an animal provides food then it is important to slow down and treat it with the utmost respect.

Donkeys and pigeons by contrast got a raw deal – I was to see plenty of dead or injured donkeys that had obviously been hit by passing vehicles. It has to be said that donkeys are stupid creatures and tend to graze in the middle of the road. Goats must be cannier because I didn't see any of them having dinner in the face of oncoming traffic.

We stopped for air at the Addis Tyre centre – 'addis' being Amharic for 'new', and tyre presumably translating as 'busted' or 'blown'.

Several locals came up to greet David and swap stories. They were all clad in rags yet had pruned themselves and their attire enough to make them look perfectly respectable.

Gar awoke and disembarked for a few moments to take a picture. Miraculously, there were no officials on hand to demand payment for the privilege.

As we moved on I caught sight of an ominous mountain range we were clearly going to have to negotiate. A great pinnacle soared into the sky on our approach to the next town, Addis Zemen, which, incidentally, is also the name of Addis Ababa's official Amharic daily newspaper.

Gar told an interesting but crude local story about the landscape of that region. On the border between Gondar and Gojjam provinces the mountains are distinctly thumb-shaped. Gojjam women are not traditionally circumcised and are supposed to have large clitorises, something celebrated in song and poems. As you drive from Gondar this rock formation is, therefore, supposed to indicate that you are entering clitoris country.

'Good news, hey David?' I responded, winking at the driver. He ignored me.

As we approached the crest of the mountain, a bus careered towards us down the hill. David had no choice but to take to the ditch on our right to avoid a collision. My nerves once again began to fray, but my concentration was quickly diverted as the view on top of the mountain began to pan out. In spite of my natural tendency to flee, the shape, colour and scale of the mountain range took my breath away. It was as if the eruption of a thousand volcanoes had been frozen mid-blast.

'Volcanic plugs,' Gar explained, slowly as if I were thick. 'You should write that down.'

'You said you'd stick to photography,' I said.

I managed to nod off, and when I awoke I had the sense that we were approaching another major town – perhaps even Gondar. Steel electricity pylons appeared, in place of striped eucalyptus trees supporting the cables.

It was also apparent we were entering the territory of Men with Rifles. A rifle appeared to be the manbag of the Gondar region.

We stopped at a crumbling ruin and I asked what it was. Having no idea, David asked a passing shepherd in Amharic. The reply was that it was the 16th century Castle of the Fasils, which according to our now totally discredited guidebook, was supposed to be in the city of Gondar itself.

As we moved on we saw three shoeless young women trying to get their two stubborn mules to budge. Despite their predicament, they smiled broadly and waved as we passed.

'Are they just friendly, or are they selling something?' I asked. But of course Gar was asleep, and David wasn't so eager to talk to me.

The crowds now gathering on the road were of a completely different tribe from the last ones we'd encountered only a few kilometres back. Their cattle sticks were of a uniformly darker wood, their cloaks almost a pure white. Once again I marvelled at the ability of these people to keep so clean. Washing powder companies should use them in their advertising: 'Tell us, how do you keep your shepherd's cloak so white and bright?'

But looking at the place I had little faith in the TV reception.

We hit the village of Maxenete, whose name was revealed by yet another bewildered villager. Two kilometres down the road, at the other end of the plain was the village of Saydar, notable for having a local population that wore no shoes of any kind, despite the land there being particularly rocky. Perhaps the cost of guns restricted the purchase of footwear?

As Gondar came within our sights, so did a massive build up of military activity.

'Maybe they knew you were coming,' commented Gar, which got a laugh from David.

On the fringe of the city's outskirts, and the location of the airport, was a comparatively modern town called Azozo. 'The first city of Gondar,' David said, suddenly talkative now that Gar was awake. 'For the past 30 years it has been a soldiers' camp.'

Many of the new buildings in Azozo were surrounded by wooden scaffolding reminiscent of the bamboo kind used on the skyscrapers of Hong Kong. Another ten or so kilometres to the north, in the valley ahead, was the city of Gondar itself. A sea of tin roofs stretched into the surrounding hills.

David took us up to our chosen hotel, the Goha, set on a private road at the peak of Genet Terara. 'The mountain that overlooks the city was known as Tigre Me'choya until the early 1980s,' Gar told his captive audience.

Despite my concerted efforts to look bored Gar continued the travelogue.

'Just over 30 kilometres north of Lake Tana and situated on a flat volcanic ridge some 2000 metres above sea level, Gondar was founded as the new capital city by the 17th century King Fasil. It served as the imperial headquarters for many generations and is surrounded by rings of mountains, which have provided military protection for centuries.'

'Do you think the hotel room will have a bath?' I asked.

Ignoring me, Gar continued. 'Gondar's predecessor was Gorgora. Legend has it that Fasil was inspired to locate his new city in Gondar because of a prophecy that Ethiopia would achieve its greatest power if its capital was established in a place whose name began with the syllable 'Go'.'

So much for prophesies.

As we pulled in to the hotel's car park there was no sign of the Hot Rock truck. Gar's expression turned from excitement to one of deep despair, whilst mine turned from deep despair to extreme exhilaration.

'This has all just been a waste of time, hasn't it?' he said, with uncharacteristic glumness.

Finally, someone agreed with me. And the good news continued: Gondar had an airport, and London was just two flights away.

We checked into the hotel at the huge price of 36 dollars per room – thirty times what we may have paid for a single room in a lesser hotel in town.

Gar started on about the price but I smiled and ignored him, paid and dumped my bags in the room. Then I left to sit and admire the view of the city, drink some ice cold beer and calculate how many hours before I would be sitting in my local boozer.

I was able to relax for the first time since I got on the plane at Heathrow, and was about to have a nice doze when I was brought to my senses by what looked like a cross between a wasp and a bumble bee the size of a small bird that was circling a foot or two above me.

I leapt to my feet. 'WHURGHHH-HHH-AARRGGGGHHH!'

'What's the matter now?' asked Gar, hardly looking up from where he sat on the terrace.

I was running around in a zigzag in an attempt to avoid pursuit by the insect. You've not witnessed sheer cowardice till you've seen me in the company of a wasp.

'I haven't got any anti-histamine!' I cried, slapping my arms about.

'You've tried pretending you're allergic to wasps before and it simply isn't true,' he retorted.

Shit. Had I?

I had assumed that since we were so high up there would be no mosquitoes. Then I noticed two large red blotches on my right hand that at first I had incorrectly attributed to sunburn. Within a short time two large insect bites were visible and growing. There were plenty of massive flies too, all with hairy armpits.

I'd forgotten quite how much I hated insects. Doubtless they speak more highly of me.

I sat down again, this time opposite Gar.

'I suppose it'd be asking too much for there to be anything to eat.'

'Plenty,' he said, sliding a crumpled brown piece of paper across the table towards me.

'It's all in Amharic,' I said in dismay.

Gar sighed. 'Other side.'

I turned the paper over and sure enough there was a list in English of unpalatable-sounding foodstuffs. I stared at it in disbelief. What the hell was hot pea flower sauce? 'I'll start with the spiced beef jerky, and then I'll have a main course of barley gruel.'

'So don't eat.'

But I had to eat something. I settled for spiced tripe with broad bean bread. Heaven knows why. I hate broad beans. Gar chose a side dish described on the menu as 'spinach like plant sauce nettle' because, he explained, he'd never tried nettle. I went indoors to the cafeteria and placed the order and returned with a bottle of beer.

Gar wanted to discuss our strategy as we waited for the culinary delights to arrive. 'Strategy' essentially meant deciding whether to hang around waiting in vain to meet the truck or simply returning home without a story. No prizes for guessing that I plumped for option two.

'The Hot Rock truck could be days getting here if it hasn't already been and gone,' I concluded. 'If we wait another few days then we will have to spend a fortune on hotel rooms.' That'd work, I thought, because if Gar was afraid of anything, it was wasting money.

After staring at maps for about an hour, Gar's

solution was to check into a cheaper hotel in Gondar itself. The National Hotel, he said, was advertised at about a quid a night. Clearly he was not quite ready to give up. Gar pointed out across the distant mountain ranges to our east. 'It's over there.'

Just then, the concierge stepped through the open French windows and approached us with a tray which he placed on our table. He was grinning. Did he know something we didn't? I stared at my plate and my heart sank.

Balancing the prospect of eating the hideous stuff in front of us with that of starvation, Gar devoured his meal, finally using strips of injera to polish clean the surface of his plates.

When I could bear it no more, I stormed off to retrieve a can of All Day Breakfast from my rucksack. Lying on my bed I digested the best meal I'd eaten since my last can of All Day Breakfast.

Still insisting that we check out the next morning, despite the fact that the meeting point with Hot Rock was the grounds of the Goha Hotel, Gar told me we would have to keep making the trek up the mountain from wherever else we would be staying in town. Apparently the Goha Hotel's staff couldn't quite grasp the concept of passing on a message.

Gar had spoken to the manager the previous day by phone, asking to leave a message for Dave Lucas, leader of the Hot Rock expedition. Gar wanted him to tell Dave that we would be arriving a day later than expected.

When Gar then asked to revise the message, the

deputy manager denied that any such message had been left.

After commiserating with Gar, I returned to the hotel room for some cigarettes. As I passed reception, I witnessed a scuffle. It was the manager, a large, gruff fellow, taking over at the reception desk, seemingly by force. I slyly told Gar he might have better luck with this new guy, more for my own amusement than anything else. Gar went to ask him if a Dave Lucas had arrived at the hotel.

'My name is Gar Powell-Evans.'

The sour manager's face didn't brighten as he picked up the phone and called the room of a hotel guest named Paul.

'Mr Paul, Mr Dave is here,' the manager said down the phone, as I roared with laughter in the background.

No matter how much one pays, the comparatively expensive, government-run hotels in Ethiopia all seem to feature regular power cuts, intolerably poor plumbing, broken tap handles, toilets that do not flush and service that involves inane grinning and nothing much else.

Chapter Twelve

Ruins and other worthless pursuits

It was mid-afternoon when we set off by cab to see Gondar, planning to return later that day to find out if the truck had arrived. My mood was improving with every hour the truck failed to materialise.

A sea of the town's inhabitants, all crying 'Mister! Mister!', was unsurprisingly there to greet us as we emerged from the hotel.

I would have offered them a couple of birr to be rid of them (and to annoy spendthrift Gar), but I was all out of local currency, so our first port of call was the bank. It was a grandiose building of Italian design overlooking a bleak concrete town square.

Two uniformed officials guarded the entrance. As we approached, Gar was ordered to leave his camera bag outside, which he pointedly refused to do. You've not seen jobsworths till you've visited an Ethiopian bank. I nudged Gar, who of course still had cash left, and he handed them each a 5 birr note.

They both looked furtively around before snatching the bribes and we were allowed to proceed on the strict condition that Gar did not unzip the bag.

We had quickly established that Gondar was another major Ethiopian city which did not deal in credit cards so we went straight to the foreign exchange counter. We pooled our dollars rather than going twice through the time-consuming process of counting them out, calculating the transfer rate, adding four rates of tax, then subtracting some percentage or other.

While we waited, we could see our papers and cash progressing through four or five different stages, forms filled out in triplicate at each stage. It was almost as tortuous as filling in a US Immigration form on a plane.

I glanced at the *Ethiopian Herald* beside us. It was dated Yekatit 8, 1994.

'Like a bloody doctor's surgery,' I grumbled.

'Ethiopia still uses the Julian calendar,' said Gar, happy to pass the time by subjecting me to a lecture on the Ethiopian calendar. 'By the Gregorian calendar that paper was printed no later than 15 March, although . . .'

Despite my total lack of interest, Gar droned on. 'The 13-month Ethiopian calendar – 12 months of 30 days and one of five – is approximately seven years and eight months behind the Gregorian calendar. They have their leap day every four years, 15 months before the rest of us.'

'Fascinating,' I said.

'Incidentally, Christmas day,' announced Gar, 'is the seventh of January in Ethiopia.'

'That answers the question, 'Do They Know It's Christmas?'' I said, to resounding silence.

Eventually our clerk, having received the order for a cash exchange, summoned us to the counter. We rose and approached the desk, where we were both ordered to present our passports again.

'Technically only one of us is changing foreign currency,' I retorted, but Gar hissed that if I made a scene he would give the street beggars my hotel room key.

Behind the clerk sat four men counting through piles of bank notes. The Ethiopian birr is not what I would call a currency. It cannot be taken into or out of the country; can only be exchanged in the country itself; and after a couple of days in one's pocket the notes deteriorate to ragged, black pieces of worthless paper which few traders will accept.

However, Gar was delighted with the total fixed commission fee, which came to 5 birr, or around 25 pence, rather than a percentage of the sum exchanged.

After two hours in the bank, we stepped blinking onto the bright African street and went to find an Internet café. Unfortunately the Ethiopian Telecommunications Corporation (ETC) had a monopoly over Internet provision, which was both expensive and dial-up. Phone calls were also very pricey and unreliable. It was like mainland Europe: the worse the service, the higher the price.

'The latest available figures suggest there are just three lines per thousand people in Ethiopia,' Gar helpfully told me.

The rate per minute charged by the Internet café for using the machines was 1 birr whether we were online or not – and most of the time we weren't. I wanted to leave but Gar of course was made of sterner stuff and continued to try and send and receive a couple of emails. The woman in the café kept insisting he was connected, even though the service had been static with no data transfer for over an hour. I began to understand why my brother, who lived in Zambia, never replied to my emails.

Finally admitting defeat, we left. Gar was eager to find the tourist office and establish whether anyone there had any clue as to how we might find Mount Wehni.

I lagged behind, not wanting to encourage him. There was so much Italian influence in the city and not just the architecture. I pitied the Ethiopians for having been occupied by Mussolini. It was the Italian fascists' beastly use of chemical weapons there (among other things) that led to widespread League of Nations condemnation and liberation by the allied forces – notably the British – in 1941. That year Haile Selassie was brought back from exile in the UK to resume power until being overthrown in 1974 by the Derg, the communist regime under Colonel Mengistu Haile Mariam who is said to have assassinated Selassie a year later. He allegedly had him smothered with a pillow and his remains thrown down a pit which was hidden beneath his desk.

As I stood on the street getting my bearings a smartly-dressed middle-aged man came up to me. He introduced himself as Gislassie Gimoriam and claimed to work for the National Tourist Office located across the street. This could have been just the man I was looking for (to organise my flight home); or someone who just fancied a free drink from a gullible tourist.

Gar asked if he knew the whereabouts of Mount Wehni and Gislassie gave a nod convincing enough to persuade even Gar to buy him a bottle of Pepsi. He promptly began to tell us all about the sights and monasteries he would take us to visit in Gondar. Gar kept trying to persuade him we were not conventional tourists and just wanted to find the mountain. 'Wehni, yes,' he repeated. 'Churches is nice – ancient tombs and monasteries here.'

'Please!' Gar said firmly. 'Where is Mount Wehni?'

He nodded. 'Is near Sudan.'

'It's not near Sudan,' I said.

'Is 150 kilometre west.'

'It's not,' I insisted, beginning to tire of him.

He thought for a minute. 'Is a drive east then a half hour walk.' This sounded promising (although a promising answer was inevitable given the number of permutations of travel, distance and direction suggested by this time).

We managed to persuade Gislassie to take us

directly to the tourist office itself, bypassing visits to monasteries, churches and ancient tombs.

'Do you have a map showing the mountain's location?' I asked when we reached his office.

'Yes,' he said, unconvincingly.

'Where is it?'

He pointed to what was apparently the only map in the building, stuck slightly askew on a once-white wall. It was a 1:1,000,000 map of Ethiopia.

We walked out and were not pursued.

Gar insisted we take a walk to see some of the ancient ruins of Gondar, calling firstly at a closed circular church. We had an eager guide lead us voluntarily to the locked doors and then demand 2 birr or we would not be able to leave. We hastened away and thankfully were not followed.

As we approached a haggard old woman standing on the pavement, she presented us with a novel approach to begging: whistling to draw attention to an opened top and exposing a saggy right breast at which she was pointing.

It was quite alarming.

'It's not exactly going to give you a stiffy, is it?' I exclaimed, guffawing happily to myself as we made our way on up the hill.

'It's interesting what amuses you,' Gar noted, unimpressed.

We carried on up the hill to the fort, where we were charged 50 birr – about £2.50 – to enter the castle grounds. Gar was incensed, because for locals the price was 3 birr (15 pence). This appeared to be the standard scale of tariff throughout the country where we were concerned. Some 40 years earlier Barbara Toy, when researching *In Search of Sheba,* had only been asked to stump up two Ethiopian dollars – around 16 pence – to see one of the churches in Axum.

Fasil Castle, said (by those who had clearly never visited it) to be the highlight of Gondar, was built in 1632 and was closed due to reconstruction – according to a gothic-looking sign which itself was carved in stone. Apparently the castle had been closed since soon after it was built. Well worth the five quid entry fee.

We strolled back into town to find a taxi to the hotel. On hearing our foreign voices, an elderly man hobbled towards us with a walking stick. His eyes appeared to have been completely gouged out.

'What does he want?' I cowered behind Gar.

An urchin nearby piped up: 'Mister, he wants you to help him!' I reached out and placed a birr note in the palm of the old man's hand and his expression, if not his eyes, lit up.

No taxi and an hour's walk later we were back on the hotel terrace again. Across the valley we could see a storm heading our way, outlined in its entirety from cloud to ground, end to end, approximately 16 kilometres away.

For some inane reason, Gar asked one of the bar waiters whether there was access by foot to the hotel up the mountainside – he called it a hill – rather than via the long road that wove its way to the hotel.

There was indeed, he was told, at the far end of the grounds. Gar set off eagerly and once again I had no choice but to follow. Of course, we got to the top as the storm hit, so there was no option but to turn around and immediately return.

Taking my first step on the descent of the mountain I slipped, gashing my knee on a rock. Notebook in one hand, pen in the other, I had absolutely no balance.

'I thought these bloody mountain boots were supposed to help me stand up,' I shouted – they were going straight to the charity shop when I returned.

I picked myself up and resumed the steep descent, falling a few more times on the way. I was in an exceptionally bad mood. I had been suckered into a climbing expedition and I hated climbing. At the same time the mosquito bites on my right hand were causing it to swell painfully. Gar was soon out of sight. Bastard.

Somehow I made it to the foot of the mountain. It had taken two hours for what should have been a half hour jaunt. Judging by the expression on his face Gar was finally having serious doubts about my ability to go hiking to find the legendary Mount Wehni.

I thought I'd try the concierge for some kind of antiseptic lotion. 'Sudocreme?' I enquired.

'Alcohol,' he replied, and showed me a bottle of what looked and smelled like iodine before making a brief phone call.

I asked for a swab.

'She's getting it,' said the concierge in reaction to my impatience.

'She' turned out to be a nurse clad in full uniform, complete with hat. Her medical duty on that occasion was to deliver a roll of toilet paper. Mission accomplished, she disappeared into the office for a few moments to register in triplicate the administration of three sheets of toilet roll and a dash of iodine, despite the fact it was actually applied by the concierge rather than the nurse herself.

I left for the terrace to imbibe some more alcohol, by mouth this time.

The storm settled in with the darkness. We were still on the terrace when all of a sudden the lights went out again. At that precise moment the hotel shook as it was hit by a bolt of lightning. One of the other guests was thrown across the terrace. He had been leaning against a supporting pillar that absorbed much of the shock. The sound was absolutely terrifying, roaring on for an incredibly long time.

I grabbed hold of Gar, shivering. After a few moments he slapped at me as if I was a mosquito, so I cowered by a rock.

Then two concurrent bolts of lightning caused another fearsome explosion, simultaneously hitting what looked like a fig tree at the crest of the mountain, and the water that had settled beside an empty swimming pool.

Gar pushed me off his lap and suggested we trek down the mountainside to get dinner somewhere in town. 'We can get in some mountain climbing practice.'

'Have you noticed the torrential downpour?' I asked, annoyed.

'You need to practise walking down mountains in the dark.'

Once again I seriously wondered why he had conned me into joining him in the first place. He knew what I was like.

The lights came on again, interrupting my quickly evolving escape plan, and I managed to convince Gar we should eat at the hotel, which continued to live up to its own unexacting standards of excellence.

'Can we see the à la carte menu please?' Gar asked.

'Yes,' replied the waiter, who duly brought it across to him. He studied it for a few moments before asking if he could have the chicken.

'No chicken,' the waiter said.

'Beef?'

'No beef sir, no.'

It transpired that yes, he could indeed see the à la carte menu but no, he could not in fact order anything from it.

Two Britons at the next table asked the same question and as the waiter obligingly fetched said menu, I turned and warned them to expect disappointment. Then the lights went out again and tea light candles were brought to each table. We finished the only available dish – fish, which seemed a safer option than the product of malnourished cattle in any case – before settling the bill and adjourning to the bar. To my dismay, we were informed it was just closing. It was 10:30 pm.

'That is deplorable,' I said.

'Good,' Gar said. 'I desperately need an early night.'

Just as we were leaving the two people who'd been dining at the next table arrived. Nadim was a doctor based in London and his friend Richard was an artist who had recently been shortlisted for the Turner Prize.

I sadly informed them that the bar was closed, but that didn't seem to faze Nadim. He helped himself to half a dozen bottles of beer from the fridge behind the bar – bottles for which he told us he had every intention of paying.

'What a life,' he said, 'holed up in a candle-lit Ethiopian bar opening bottles of beer on our lap so the barman doesn't notice we're drinking.' I looked over at the barman. He was unlikely to notice anything while fast asleep on a sofa at the far end of the bar.

Just then Nadim noticed that his actions had in fact been clocked. 'Leave this to me!' he commanded and, turning to the approaching waiter, reached in his pocket and brought out two 10 birr notes.

The waiter just looked at them.

Nadim brought out a couple more and thrust them into his hand, saying: 'For you!'

This time the man took them. Transaction

complete, Nadim first gestured at the beers he had already procured and asked to pay for them, then asked us what we wanted to drink. The waiter-turned-barman was in the process of fetching the round of drinks when the barman himself awoke, crossed the bar and said: 'No!' looking daggers at us all. The waiter tapped his shoulder and waved some birr, splitting the bribe between them. He then resumed his duty while the barman went back to sleep. How very civilised.

We supped the local gin as Gar carefully explained to our new acquaintances the complex dilemma confronting us. What Nadim then had to say was potentially to rescue Gar's trip, at the same time scuppering any plans of an early end to my hell.

'We have a car and a driver which we have paid for but no longer need. You're welcome to them,' he said. He and Richard were heading off east the following day, to the Dalol depression in the Afar region, the lowest place on Earth and every bit as warm as Death Valley in California.

Afar, he told us, was where traces of some of man's oldest ancestors have been found, including the three million-year-old Australopithecus Afarensis, better known as Lucy, and the four and a half-million-year old Homo Ramidus Afarensis.

Gar was beside himself with glee and quickly accepted the offer.

To match my mood, the fearsome weather continued its attack. Rain hammered on the roof and window panes and lightning streaks made like a disco strobe.

I downed a long swig from someone else's bottle of Bati Beer. The waiter who was now our barman was fast asleep too and Nadim helped himself to more bottles from behind the bar, leaving the money on the counter. I had to hand it to the Ethiopians for their diligence in honouring their bribes.

Finally, I headed off to my room and passed out, but was awoken later in a state of panic at loud knocking. Shit. I must have missed check-out time at the hotel.

But no. It was Gar, shouting over and over again that the truck had arrived.

I was certain it was a nightmare. The power was still off and I banged my toes on my rucksack as I staggered across to open the door.

But it was no dream. There stood Gar, grinning and clapping his hands. It had just gone 4:30 am, and the Hot Rock guys had arrived.

The expedition was still on. My heart sank even further.

Chapter Thirteen

Nutters and a truck

The next morning, Nadim walked over to introduce us to his driver. I desperately wanted to take that easy option but could see no choice but to turn it down in favour of a truck heading for the wilds of Ethiopia. I hesitated, then said: 'Thanks for the kind offer. Things have taken an unexpected turn.'

'For the best, I hope?' replied Nadim.

'Not really,' I mumbled.

The first 'Hot Rocker' I met was Dave. He had a broad smile and far too many teeth. Originally from the Isle of Wight, he had a broad West Country accent. He was leader of the three-year global expedition (now just fourth months into its world tour), and described the expedition as 'the most exciting climbing road trip ever undertaken.'

It planned to take in 55 countries, 100 000 kilometres of road (or track), 500 climbing areas and 'improbable amounts of stories, beers and laughs along the way'.

Improbable amounts of beer I could deal with. As for the rest . . .

Its route would cover the length of the Nile, from the start of the Andes to the end of the Rockies, across the Himalayas and around the entire world from East to West. Once finished, the so-called Hot Rock truck would become the first convertible truck to have made it from end to end of all six continents, according to Dave.

Its first trip had taken it from Cape Town to Nairobi. Its second ran from London to Hong Kong – the Silk Route. On its latest journey it would drive to many unclimbed mountain peaks around the world. The truck could carry up to 35 passengers.

It was only 9:30 am, but as the expedition had just entered Ethiopia after two months in the dry country of Sudan, Dave ordered himself a beer.

Gar eagerly showed him the maps we had found, highlighting the area the mountain was believed to be situated. Dave appeared delighted with the research already undertaken. His face lit up when he saw the pictures in Pakenham's book and his delight grew when I showed him the passage explaining that even good ol' Pak had failed to land in a helicopter. There was further joy when Gar revealed we had learned from Tony Hickey: that the 1999 Royal Marines expedition had been aborted.

Gar and Dave then started to talk about the various climbing routes they could take to the top. They studied photos of the ominous Wehni mountain taken from a variety of angles: surrounding hills and, in one photo, from the helicopter commandeered by Pakenham.

The state of complete relief in both Gar and Dave was incredible to see: Gar because he had met up with the expedition; Dave because he was in a bar and not a Sudanese desert. They talked enthusiastically about how and where they had already climbed; how they were going to climb; and about the kit they had brought with them – full lead rack, including cams, rocks, hexes, quickdraws, screwgates, slings, ascenders, descenders and a portaledge.

I had no idea what they were talking about. I just wanted to put my hand up and ask if I could go home early.

We paid the hotel bill. The manager refused to give us the discount we had demanded to compensate for the lack of power. I suppose it made good commercial sense. I'm sure we weren't the first to have made such a request.

As the three of us rolled down the mountainside to join the rest of the expedition (in a cab that didn't appear to have any brakes), Dave reminded us that they had all just emerged from a dangerous and thoroughly exhausting two weeks of hell in Sudan. 'Treat us gently,' he warned.

Their troubles had apparently started in Sudan when the truck broke down in Wadi Halfa, but it could have been a whole lot worse. As luck would have it they were just four kilometres from an old goldmine in its final stages of use and whose mechanic, Rafael, was said to be the best welder in Africa. 'We were having to drive at one kilometre per hour because the springs were f*cked,' said Dave. The truck received a fresh coat of paint while they waited, including the inside of the cupboards, which had become almost black with dirt.

Riveting stuff.

Our cab pulled in to the Terara Hotel's grounds and I caught my first sight of the truck.

It was like nothing I could ever have imagined and certainly the largest road vehicle I'd ever seen.

A huge, red, converted Scania 112 articulated vehicle, with two decks of purpose-built, spacious accommodation for 35 passengers on top, and every conceivable piece of equipment below. It appeared to accommodate anything one might need for travelling around the world, right down to its own bar, a 'sin bin' (for couples desiring a bit of privacy), a coffin, a compartment with four spare wheels and a firewood store. At the rear end of the truck was a climbing wall – a useful feature in case you were stuck for two weeks in the Sudanese desert miles from any rocks, apparently.

With a wheelbase one and a half times the length of a conventional truck, one outer wall of the beast was decorated with an outline of the world and a dotted line indicating the Silk Route, while the other side bore a caricature of the Silk Route, featuring the Taj Mahal and a desert scene.

I went through to the hotel's garden where I met those from the expedition who were neither showering nor out buying beer, cigarettes or other provisions. They were almost black with filth and looked shattered, just as Dave had warned us.

At first we didn't arouse a great deal of interest in the climbers, whose topics of conversation were limited to the rainy season coming early and the bandits they were likely to encounter when they reached Kenya.

'It'll be like Iran,' said Wayne, a Hot Rock devotee who both shared the driving and participated in the climbing. His fellow driver Fi had been driving international expeditions full-time for five years but did not climb. Wayne told me he had been shot at on Hot Rock's first expedition two years earlier: he spent the night on an Iranian mountainside and made the mistake of turning on his torch.

As he climbed further up the peak to escape the machine-gun fire, he had encountered a troop of baboons and had to descend again rapidly.

Despite this, Wayne's major concern was not stray bullets or beasts. 'The problem with Wehni will be snakes. Snakes can climb,' he said, before describing how he had once climbed a mountain to get away from some threatening-looking snakes, only to find 100 metres up that he had been overtaken by one of them.

I discovered Wayne came from Nottingham. Apart from his strong regional accent, he was the spitting image of British comedian Al Murray. He had a distinctive patch sewn onto his trousers commemorating an accident at the base of Mount

Kenya. 'I bent down to pick up a rope, farted and shat myself,' he explained. 'I took off the trousers, cleaned myself up, cut out a patch for the memories, sewed it on and went on up the mountain.'

Sewing and climbing *sans* trousers. 'That would be my reaction after I shat myself too,' I told him.

Turkey had been the highlight of their trip so far. 'In England you know everything has been climbed hundreds of times but you could spend the rest of your life in a small part of Turkey climbing nothing but virgin rocks,' said Rex, a bomb disposal and mountain rescue expert who had quit the army to join the trip.

Several of those present had been involved in the construction of the truck, which had taken place in a barn in Banbury, Oxfordshire. It had begun with the process of stretching out the truck's wheelbase. The main body of the truck was then built from a tractor unit that was chopped in half and stretched. The design was the brainchild of Stuart 'Stiggy' Marlow, founder of the whole venture but who was not on this leg of the truck's global expedition.

Talk turned to the fact that Ethiopia was extremely mountainous and that therefore the progress of the global expedition would be slowed to a crawl for a few weeks.

I was then introduced to Johnny 9.5, an epithet won after cutting off half of one of his fingers with an axe on a previous Hot Rock expedition in India.

An amiable young chap, Johnny was an engineer for Rolls Royce prior to joining the expedition and had designed the steps for the Hot Rock truck. As vehicle stairs go these ones were remarkable – even I managed to climb on board without assistance and I found it hard enough getting into the passenger seat of a conventional saloon car.

Johnny had turned down a redundancy package the previous summer, believing that the shares he was sitting on would see him right for a long time to come and apart from anything else would help to fund his Hot Rock expedition.

He was also rated 26th in the Tiddlywinks World Championship league. Despite such gifts, he did not plan on climbing Wehni, personally ranking himself as 'in the lower middle of four standards of climber', whatever that meant. 'Basically I'm the sort of climber that prefers technical rather than long, hard climbs,' he said. He could see from the pictures that Wehni would be a 300 to 500 metre vertical ascent and therefore not the sort of climb he favoured.

Yet Gar wanted *me* to give it a go!

Manne was from Sweden. He had chosen to join Hot Rock for a few months rather than taking up the offer of a role in a Jackie Chan film. Before joining the expedition he had been doing his national service, reaching the rank of sergeant, in charge of ten men.

'Me and my ten men will clear up this country, won't we?' he said to hysterical drunken laughter.

Adam (the group called him Daddy) – in his mid-fifties and the only person there older than me, was himself mildly intoxicated that night.

He was called on by the group to tell a joke they had evidently heard him tell many times before, and one that clearly nobody but Adam seemed to understand.

The expedition's doctor, Lisa, then announced she had malaria. Slightly less laughter.

The conversation turned to me and Gar. We explained that we were joining them on this leg of their trip to photograph and write about conquering Mount Wehni. Gar told them a little about how, we believed, nobody had scaled the mountain for hundreds of years since it was used as a prison.

'Presumably there will be skeletons on top,' said Rex.

'And gold,' added Becky hopefully. She had quit her marketing job at Wella to join the expedition. It was indeed believed by many that there was much gold to be found on the roof of Wehni. She left for the bar with that thought in mind.

I explained to the others that after enduring the discomfort of the bus journey from Addis to Bahir Dar we had resorted to splashing out on the luxury of a minicab for the final leg of the journey to Gondar. I wanted to make them all aware that I did not necessarily share their spirit of adventure – not if it was going to hurt – so I drew the laminated note from my money belt and they passed it around. It was caked in dried sweat and in need of a good clean, but failed to impress.

Rex, who felt it important to make the point that someone had been shot by bandits on the same route only the night before, interrupted my campaign. I persevered. 'I didn't even want to come,' I explained. 'This sod dragged me here.' I pointed at Gar.

The tense mood began to lift. For them, anything different was good. Rex tried to turn the conversation to the dangers of the flash floods in which they had almost drowned in Turkey, but the mood was determined to change and no one responded.

They turned to some of the lighter stories of the trip so far. 'In Muslim countries they just walk across the road without looking. They see it as a win-win situation. They may make it across, but if not then they go to meet Allah,' said Mark who, at just 20, was the youngest member of the team.

Fi returned from the shower looking a completely different person without the weeks of Sudanese desert caked to her. I saw that she was, in fact, blonde.

The others left for a shower one by one and as each returned I was unable to recognise them – something of a nuisance since I'd worked so hard to learn all their names.

A distinct mellowness began to set in among the group. Some left to shop while the core remained talking and illustrating the tensions to which Dave had alluded – the dangers, unpredictable hungry wildlife, falling rock and gear placement.

Naturally, I found it extremely hard to comprehend their enthusiasm.

'We headed across Europe to Greece, stopping off in Meteora before hitting Turkey. Braving the cold, we still managed to climb and bolder at some excellent European spots and also slept on a couple of beaches,' said Dave.

Turkey had proved no warmer than Europe and after being almost washed away in a flash flood, I was told, they headed south to Syria and Jordan.

'We spent Christmas in Petra,' said Mark. 'Think Indiana Jones and the Last Crusade . . .'

Fi interrupted him sharply. 'I actually spent the day fixing the truck with Wayne and Dave,' she stressed.

'Yeah, then we headed off to the magnificent climbing venue of Wadi Rum,' Mark continued, opening a packet of duty free cigarettes. 'After a crazy, camel-intensive New Year out in the desert, we crossed the Gulf of Aqaba and hit the Sinai in Egypt, and the beach resort of Dahab.' Here they had to endure scuba diving and camel trekking.

Reminiscences over, they began to discuss the dynamics of the varying ways in which kids in Ethiopia beg for money. Fi, just 30 but already an old hand at Africa's evolution, reflected: 'In 20 years time they will be like the Kenya kids, hurling stones at you.'

I sat and listened. Not since stumbling accidently into an AA meeting had I felt so out of place.

Dave returned and led Gar and me to the truck for a tour.

The ceiling had a huge map of Africa marked with the route the truck had travelled so far. The map was replaced each time it entered a new continent.

'These are the keys for the various compartments. The blue key's for the baggage doors on the right, the red one for the equipment stores on the left,' he said. At least I think that's what he said.

The food store contained such luxuries as 7 kilos of salt, 5 kilos of mango chutney and enough powder to make 288 litres of soup. The mobile office contained the satellite and mobile phones, a fax machine and various fake rubber stamps like those for which Gar and I had found a need in our encounter with the Ethiopian Mapping Authority. There was also a miscellaneous section with four sand ladders, an inflatable three-man canoe with three paddles, a canoe pump, a mountain bike, volleyball net and of course the first aid kit.

We all assembled around the truck at 5:00 pm–dinnertime. It was my first sight of the co-ordinated routines the expedition followed. By this time the two whose names had been on the rota for cooking and cleaning up that day had prepared a vegetable curry and pasta.

Washing up, meanwhile, was simplified. Three tables were brought from the kitchen compartment of the truck and three plastic tubs were lined up. The first had a detergent solution, the second a sterilising agent and the third was simply chlorinated water in which to rinse said items. Everyone followed this routine in turn before and after each meal so that, apart from returning the folded tables and the crates of food, plastic plates and cutlery, there was little domestication required.

Just like being back in primary school.

Towards the end of every day or two there would be a thorough clean-up in the upstairs living area of the truck itself. All personal items on the truck had to be taken off before a team would enter and clean inside. Everything that was not stashed away in lockers would be placed in a pile and then auctioned to the group. (To Dave's dismay, two Sudanese swords he bought in Kassala had been sold for 9 pence one evening.)

The expedition had essentially requisitioned the hotel, its staff and facilities and was pouring a fair amount of money into it in the process. I wandered about, a little at a loss as to what to do. I was a slow learner and it would take a day or two before I was sure how to avoid assisting in any way.

After tea Gar left for a few minutes, returning with 400 Nyala cigarettes (enough to last the trip) for the grand sum of three quid. There were two products in Ethiopia that seemed to be named after the nyala (a kind of antelope found in Southern Ethiopia): cigarettes and insurance.

Dave summoned us all to gather by the truck for an update on the plans. The two-day drive to the north of Axum (on the other side of the Simien Mountains) would take us to an area of spectacular climbing. There we would spend three days before returning, possibly via Lalibela.

There was some good news, though.

The truck had to be in Kenya just six days after Lalibela, so I calculated that – provided we were still alive – there would be little chance of extending our stay.

Axum is said by Ethiopians to have been the capital of the Queen of Sheba and the place from where she set out on her legendary visit to the court of Solomon in Jerusalem, although there is scant evidence to support this. All the gifts she supposedly brought to Solomon, for instance – gold, frankincense, spices and so on – were natural resources not of Ethiopia but of Yemen, where the land of Sheba itself was situated.

The Ethiopian variant of the Queen of Sheba legend goes that Solomon seduced her and she gave birth to a child named Menelik, destined to be the founder of the Solomonic dynasty (whose last representative was Haile Selassie). It's all a bit iffy.

Axum, however, is certainly where the Ethiopian Orthodox Church was founded early in the 4th century AD, during the reign of King Ezana. Ethiopians also believe Axum to be the location of the Ark of the Covenant, guarded by the only man entitled to see it – a (really old) monk armed with an old wooden cross.

1700 years later, UNESCO designated the ruins of Axum a World Heritage site. Ethiopia didn't get another look-in from UNESCO's World Heritage programme after 1980. (For a programme designed to award Heritage status according to merit, there is something deeply suspicious about the fact that the first ever World Heritage award to be given to Afghanistan was announced in June 2002.)

Dave moved on to some of the more abstract aspects of the trip. 'So you've met these guys – this one writes,' pointing at me, 'and this one take photos,' he turned towards Gar.

Meeting over, I asked a few of those who were on the truck for their views on the expedition so far. 'Hard going, but fun' seemed to be the general view. I found this remarkable given that they had spent the past two weeks on an unscheduled two-week dig through the Sudanese desert and felt they had to be either insane or simply lying.

I sat down against the hotel's exterior wall to talk with Dave. He had a degree in marine biology and had worked with underprivileged kids in the northeast of England, and as a butler. He had also worked in several bars in London's Docklands. Now, at just 24 years old, he was displaying the potential of an effective senior company director. I suspected he had the ability to step into the shoes of somebody twice his age and shake up a failing brand.

'When you get back from this trip, head into the City of London and you'll be able to name your own price,' I told him, but he just wasn't interested.

'No, if I am instrumental in getting just one person on this trip to achieve something better in their life – in making them realise happiness – that for me is success,' he replied.

The crazy fool.

The expedition had fewer participants than I had expected. Dave explained that the truck was only filled to half its capacity, but would be picking up a lot more people in Kenya for the next leg of the trip: passing through Nairobi and heading for Cape Town.

It occurred to me that, compared to Africa and, in particular, Ethiopia, the rest of their trip around the world would be a doddle.

And that Gar had lured me to the worst possible location of the lot.

I drank very little that night, keen not to stumble intoxicated across anything dangerous such as a scorpion, a snake or any of the varieties of venomous spiders that were rumoured to exist in that part of the world. I was feeling a little shell-shocked. Every one of these people had come with a passion for climbing and they had all had thrown themselves into the spirit of the expedition. I, meanwhile, wished to throw myself off a proverbial cliff (given I couldn't get up to the top of a real one).

I was the last to leave the bar as I scrawled a few notes about the past couple of days. The waitress who had been boisterously joining in the fun asked me for my pen. It was not mine to give away, I said. 'It remind me of evening,' she said, as she took it from me anyway.

I crawled on to the floor of the truck and shut my eyes, only to be awoken a few short hours later by the sound of religious chanting coming from the street.

I got up and stumbled outside. It was 5:00 am and people were beginning to prepare breakfast. I needed the loo but did not wish to piss outside in the dark in case I hit a snake, which would presumably hit me back. The sun wasn't to rise for another hour.

I saw Gar emerge from his tent and I went over to him to plead that it was not necessary for me to join the trip on its excursion to the border and its 'spectacular climbing'.

'I can stay here till you return in a couple of weeks.' I was almost on my knees begging.

Seldom one for putting his foot down, Gar, on this occasion, put his foot down. 'You're bloody well coming with us,' he said.

At that moment, a dozen of the others emerged from their pits. I put my hat on, as much as anything to disguise the fact that my hair was filthy, and cleaned my teeth. I was starting to smell like a dung heap, but I could see that showering in the hotel was going to prove impossible in view of the queue for the bathroom that had already formed. So I joined the other queue, for tea and coffee. Five minutes later I was about to be served when the boiled water ran out. At that moment we were ordered to hurry up and pack up the truck.

Chapter Fourteen

Dangling on the edge of sanity

In spite of my foul mood, setting out for the first time on board Hot Rock was, I have to admit, an experience I found briefly enjoyable.

Of course, I had to remind myself I was hardly in safe hands – with their bizarre taste for outdoor adventure, most of this lot seemed overly anxious to meet their maker. Still, standing high above the street on the imposing truck with the warm air brushing my face, I forgot my misery and impending death for a few moments. I didn't have to do anything but stand at the front, behind the cab with the roof slid six or seven feet back, and experience the awe and disbelief of the native Ethiopians. Maybe this was how the Queen feels when she visits the colonies? (Although I suspect she gets bullet proof glass, which was unfair. Of the two of us, I was far more likely to be shot. From inside the vehicle. By Gar.)

A great sensation it may have been, but I couldn't escape the incongruity of my own presence on board. For some unknown reason the mountaineers accepted me, but my enjoyment was to be short-lived.

Out of Gondar the scenery became more lush and the roads narrower. The truck was a huge vehicle and up ahead was a rather dramatic-looking, hair-pin turn.

I jumped down from my perch and found Gar. He was investigating a small camera malfunction.

'What kind of turning circle does this thing have?' I asked worriedly.

'Don't start,' snarled Gar. Clearly he had more important things than death on his mind, like how to get a minute piece of fluff off the lens of his SLR.

'But you should see the roads up ahead.'

Gar sighed deeply. 'Get a grip, will you. Haven't you been listening to these guys? They know what they are doing.'

Dave, who had overheard, told me the truck had a very small turning circle. I replied that unless it could levitate, we were in trouble.

Flickering of eyelids all around. I slouched back to my perfect view of disaster. A few minutes later I was delighted to be proved wrong – the Hot Rock truck managed the turns the way I do a packet of HobNobs. Quickly and efficiently.

My thoughts turned to other potential hazards. For instance, the United Nations estimates there are somewhere between half a million and four million unexploded mines in that part of the world. Mines! New sites are still being discovered every day, following decades of fighting in the area. A number of Ethiopians still get killed every year from Italian ordnance.

I approached Gar and Dave again.

'About those mines . . .'

A strange strangled sound burst from Gar, but Dave stayed calm.

'Don't worry mate. A guide has assured me there are no mines on the Eritrea border.'

Somehow, hearsay from a man Dave had met pushing a donkey through Gondar seemed able to override every string of common sense that advised against travel to the border region.

I told myself that I wouldn't be joining them on their off-road treks into potentially mined stretches of land anyway, so Dave would be given ample opportunity to disprove the no-mines theory without me.

As with most other aspects of my life until then, it turned out this supposition was incorrect.

In the meantime, I had a new threat to engage me. We were entering the stretch described as dangerous – even by the guide who had no problems with mines.

The road was just as wide as the truck, most of it bordered by sheer drops of 500 metres or more. However, on the plus side the ride was smoother than the one we had taken in the minicab to Gondar – and immeasurably smoother than the bus we had taken earlier that week from Addis Ababa to Bahir Dar.

I thought about Liz sitting in our cosy little place in London, and wondered if, in my hour of need, she'd remembered to tape EastEnders for me.

Gar and I were the only people with spouses back home. Technically Rex was still married but his divorce was imminent. 'I hope she sees what I'm doing: making history,' he said.

'How's that?' I called, bulging eyes still on the road.

'Basically it's a journey around the world at ten miles per hour. That's why it's going to take three years.' (He wasn't joking. The average speed of their journey was to be illustrated the following week when, back in Gondar, the truck and its occupants would become reacquainted with a lone cyclist they'd last met two months earlier in Wadi Rum, Jordan.)

At the crest of a mountain peak stood a village where the stench of what seemed to be pot was incredible. We passed through a dense cloud of smoke that engulfed the whole of the built-up area. The same experience was to be repeated several more times. Perhaps it was indulgence in the drug that gave so many of the Ethiopians we encountered such radiant, smiling faces. Most people we passed would stop to wave. When our own smiles met theirs, their faces would beam and their arms wave all the more frantically, maybe to indicate they had run out of pot. Later, Gar ruined the image of the stoned Ethiopian for me by announcing the smell was burning eucalyptus.

To calm me down (and shut me up), Gar told me both Wayne and Fi were highly experienced truck drivers. Fi was arguably the more experienced, with five years of belting around Africa and Asia under her belt. So it was lucky she was at the wheel when we hit what appeared to me to be an impassable corner and the end of the trip – at least for me.

We had stopped to look at some monkeys that were running down the mountain. Ahead of us two of them were shagging. It was the closest thing I was going to come to porn for a while, so I leaned over for a better look. Then, as we rounded the hairpin bend, there did not appear to be the space for the truck to make it round the bend without at least one wheel dropping over the edge. Fi slammed on the brakes and I was instantly introduced to one of the disadvantages of an open-topped truck; I was flung through the window to find myself dangling precariously over the cliff edge.

'Arghhhhhhhhhhhhhhhhhhhhh!' I yelled, for obvious reasons.

No one (including Gar) looked particularly perturbed.

'Hold on mate,' called Dave cheerily.

'Yeah,' muttered Gar facetiously. 'Don't let go.'

'You think?' Bastard.

Then there was a horrifying sound of crunching metal. I tried not to glance down at the 200 metre sheer drop below us as Fi reversed back along the cliff edge to try a second time, pushing the vehicle's turning circle to the extreme. From my too perfect vantage point I could see one of the wheels was hanging over the edge.

Holding tight to the rails, I glanced around me rapidly in all directions. Johnnie happily beating Mark at tiddlywinks, Kate clinically addressing some laceration to her foot, Rex waving at a group of passers-by and the rest absorbed in books.

Total and utter bastards, all of them. 'Don't worry about me, although I am, in fact, too young to die.'

Although a spring chicken at 30-something years, I was still the second oldest person on the trip. Everyone else apart from Adam was at least five years younger. This was underlined when Rex asked me if I had any preferences for music. 'Hardcore or dance?' he asked. At first I was a bit worried he was asking me for a date. Anyway, I knew I would dislike both but had no way of telling the difference. 'Whatever,' I said.

Back to my impending demise. Finally, my physical terror was noted by Rex. 'Great fun, this!' he said, but in jest rather than malice. I didn't respond. My teeth were clenched as tightly as my hands which gripped the sides of the truck.

As I swung over the pit of doom I wondered whether I should jump when the inevitable moment came.

Knowing my luck I would land in a snake pit.

Miraculously, on the fourth attempt Fi managed to inch the whole of the truck safely around the bend. She stopped so that I could scramble back on board. No one said anything and I sat, seething, on my bench, telling myself that porno monkeys or not, I would not lean over the rail ever again.

After that I couldn't relax. My laminated note was close at hand and I pondered whether my childhood head injury could persuade Fi to turn the truck straight around and allow me to seek medical help.

However, as I made my way to the driver's cabin, Gar spied the note and told me to grow up.

'I have mental and physical retardation she should know about,' I argued.

'That has nothing to do with your accident,' replied Gar. 'Now sit down!'

So I did.

At a place called Limalimo there was an explosion beneath the right hand edge of the truck.

'A mine, a mine!' I called out hysterically.

'A burst tyre, Bill.' Dave patted my back. 'Fortunately there are four pairs of them supporting us.'

We (and by that I mean everyone but me) stopped to change the wheel. The spares were stored in a compartment about five feet above the ground and each one had to be rolled carefully down a chute, ensuring nothing stood in its path.

A crowd inevitably gathered but less out of curiosity and more from a desire to extract money or pens from us.

Nevertheless, I allowed myself to be escorted to a nearby café by a villager named Anteneh. Like so many Ethiopians I was to meet he was disarmingly polite and impressively well-educated, although obviously he hadn't the slightest idea how to spell Anthony. His ambition was to go to study in a university in the UK.

'What for?' I asked. He would probably not learn anything there that he hadn't already been taught at home.

He looked surprised. 'To learn, of course.'

'Have you seen the state of the British education system? Gone down the pan. It's true. You can get a 2:1 degree by turning up at the uni bar nowadays.'

But he refused to accept this. For my part I was surprised to meet so many educated people here when school enrolment in Ethiopia was low, even by the standards of the world's least-developed countries. Barely one in four children attend primary school, 15 per cent attend secondary school – and only around 1 per cent go on to further education. Yet, people far smarter than I revealed themselves at every dusty turn.

The new wheel secured, and Anteneh paid for his time, we boarded again and headed off, only to find the road surface deteriorating dramatically. Even though we were only crawling along, the truck bounced about like a dog on a wasps' nest, the top of the truck knocking the knotty eucalypti lining the roadside.

I stayed well inside, even when we hit an area called Dibe Bahir at the foot of Mount Limalimo, where a troop of macaques monkeys were prancing around suggestively on the rocks.

My joy knew no bounds when, a mile or two beyond that, we saw dozens of huge vultures tucking into the corpse of a large cow which had clearly been hit by a passing vehicle. Gar threw me a glance, as if to say: but for the grace of God . . .

As we drew closer, the massive birds of prey glared at us Gar-style, until, with just a few feet between the truck and them, they slowly took to the air and circled high above us, poised to return to their feast once we had manoeuvred our way past. The stench of the decaying creature was unbearable – given I had been walking around covered in shit for a few days, that was really saying something.

My frayed nerves continued to take a battering. The edge of the road seemed to have the fragile texture of a sand dune as we neared a UN truck that we met on a hairpin bend. We had to pass on the outer side of the road. Quite how we managed to do that and live is beyond me. I clenched my hands and arse as I heard the sound of the exterior of the other truck slowly tunnelling its way into the rock face and began to pray like a single man confronted with an altar.

Finally, when we were out of immediate danger, I opened my eyes and told Rex how surprised I was to be alive. He snapped: 'In all their years of driving neither of the drivers has brought a truck over the edge of a cliff!'

'At least, not as far as you know,' I retorted, but he was already busy with a pad and paper, preparing some other near-death experience, leaving me to contemplate the true meaning behind his words. Perhaps they had been over the edge of cliffs hundreds of times but just wouldn't admit it. And we were only a fraction of the way into this journey. F*ck. Double f*ck.

Then ahead of us, through a gap in the peaks ahead, was a staggering view of flat-topped mountains, featuring the occasional chimneystack of rock soaring into the sky. Momentarily distracted from my plight by its beauty I thought of asking Gar to take a picture but what was the point? He'd only tell me to stick to writing again. Or just to stick it.

The distraction did not last long. It dawned on me that if the road was cut off at any point, we would have no option but to reverse the length of the entire route back to Gondar. It didn't bear thinking about. It would take at least a week.

To my great delight, we began to see increasing numbers of men en route, armed with AK47s or similar rifles. 'They're the same type of weapon as the ones they used to shoot at us in Sudan,' Rex remarked happily, as if recounting a special memory. I discovered later that people in the Ethiopian countryside have always carried weapons. Before the influx of Soviet military hardware in the 1970s and 80s there were apparently a large number of old muskets to be seen.

After the next stop Fi passed over the driving to Wayne and came to join us on the top of the truck. She proceeded to tell stories of other frightening overland truck experiences.

I interrupted her monologue. 'Why they should be called 'overland' trucks. Is it to differentiate them from a subterranean breed of vehicle?'

There was silence. Gar told her to ignore me.

'I was driving an expedition through Kenya once when a big lad on the truck was shot and killed by a poison arrow,' Fi said. 'In Gabon a man was held at gunpoint while a woman was raped.' Her face animated like a single mother with a winning lottery ticket, she continued, despite my dwindling consciousness. 'When the truck reached Katmandu, we learnt that the company I worked for, Encounter Overland, had gone into liquidation and it was going to be up to me and every other member of the expedition to find our way home – or would have been had the company not been bought by a rival.'

You see what I was dealing with? Thinking things couldn't possibly get worse, we stopped at a place called Mattsertm where I was introduced to a man whose job it was to attach rubber bands to the testicles of the feral dogs of Abyssinia. Why? In order to prevent them from mating the endangered remaining population of the region's wolves.

Gar asked to demonstrate the procedure on me, which met with uproarious laughter, even from the testicle band man who could barely speak English.

To top it all off, I was informed we were now entering termite country. Wayne cautiously drove the truck at a crawl across a fragile-looking bridge that crossed the river Tekezze, a major tributary of the Nile, whilst I held my breath.

It was getting dark. We stopped to camp, or at least they did; I was going to sleep on the truck. It was parked in a relatively sheltered flat roadside area about half an acre in size.

Before disembarking, Dave warned the less cautious of us about the perils of snakes. Fi probably used them as pillows. 'We are now in serious snake territory. They will not attack you unless they feel threatened. Some of them are nocturnal so be very careful if you go for a pee in the night . . .'

For God's sake. Night snakes ready to gnaw on my willy. As he spoke, I became more and more aware that I had made a mistake of unspeakable proportions. I looked angrily across at Gar and wondered whether I would ever forgive him once – if ever – we made it back to London. I wanted to slap him, but my hand had swollen to twice its normal size from various insect bites and the pain was becoming unbearable.

'Look!' cried Rex, pointing to a nearby tree. I looked across and saw, on an isolated tree a hundred or so metres from the truck, a brownish creature with a distinctive long mane. I was later to come to recognise it as the indigenous Ethiopian baboon, or gelada.

'Are they dangerous?' I ventured hopelessly.

'They'll rip your f*cking arm off.'

Of course they would. 'I'm sleeping on the truck.'

Rex grinned. 'They climb stairs you know.'

Chapter Fifteen

Night (and day) terrors

I awoke suddenly at 4:00 am. The first thing I did was sigh with relief that the nightmare I was having – about being stuck holding onto the edge of the truck as it toppled over the edge of a termite-ridden bridge – was not real. Well, not entirely.

The mosquitoes had stopped feasting on my flesh and the clouds had gone, revealing the stars – quite attractive, if you like that sort of thing. Which I don't. I began to nod off and then sat up again with a jolt. There were voices coming from the roadside a short way from the truck. Concluding that they were not the villagers in whose civility Dave had been so confident, but bandits who had come to rob the truck, I began to panic.

Not since the monkey porn incident had I felt such terror. Presumably these bandits were all carrying machine guns. I looked out and saw the light from five or six torches pointed straight at our vehicle. Trembling, I crawled under my blanket and prayed. Finally, someone up there listened because, to my great relief, the volume of voices decreased and the group continued on its way.

Like other groups we passed on our journey, they must have been heading to the next market town. Presumably they had a hell of a long way to go, too, given the early hour. After that I stayed awake and by 7:00 am we had packed up the truck and departed.

It came as no real surprise that the second day of the drive north was even more terrifying than the first. I sat in fear, pondering the prospects of survival while staring down an endless precipice. We seemed to be entering a new tribal district. Apart from ourselves, abandoned Russian tanks and the occasional UN truck, this could have been the Middle Ages. With less armour for protection.

As we crossed the final, long plain that led to Axum, we saw a large gathering a hundred metres off the road. Most of them were jostling for shade beneath a large olive tree, some were leading goats. A priest in a shamma – a traditional white cotton toga – stood to address them. It was late morning on Sunday and I guessed this was an open air church service. I wasn't sure what the goats could contribute, other than a hearty lunch after the event.

We left the gathering and I guessed we were not far from the next big town as the roadside population rose considerably. I steeled myself for the long, precarious mountain descent that would inevitably follow.

Eagles glided high above the next town, Alogean. From the safety of the truck window I saw my first camels of the trip, about 15 of them. I didn't bother asking if they had a tendency for violence. Rex would no doubt tell me they would rip my testicles off if I gave them the chance.

Then I saw yet something else I wished I hadn't. A child lying (presumably dead) on the road, his upper body covered in a white blanket. There was a pool of blood beside him. On closer inspection it seemed he had been mown down by the bus that stood parked by the road some 20 metres further on. A shocked-looking group of onlookers stood nearby.

Gar appeared next to me. 'If the usual form of vengeance that is said to accompany situations like this is sought, they will soon be putting an end to the bus driver's life. Eye for an eye and all that.'

'But he wouldn't have meant it,' I cried. 'We should stop them.'

Well, not me exactly. One of the others.

'Good idea. Why don't you offer yourself instead?' Gar suggested, shutting me up.

The final approach to Axum took us through lush vegetation and what appeared to be a man-made eucalyptus forest. I vaguely recalled my wife Liz saying at some point that deforestation in densely populated areas of the Ethiopian highlands has over the years resulted in severe soil erosion. I also vaguely recalled promising to call her the previous day as well.

Looking about, there seemed to be a great deal more industrial and commercial activity in this region. The farms appeared to have rich harvests; we could see steel electricity pylons presumably carrying power north to Axum, and a broad river flowed through one end of the town.

Gar regaled all with the details of Axum. 'In the 3rd century AD, Manne the Persian writer rated Axum and its empire as one of the four great kingdoms of the world, along with China, Rome and, of course, Persia. It's true that Axum was one of the most technologically advanced civilisations of its time and one of the largest forces of world trade during the first few centuries AD. It was also only the second kingdom after Armenia to adopt Christianity as its principal national religion.'

About as thrilling as listening to Radio 4 in an obscure Chinese dialect.

A little more interesting was the fact that Ethiopia was still running a petition for the return of the 200 tonne Axum Obelisk, looted by the Italians during their occupation before the Second World War. Italy signed a 1947 treaty compelling it to return all looted items. Needless to say it didn't. Precisely 50 years later a second treaty of this kind was signed by the Italians obliging them to return the obelisk by the end of that year and Ethiopia even printed postage stamps to mark the return of the Obelisk. The heavy beast was finally repatriated in 2005, but only after being damaged by lightning, the irony of which was wasted on the Italians.

The city of Axum – often spelt Aksum (probably by fools who have been educated in the modern English school system) – greeted us with the sight of a huge, fenced-in cattle ranch and a haze of TV aerials. These were disproportionate in number to the rest of the country, where only half a per cent of the population owns a television.

We parked up beside the Abeba Hotel. Things were picking up, I thought, this structure looked as if it might just keep the snakes out.

Despite the fact that Axum's apparently triumphant football team was marching through the city centre followed by a cheering crowd, we still managed to draw the usual curious throng of people desperate for a look at Westerners crazy enough to journey amongst snakes and rutting baboons.

Nevertheless, feeling brave, I set off by myself to buy some fruit in the marketplace.

An English-speaking local, Tesfay Kahssay, immediately latched onto me. At first I suspected he thought I was disabled – thanks to the fact that my limbs were swollen to twice their size from bites and scratches, my glasses were broken, and I hadn't washed properly since I had left London – and felt he was doing his good Christian duty to help the afflicted.

He showed me round, took me to buy a cup of coffee, helped me haggle for some overripe bananas and then accepted the offer of a further drink in a bar near the truck for his troubles, counting out my money for me helpfully.

Kahssay had what few Ethiopians are foolish enough to suffer: a hangover. He insisted on a Pepsi, but I explained the principle of 'a hair of the dog' and he relented and accepted a Meta beer.

Like many other Ethiopians I was to meet, Kahssay was after a sponsor in the UK so he could gain a visa to attend university there. When I told him I was not in a position to do so, he suggested I might find someone who would be able. I told him I could count the number of friends I had on one finger, but he wrote my address details down on the back of his Holy Bible anyway.

He was interested in the expedition but apparently had no idea of the existence, let alone the whereabouts of Wehni. 'It may be you cannot all climb it. You have ladies with you and it is forbidden to climb some mountains because of the monks.'

I explained that the only monks we would find at the top of Wehni would be long dead, since it had last been inhabited about 200 years previously.

'It's not the Debra Damo monastery you want?'

'No, Wehni Amba.'

This was indicative of the type of confusion we kept encountering in our quest to find the fabled mountain. We would be given directions that would leave us satisfied that we knew where to head, only to find them to be completely wrong.

When I told him I was the resident writer on the truck, Kahssay began to tell me more about Christianity in the region, despite my total lack of interest. There are three types of cross in Ethiopia, for instance. There's the Axumamite cross, the Lalibela cross and the Gondar cross. 'It all depends on the kings,' he said.

Although he was Eritrean, after finishing at Semehar High School he had moved to Ethiopia to escape the war. 'I was able to do so because my parents are from Ethiopia,' he explained.

'Despite this, you and most of the other people here still manage to look overwhelmingly happy,' I remarked.

'We are happy because the Lord is merciful,' he explained.

I told him he wouldn't think so if he were me but he just laughed.

Warming to the subject, and because my beer glass was empty, I asked if there were any conflicts between the Christians and Muslims of Ethiopia.

'No,' he replied. 'We do our celebrations together. Ethiopia is credited by the Islamic world as being a sanctuary for the first Arab followers of the prophet Mohammed fleeing persecution.'

Addressing issues of my own personal safety once again, I asked my new friend about bandits in the northern area of the country.

He was vaguely reassuring. 'You have already passed through the most dangerous region south of Gondar.'

And would soon be passing back through it again on our way back south.

Later I discovered that Barbara Toy (*In Search of Sheba)* wrote: '*News came through that shiftas had held up a busload of people coming from Gondar to Axum and killed four passengers.'* Admittedly that had been 40 years earlier, but it was enough for me to reserve judgement on Kahssay's optimism, especially when Gar reminded me that Tony Hickey had himself been attacked by shiftas there in the mid 1970s.

I paid for the drinks and returned to the truck, where a boy of around 12 (and one of an astonishingly high proportion of young polio sufferers in the town) told me he was collecting coins but had none from England.

Feeling buoyed by a bandit-free journey ahead, I boarded the truck to ask if anyone had any loose English change, and Kate produced a 2 pence piece for which the child was most grateful.

'You play football in England?' the boy asked, pocketing the money.

'No,' I said as I climbed back on the truck, only realising too late that he probably hadn't been asking about me personally.

We moved on towards Wehni. I sat at the open end of the truck and broke open the bottle of beer I had brought with me from the café. Loud but slow and relatively melodic heavy metal was playing through the truck's stereo system.

Rex was at the front of the truck waving to everyone we passed. A natural high prevailed, helped by the fact that the garage mechanic had not only changed the tyre but had fixed bolts along the roof, preventing it from banging loudly whilst open.

Helped along by the beer, I feel asleep.

The comparative peace was welcomed by everyone on board.

Chapter Sixteen

Climbing out of my mind

Finally we reached the area of rocks that the rest wanted to climb, which meant that my day of reckoning, or at least of running screaming into the desert, was nigh.

'Every peak will be riddled with vultures,' Dave said excitedly, in the tone one would use in the unlikely event of being offered an all-night nookie session with an undiscriminating Vogue model.

I didn't care since I wouldn't be climbing.

The truck parked on an open patch of flat ground. Everywhere I turned I saw craggy, sinister-looking rocks soaring into the sky.

A large group of children spontaneously appeared from God knows where – we were not close to any village. With them was a man with a Kalashnikov over his shoulder. He approached Dave, recognising him as the group leader, and Dave explained the purpose of the visit. It turned out the man apparently owned the land, and a deal was brokered that allowed us to stay.

Meanwhile the children helped out those who were putting up their tents. I put to good use my talent of doing absolutely nothing while looking remarkably busy.

As I was staring deeply into my rucksack for no apparent reason, Hazel, who was on truck duty that evening, asked me if I would be sleeping in the vehicle that night.

'Of course.' No way was a thin wispy tent shelter protection enough against snakes and vultures and whatever else Ethiopia planned to throw at me.

'Excellent,' she replied, 'then I can sleep in my tent.' She clearly hated sleeping on the truck. Or maybe that was just sleeping on the truck with me. Ethiopian fare wasn't exactly conducive to healthy bowel activity.

The relaxed mood of the group continued throughout dinner and long into the evening. I even enjoyed myself a little as I had an audience for whom many of my jokes were new. I cheered back down again when Fi began telling stories about the scorpion and snake bites she had encountered as an expedition driver. It was like an addiction, these stories of peril. In fact, I was beginning to suspect some were told just to see how I would react.

Which was daft, seeing as I reacted in the same way each time. Writhing in fear and clinging desperately to whoever was closest.

The lights went on as darkness fell and I noticed there were no bugs or mosquitoes gathering in the beams. Christ.

'Are they all gathering for a mass assault?' I asked.

'Idiot,' said Gar.

'It's because we're so high up,' Wayne explained.

The crowds of onlookers continued to grow to ridiculous numbers. I was escorted by about twenty people when I went to take a leak but they disappeared again when I had a little breakdown and screamed that I just needed a moment to myself and that considering we were in expansive countryside, why on earth would they . . .

Gar appeared and pointed out I was yelling into thin air. 'Clearly they realised watching you take a leak wasn't imperative viewing.'

Back at camp conversation stalled so I asked Dave if there was still a danger of snakes in this area.

Gar choked on a Pepsi. 'God, you really are –'

But Dave ignored him. 'According to the chief there are none.'

I wasn't convinced that the chief, whoever he was, could make such a claim. Unless he had a global positioning and tracking system on all local reptiles, I wasn't having it.

I slunk off to bed before I could be suckered into a chore or two, but just as I was getting comfortable, Gar came up to me on the truck to advise me that I'd need a sleeping bag that night.

I scowled at him. He knew very well that I preferred to sleep on the truck. I couldn't work out why Gar was so infuriated with me. After all, I was just being myself. And I *had* been the best man at his wedding. Surely that counted for something?

'I'm sleeping here, I told you.'

'But the weather might turn and . . .'

'Leave me alone, Gar, will you.'

Turning back to my bed, I realised that Tom, the crafty bugger, had taken occupancy of the back seat of the truck, which meant I had to sleep open to the elements; far too close to camping for my liking.

The roof at the front was fixed wide open with six bolts since the semi-repair earlier that day further south in Axum and there was no way I could close it by myself. As the night wore on the wind began to howl and the temperature plummeted. I realised that Gar turned out to be right. I did indeed need my sleeping bag, which was locked away somewhere in the lower part of the truck. It was a lesson I wouldn't forget: you cannot sleep in the open in northern Ethiopia at 3000 metres above sea level in a T-shirt – it was like counting in the New Year at Big Ben wearing only a G-string and a smile.

I whiled away the long, chilly hours in extreme discomfort, shivering and wondering if I could make it down to find the sleeping bag without waking everyone else up. Of course this was not possible. Given that they were all to be up exceptionally early to climb some highly dangerous, challenging rocks, and that I was only there for the ride, I had no choice but to curl up and endure it.

It gave me time to worry some more. Despite being afraid of everything from inanimate objects to the smallest insect, I had the awful feeling that the Hot Rock team continued to assume that as the writer, I would be climbing up that insanely sheer cliff face with them.

The crew rose at about the same time as the sun the following morning to discover me shivering and semi-comatose on the seat.

'Christ, Bill,' said Adam. 'Use your sleeping bag mate, or you'll be too ill to climb.'

The first thing I did was to try and get myself a hot cup of coffee. Gar was nowhere to be seen while I was queuing, yet he miraculously materialised in front of me with a steaming mug of perfectly brewed coffee moments before I reached the front of the queue. 'Enjoy your slumber?' he toasted me with his mug.

I could barely stop my hands shaking from cold to give him the single figure salute, so I ignored him.

I was looking forward to a day in the sunshine on campsite security duty (doing nothing) when I saw Dave's illustrated plan for the next few days. It featured the campsite and 11 surrounding climbing routes (not to scale).

The idea was to do some practice climbs before the big mama of rock faces – Wehni. The climbers' times and routes were then numbered on the facing page. To my horror I saw my name written down for that day's climb with a return time of 7:00 pm.

'I'm not going,' I said to Gar. 'Oh yes you are,' they both said.

'I can't bloody well climb,' I pleaded.

'Just join us for the first leg up to there,' Dave said, pointing to a steep 500 metre mountain wall just sloping enough as not to require ropes. Jutting out from its top was a vertical volcanic plug. 'Won't take long. After all, you can't write about something if you've never done it.'

Try me, I longed to say. I almost exclusively write from a position of nil experience.

'I'm not going!' I said again, a little hysterically, but then Fi appeared and I didn't want to completely embarrass myself by making a swift exit into the uninhabited wilderness, so I followed Dave and Gar tentatively, hoping Fi would vanish so that I could run screaming into the day.

But before I knew it, the three of us were heading off up a mountain. It took me about fifteen minutes to re-tie the mile-long laces on my hiking boots, during which time Dave and Gar were already 50 metres up, dangling off ropes.

I stepped gingerly onto the first rock, and to my horror there sat a fat snake. It looked me up and down as if to say: 'You, up there? Never going to happen my friend. Let me take a bite out of your gonads instead.'

Being only inches from certain death put the speed of Andrew Murray into me. I leaped up to a height of about 20 metres in seconds, at which point Dave and Gar turned around.

'Good on ya, Bill,' yelled Dave.

'Unbelievable,' said Gar.

Then I began feeling profoundly unbalanced. I tried to move ahead but boulders that looked secure titled backwards and I repeatedly lost my balance. At one point, reaching urgently for the ground my hand came to rest on a patch of thorns.

'Argggghhhhhhhh.'

'I knew it.' The faint sarcasm of Gar drifted downwards.

Everything on that mountainside was covered in thorns, including Gar.

An hour passed during which time I didn't move. Gar was sitting with Dave, smoking cigarettes a hundred metres or so ahead, waiting for me to catch up.

'Will you come the f*ck on, Bill.'

I deliberately leaned back, to show Gar I wasn't going to be bullied, when I noticed, about a second too late, that there was no supporting pile behind me. Unable to counter my backwards descent I rolled towards the base of the mountain like a Malteser on a slalom, and crashed back onto flat earth.

There was silence for a moment, then I heard the sound of unfettered laughter from above. Finally, Dave said: 'You okay mate? Lucky you were wearing your rucksack.'

The rucksack had cushioned my fall, but from their vantage point, they couldn't have known for sure. Bastards. I was actually quite winded.

Dave called out again: 'Don't worry, your climbing skills will improve.'

My mood wasn't improving, however. 'Going

back to camp,' I announced, and started walking away from the grey nemesis in front of me.

A chorus of objection rained down, but I continued moving slowly, with a slight limp for effect, back towards the relative comfort of the truck and its surrounds.

Then I heard something reasonable. 'At least wait with our bags. This face is so sheer we can't take all of our stuff with us.'

I thought – stupidly, as it turned out – that I would be safe enough simply sitting with a pile of gear at the base of the mountain, so I made a show of reluctance, then slunk back to accept the backpacks that Dave and Gar were lobbing off the mountain at me.

'Get the walkie-talkie out of my bag,' said Dave. 'We've got one here, so that we can stay in touch.'

He instructed me to check there wasn't anyone else on the airwaves. Listening intently for militant extremists, who would, in all probability, issue immediate and severe retribution to illegal airwave takers, I called up to Dave that everything seemed all clear.

They set off again and were out of earshot when a splurge of Amharic suddenly blasted through the speakers. Shit. I quickly threw down my walkie-talkie and promised myself that unless Dave and Gar were in severe danger, I wouldn't use the thing, lest I attract the indignation of a proprietorial warmonger.

I glanced up at the rock again but I couldn't bear

to watch as Dave climbed like a spider up the vertical wall of the rock to the first point at which he banged in a peg. It took an hour to secure it. I meanwhile realised one of the reasons my feet might be in such pain was because I had not removed my shoes in several days.

I took them both off and a warm mist formed a few inches above them. Both feet were a sickly white, like dough that had yet to set.

By now, the remains of any protective shadows had disappeared and for the next few hours the sun shone directly overhead. I felt as if I was in a furnace (or the tube in August) – as did Gar, who reported 'it was hot as f*cking hell' on the walkie-talkie, as he stood on the first rung waiting for Dave to move out of his way so that he could start his climb.

Of course I didn't answer.

'Bill, you there?'

I waved at him, but then pressed myself back against the rocks in case a missile launcher suddenly appeared and took Gar out.

The hours passed as the two progressed up the rock face with an agonising sluggishness. All I could think about was how I was committing myself to skin cancer.

I found a tree about a hundred yards away where I proceeded to stand for the rest of the day in whatever shade was formed by its half dozen leaves. I drank my way through two litres of water as my legs began to give way.

Four hours had passed and Gar and Dave were

still a long way from the top. Gar didn't appear to have even made it halfway.

Lisa, the doctor from New Zealand, and Adam then appeared from nowhere en route to their next climb.

'What are you doing here? Problems?'

Many, but there wasn't time to go into them at that moment.

I indicated the backpacks. 'Someone had to stand guard.'

'So that wasn't you we saw tumbling backwards onto your backside then?'

'No.' Yes.

'You really can't climb, can you?'

Obviously. I had never made any claims to the contrary. Still, at least I wouldn't be expected to try Wehni if I couldn't make it up this insignificant rock face, would I?

Lisa patted me on my wringing wet back. 'Don't worry, you'll learn as you go. On Wehni we will all be there to help you.'

I didn't even bother to answer and they strolled away down the mountainside. As they left, I heard Dave shout down to Gar to proceed up the next pitch. Gar clearly could not hear because of the rock protrusion between the two of them that must have muffled the sound, so I shouted the order up to him from below.

I could not believe that either of them was having what could be called fun.

Gar embarked on his next ascent and I heard

him curse: 'F*cking hell – how am I meant to get up that?' I decided against relaying that to Dave.

I looked across the valley and wondered whether they would make it down before dark, and how much longer it would take us to get back to base camp.

'Ow!' cried Gar suddenly. I looked back up the rock and saw him swaying loose on a rope in high wind. He was stuck and a small slither of satisfaction pinged the small space between my ears. I spent a few enjoyable minutes watching him dangle, before he managed to grab hold of the rock face again and boredom ensued once more.

Another hour passed and in a further two it would be dark. It was not like Gar to curse but I could hear him repeatedly swear in tones of anger. I told myself I shouldn't be smiling broadly at the wide range of expletives, but it didn't stop me.

A few minutes later I looked up again and could see he had made great advances and Dave was out of sight, presumably having made it to the top. The shouting was now conducted in tones of desperation. I pretended not to hear and looked away from the rock. They were out of sight anyway and there would have been nothing I could do in the event of them falling other than to have picked up their lifeless bodies – although that task may have been difficult given I was dehydrated and weak and my legs had cramped up.

I assumed they were going to have climbed back down via the same route so I was somewhat taken aback when, a few minutes later, they suddenly appeared from nowhere at the foot of the rock. They were talking to each other excitedly about hard E4s, 5Bs, some 6s and a 5C. They had either discovered a dumped load of ageing vitamins up there or it was rock talk. Either way, I couldn't care less.

On the way back, with paths spreading in various directions, it was unclear which path to take.

'So, now we're lost?'

Gar glared. 'Shut up, Bill. For someone who has sat on his arse for hours on end, you of all people shouldn't be tired.'

Whilst I pointed out that there were some rather attractive tree stumps Gar could impale himself on, Dave greeted some passing women with 'salaam' and asked in sign language which route to take.

Despite the sign language being totally unintelligible, one of the women gestured to her son to escort us. In appreciation, Dave took a Polaroid shot of her, and mother and son both became delirious with excitement on seeing the result. I wish my wife would have been happy with an instant snap as a gift. Last Christmas I bought her a soap holder in the shape of a leaf and she looked at it as if I'd scraped it off the front lawn.

As we followed our young guide down towards the camp a dog began to bark ferociously. I picked up a rock with which to threaten it – the way I'd been told to deal with potentially rabid dogs – but it kept coming.

'Argghhhhhhhhhhhhh. Is it salivating?'

But Dave and Gar and the guide continued on in front of me, probably engaged in a sign language conversation about what a twat I was.

When the dog was about one metre away (my mad stone-waving having nil effect), I decided to bolt for Gar and Dave in the hope that I could jump in front of them and the dog would ravage one of their gonads instead of mine.

I counted to one, then ran like a lunatic and heaved myself in front of my compatriots, who stared at me as if I had just beamed in from outer space, or Hull.

'What the hell is your problem?'

I was so out of breath I couldn't speak. 'DOG!' I pointed.

They turned around but the scrawny animal had disappeared. Dave shook his head and mumbled something like, 'the writing had better be good.'

Life really sucks when you can't even rely on a rabid dog to behave predictably.

We finally made it back to the truck as the sun was setting. Looking the roughest and most jaded of anyone there, I resembled a refugee who'd just bolted from under a trans-continental train – while it was still moving.

However, I felt I had achieved something very special that day. I had illustrated the entire scope of my physical agility and as a result there was less threat that I would be called upon to climb for the rest of the trip. Especially not up a sheer face like Wehni: one that held infinite possibilities for permanent paralysis or death. Dave now knew I was incapable. Not a wasted excursion then.

Two other Hot Rockers turned up. 'It was a half-twister . . .' one began. I couldn't figure out if they were talking weather or mountain and couldn't care less anyway, so I wandered off to prepare myself for another night in the wild.

I stepped outside to take a leak before securing the most comfortable position on the truck. I walked round to the other side, found a comfy spot and was in mid-pee when from about two metres away came a blood-curdling howl.

I looked up, wetting my shoes. Almost beside me was a wolf, its ears pointed at the sky. Scared out of my wits, I turned around as slowly as possible, before racing back up the truck's steps, trousers sprinkled with urine. I could hear Gar laughing uncontrollably from above, where he was making himself comfortable on my back seat.

I was giving him the middle finger salute when Fi came out of her tent to scare the wolf away. She patted my back and looked down at my trousers.

'God, you were frightened, weren't you?'

I tried to claim I hadn't pissed myself but Gar's guffaws blocked out my protestations.

It took such effort to unload my rucksack from the tall locker doors on the outside of the truck that I had resisted changing my clothes for as long as I could. I felt more content to smell like a flea-infested tramp than to indulge in the tiresome activities of dedicated outdoor campers. In any case, I'd probably end up losing the locker key and incurring the wrath of the rest of the expedition.

It was approaching midnight and my underpants were entering their eleventh day, my socks their eighth. Urine on my trousers was hardly going to make a dramatic difference to the overall impression.

I lay down on the uncomfortable back seat and drifted into sleep.

At about 2:00 am I awoke to an unfamiliar sound. I peered through the truck window to see Dave come out of his tent and throw stones at a hyena. At first I thought I was still in the nightmare I was having, but a mosquito took a shark-bite sized slice out of my arm and I realised that I was, in fact, awake. Then the hyena ran away, Dave took a piss and I stayed awake for the rest of the night, fearful of the next onslaught from the animal kingdom..

Chapter Seventeen

A grim fairytale

Plans were afoot for those not climbing the to head with the truck to Yeha, another of Ethiopia's oldest known cities. It dated back to the 8th century BC and was supposedly established shortly after the Queen of Sheba's reign. Yeha lies just over 50 kilometres east of Axum, its successor as the country's capital.

'This is one of Hot Rock's great selling points,' Dave explained.

Yeah right.

Gar was trying to persuade me to go, but I was exhausted and quite frankly, couldn't be fagged if I ever saw another bloody ruin as long as I lived.

'Besides,' I argued, 'I'll be more use guarding the tents.'

'Agreed,' said Dave, 'we don't want the place torn about by the wild animals while we're gone.'

'Alright,' I said hurriedly, 'I'm coming.' Me alone with the rabid wildlife and no girls to protect me?

Hardly.

First of all we had to drop off a climbing group at the foot of their appointed rock a mile or so down the road. They jumped out, and Fi, who was driving, had to undertake a major ninety-three-point turn. I was too nerve-racked to stay on the truck during what I perceived to be a terrifying manoeuvre, so I leaped from the vehicle and pretended to take a leak. In the event, although the truck didn't actually keel over, it managed to pick up a rock, which became jammed between two of its rear tyres.

'This is what happens when you do someone a favour,' said Fi lightheartedly as she disembarked to deal with it.

Stone finally extracted, we both climbed – in my case scrambled – back on board. I joined Fi in the cabin, but regretted the decision when she began a convoluted story about her Hot Rock history and her previous position. The first company for which she worked as a driver, Encounter Overland, was at one stage the only commercial overlanding company. A market was soon created with the formation of Dragoman, Exodus and one or two others.

'These all ran the route between Nairobi and Cape Town,' she said. 'Then there was expansion into the Middle East; Istanbul to Cairo became a popular route. It's a shame, because I love the Middle East and things get ruined with tourism.'

Apparently, she had grown tired of many of the kind of passengers that would join these 'overland' journeys. 'Usually people from professional occupations – lawyers, accountants and the like. I got sick of them, having to make them do things. They assumed it would all be done for them and they didn't like it when things went wrong, moaning about stuff that they could easily sort them out themselves.'

I squirmed uncomfortably. Was she referring to me?

'You *usually* get a better clientele with Hot Rock,' she added.

Yes, definitely referring to me.

She sounded the truck's horn, known as the Nine Tune Invader Series Air Horn, which played from a combination of five horns. It made an impressive noise and donkeys, men and women dispersed ahead of her. 'If I get really annoyed then the Mega horn doubles the decibels and does the trick,' she told me.

She stopped the truck to let two unarmed native hitchhikers climb up the side of the truck for a free ride the rest of the way to Yeha. I took the opportunity to escape for a doze.

We arrived in Yeha. Little is known of the history of the ruined pre-Axumite city and the lack of attention towards the preservation of what remains is scandalous. If you care about old cities, that is.

I was amazed it had ever been a capital city. It had a market about the size of a supermarket car park, but without the tarmac. All kinds of goods were for sale – vases, fruit, coffee, clothes, tea cloths and some pretty ugly-looking vegetables (takes one to know one, as they say). At one end of town were a few ragged stone buildings which served as stores. At the other, the entrance to the church of Abuna Aftse and a temple predating Christ, but which had been adopted by Christianity.

Outside the monastery it said: 'Enterance (sic) to visit Yeha for one person 50 birr. Thank you for not smoking.'

Tourists were mighty popular here, illustrated by the fact that every single child and young adult, on seeing our white faces, ran towards us loudly shouting to give them money.

I went on a quest for a bar that might provide some off-street relief from the din. It was a while since I'd had a beer, but just about everyone I asked shook his or her head when I asked if there were any bars in Yeha.

Or replied: 'Money! Money! Money!'

A group of inoffensive, English-speaking teenagers offered to show me the historic sights of Yeha that didn't require an 'enterance' fee, for the princely sum of 3 birr.

'Let me guess, your houses? The local toilet block?' I replied.

They insisted they were on the up and up and led me to the ruins of what had probably been quite a large temple outside the 50 birr zone. Looked like roadworks off the M25 to me.

'This temple,' they told me, 'dates from 2000BC'.

'Oldest temple in Ethiopia,' said another of the youths, who I think was called Solomon, pointing at the pile of rocks.

'Is this really all I am going to see for my 3 birr?' I asked them.

'No,' said the oldest, also Solomon, who was wearing flip flops and a Simpson's T-shirt. 'There is much, much more.'

They took me to see the rest of the city, which just seemed to comprise the street via which the truck had entered and a few tracks running off it. They showed me a school where they would be going that afternoon.

'Morning is Year One to Year Seven,' explained another Solomon. 'There are an average 47 children per teacher in Ethiopia.'

Much like the UK then.

They then led me to a side street – like almost all streets in Ethiopia, its surface mud and rocks – and to the entrance to a garden with a pathway leading to a tiny brick house. The gate was fastened with a gleaming Yale padlock.

'Oh, my mum must be out,' said one of the Solomons.

I knew it.

They then took me to see the police station. A stone building the size of a small bungalow with its windows bricked in, it too was padlocked.

Realising I'd been had, I decided I might as well make use of the Solomons and do some shopping. I needed some matches so they took me into the market and found a woman sitting on a blanket selling, among other things, some matches.

'2 birr for a box,' said a Solomon.

They normally sold for .04 birr, but I handed him the cash, which he pocketed before deftly swiping a box for me while the stall owner was not looking. I could learn a lot from these kids.

Eventually I paid off my guides. Despite demonstrating an impressive range of skills, they were starting to exhibit behaviour that might get me arrested.

I wandered off through the market to find the others. An old man with one tooth took my arm and pointed across the vaguely square market. He reminded me of the guy at my local off licence – the one who banned me for arguing with his wife. (I had the last laugh when his takings plummeted.)

'Your friends,' he said helpfully.

I looked over, but Fi and the rest were busy shopping and clearly in no hurry to leave.

The one-toothed man and I eyeballed each other.

'I don't suppose you know where I can get a beer do you?' I asked.

He nodded and beckoned me to follow him up the main street again, telling me he knew an 'inn'.

We walked through a broken gate and into a tiny, ancient stone building with a thatched roof.

Inside there were three middle aged men seated on stone seats and a woman, who stood stirring a large black cauldron. At her feet was a small black kitten.

I had unsuspectingly walked into a Grimm's fairytale.

'Sit,' the old man said to me. I did as I was told.

The woman picked a dirty-looking plastic beaker from the floor, ladled some kind of liquid into it from the cauldron and passed it over to me. Then she kicked the cat out of the way, hissing: 'Puss!'

I looked anxiously at the contents of the cup I was now holding. Ironic, wasn't it. I dedicated so much time worrying about the more traditional ways to perish, when in the end I would be poisoned by a witch in a hut in Yeha.

'Drink!' said the man. 'Is tella!'

Unbeknownst to me at the time, a glass of tella, or talla, was a drink traditionally brought to guests upon their arrival at another Ethiopian's home.

Given the choice between a drink or ending up in the cauldron, I took a sip. It appeared to be made from some kind of barley and had a vaguely alcoholic bitter-sweet flavour to it. A few sips of this tella were more than enough for me, but I felt compelled to stay in case making any form of dramatic movement reminded them they hadn't been to the market to buy their supper and I would probably do for a meal or two. If they held their noses.

Of the three other men in the room, two looked in my direction as if I wasn't there, while the third managed a smile and the occasional nod of his head when I caught his eye.

A few minutes passed, after which I didn't feel so uncomfortable and threatened, except by the tella, which I pretended to sip. Then, through the open window I saw the expedition gathering outside the truck at the other end of the market square. I pointed at them, gave 1 birr to the woman who'd served me, nodded my thanks with a somewhat nervous smile and left.

As I approached the truck Dave called out, 'We found a pub that serves Stella!'

'Me too. You didn't drink it, did you?'

'Yes,' he replied. 'Why wouldn't I? It's not like it's that foul tella or anything.'

Oh. Stella. As in the proper beer. Bastards.

Later, I discovered it goes against tradition to exchange food and drink for cash in Ethiopian homes. So presumably I'd been ripped off yet again.

Of course, that tradition may have been modified over the years as the country's population exploded. In the early 16th century the soil was so fertile and food in such abundance in the highlands of Ethiopia that, according to the Ethiopian monk Brother Thomas of Agnot, Ethiopians spent 'nothing' on their meals.

This might explain the lack of work ethic among many Ethiopians: there was no actual need for them ever to have done so until recently. What excuse the millions of unemployed English have I can't imagine.

I wandered back towards the monastery to establish why a large group of women had suddenly begun to wail at the top of their voices. I was still wearing my urine-stained trousers but surely I couldn't look that bad?

Peering rather than passing through the gates to save myself 50 birr, I had a bird's eye view of a bizarre funeral ritual that was taking place.

A coffin supported on wooden legs contained the body of a woman. A crowd (oddly not offended by Gar and his camera) stood nearby, carrying out ritualistic, apparently emotionless mourning. This went on for some time before most of the voices fell silent and a bell began to toll. When it stopped, everyone around the coffin ran like the wind to the walls of the monastery, women to the left of the door, and men to the right. The children gathered on the steps.

I stopped a sombre-looking priest who told me the coffin bore a local woman who was shortly to be buried in front of her own house.

That explains why I noticed so few cemeteries during my travels.

According to the early 17th century Jesuit Manoel de Almeida,. a traditional funeral comprises mourning for the deceased that continues for hours into the night, followed in the run-up to dawn by 'lamenting loudly' until 'broad daylight'. Gar told me later the 18th century French traveller Charles Poncet observed similar rituals: *'When any Ethiopian dies you hear on all sides most doleful howlings. All the neighbours assemble in the house of the person deceased and join in their bewailings with the kindred they find there.'*

We weren't hanging around long enough to see whether these customs had survived to the early

21st century. Instead I underwent further forced exercise by once again climbing up into the truck's cab for the journey back to camp.

As the engine started there was banging on the roof. Fi braked.

'Have you got Bill?' Dave shouted. I swore I heard Gar add, 'not that it matters.'

'Yes!' she said and drove away.

I shuddered at how easy it could be to get lost or abandoned in the middle of nowhere. Or worse, in a hut with a witch, a cauldron and tella.

While in Yeha, Fi told me she had stepped into a small shop on the perimeter of the market to buy a drink. The woman who served her had a newborn baby in her arm and Fi had some new baby's clothes on the truck given her by a friend whose child had grown out of them, and this was the ideal opportunity to give some of them away.

I asked her what she thought of the suggestion that it is better not to give such impoverished people things like money or sunglasses.

'I think you have a right to choose,' she said. 'It's not for us to say that people should live in poverty.'

'Or indeed Birmingham,' I said.

We arrived back at the campsite and Gar and Dave decided to set off on a climb.

'Want to come?' said Gar sarcastically.

I almost said yes, just to spite him. Almost.

I sank onto a mat near the truck and dozed, only waking when the man who owned the land on which we were camped turned up for the second time. On this occasion he pointed at Wayne and asked him to take a Polaroid photo of him. Wayne obliged and the man left looking pleased with himself, the photo wedged into his bullet pouch. Another night of free camping secured.

If someone gave me a picture of myself I'd throttle them.

By 7:00 pm darkness had fallen and Gar and Dave were still not back from their climb. This was promising. If they delayed their return long enough then perhaps it'd mean we were not going on to Wehni after all.

'Safe is Dave,' Wayne assured me. 'He'll bang in a couple of bolts and they'll sleep the night up there.' He left for another crap. On returning he announced that he could see that Dave and Gar were indeed on their way back.

I didn't comment. The long hike to find the lost mountain loomed once more.

I climbed on board the truck. So much for there being no mosquitoes at high altitude – a colossal one flew in and tried to bite my right ear off.

Dave stepped onto the truck, which promptly filled with a familiar smell.

'You've been walking through goat piss, haven't you?' I said.

'No – it's my armpits,' he replied, wafting them at me. He was right.

'I don't suppose you left Gar stranded on a sheer cliff face?' I asked, only to find Gar standing behind me, a murderous look in his bloodshot eyes.

After dinner – vegetable curry and pasta yet again – Dave told the group what was planned for the next few days. He updated everyone with the latest news on the likelihood of the whereabouts of the legendary Mount Wehni. He'd apparently met a local who claimed to know where precisely it was – news that was later to prove hopelessly wrong but which served to cheer some of us up at the time.

Not me, though, because I worked out that at the rate of progress that Dave was predicting, we would not be back at Addis Ababa until the day after the expiry of our open tickets back to London.

What if I were stuck in Ethiopia for another month? Or even two? I was desperate to call Liz. Someone had to save me.

Still calculating, I realised that in six days' time, we should be at the mountain. If we ever found it. The date for our return to London seemed to shift further and further away. The length and complexity of the trip back from Wehni were fatal to my cause. Why, I asked myself again, had I agreed to go on this godforsaken trip?

Oh yeah, I was pissed at the time.

Speaking of drink, that night we treated ourselves to some warm beer from the limited stocks of the truck's bar. It was to be another late night but at least this time Gar had finally lived up to his promise and gone early to his tent.

I eventually fell asleep at the back of the truck, vaguely wondering what my hair looked like. I hadn't washed or even seen it for well over a week.

Chapter Eighteen

Chapter and curse

I woke up late the next day, as did everyone else. Those of us who had indulged in tella the previous day were sick, most notably Dave. Johnny and Mark were cooking breakfast. I had two eggs and there was still enough hot water for me to have a cup of coffee.

After breakfast Rex was on the truck looking for a needle and thread. A voice from outside suggested aloe vera, which grew in abundance around there and was supposedly perfect for sewing.

Johnny and Mark, meanwhile, had finished cleaning up and were playing tiddlywinks. Johnny's technique and accuracy were amazing and I was surprised he was ranked as low as 26th in the Tiddlywinks World Championships. 'It wasn't hard to get to 26th. You just need reasonable dexterity,' he said modestly. That ruled me out then. 'Americans love it the most. They'll fly over to London for a weekend championship before flying back Sunday night,' he said.

As well as participating in climbs, Johnny was

also playing the role of international ambassador for the English Tiddlywinks Team. Even though he was not officially a paid-up member of the English Tiddlywinks Association, he was given special dispensation on the grounds of his PR skills. 'There is no African Tiddlywinks Association. I'm here to spread the word,' he explained.

'How lucky is that?' began Rex, though it quickly became apparent he wasn't talking about tiddlywinks. 'Some guy at the rock yesterday told me to come round for tea at three this afternoon. Job's a good'un,' he added, in his trademark way. He was what a senior colleague of mine in the press would describe as a 'cheeky chappy'.

I stepped down from the truck and was immediately alerted to the sound of a helicopter overhead. For a few seconds I froze, realisation dawning that I didn't have time to spell out HELP! in pebbles before it passed out of sight.

My eyes darted across the plain, desperately seeking something that could attract my potential rescuers. Like a Harrier, the chopper slowed and hovered over us. As it dipped forwards, backwards and from side to side I could clearly make out the letters U and N through my grime-coated glasses.

I waved frantically with both arms, but it drifted away towards the distant mountain range, its propellers making the sound of a pump-action shotgun.

I looked back down and saw Gar. I shrugged at him and he shook his head pitifully.

So I was back on my solo mission to escape. As each day passed I felt the agonising certainty grow that I'd be roped in to climbing the godforsaken mountain if ever they found it. I was destined to end my days decaying in a dried pool of my own blood on an inaccessible ledge 1000 metres closer to God. The only positive thing about this shit-a-brick terror was that it put me off my food, preventing me from prematurely dying of food poisoning.

It was 9:00 am and the sun was already scorching. 'We're setting out at noon!' cried Dave. I looked up, puzzled. I'd come to know that noon meant the sun would be close to its most glaring. Then I shook myself, appalled by the thought that I was beginning to care about what these people got up to on their ludicrous expedition. I stood up and walked over to help myself to the last of the hot water from the makeshift fire.

Rex, himself as yet unfortified with coffee, looked at me knowingly and began to regale me with stories about his time as a bomb disposal expert. I had little choice but to listen politely. 'Could be tough,' he said, dramatically. 'UXB – hit the timer with a hammer and you'd had it,' he said. 'I lost ten good friends to those pricks in Northern Ireland.'

'Terrorists?'

'Yeah, man, and it all comes down to religion. That's why I'm an atheist,' he said angrily.

It wasn't all anger, though. He told me how one morning a child had walked into a school – he wouldn't say which – announcing to the classroom:

'Look what I've made!' 'This was just after How to Make a Pipe Bomb had been posted on the Internet,' he said, grinning.

'We were summoned to the school. The headmaster asked me if it would make a noise. I said no, just a small hole in the playing field. He called the rest of the school out to watch and learn. We put 400 volts through it and it caused a massive explosion creating a 25-foot crater.' His grin grew suddenly wider. 'This bastard little kid had got the mix spot on. If it'd gone off in the school it'd have blown it half away. The headmaster tried charging us for damage. He'd rather it had been me than his precious playing field.'

Rex picked up his leather hip flask, unscrewed the lid and took a long and evidently satisfying swig of liquid. It was the perfect opportunity to ask about the mines that were supposedly lying unmarked in the region designated for climbing that week.

'Sod's law someone here's going to tread on one, and I haven't got the equipment to deal with it,' said Rex, sounding like Mrs Joe in *Great Expectations*. But then, just as suddenly, he was Rex again. 'Did you know, the kit for defusing a UXB costs eighty grand? It's all got to be nonmagnetic,' he said.

The things you learn.

News began to spread that five members of the expedition had gone down with food poisoning. The team's doctor, Lisa, diagnosed it as *giardia lambia*, an organic sporozoan found in water, often known as beaver fever. (Don't snigger.)

Its incubation period can be weeks, she said, after which its symptoms are profuse watery diarrhoea, abdominal cramps and bloating. Sounded delightful. Lisa suggested they had picked it up in Sudan.

'I refuse to blame them fruit juices we had in Kassala,' protested Wayne, who had been suffering quite badly for the past few days. 'They were just too good.'

An Australian voice piped up. 'No, mate!' Mel was charged with the role of filming the expedition. As usual she was trying to clean dirt from a camera lens. 'I blame the bug on your tendency to eat leftover food,' she said.

'Some people are naturally immune to it,' announced Lisa. 'I don't have it myself.'

No, she just had malaria.

Gar and I did not have it either. 'It can take months to clear. I had it once and was passing blood every 10 to 20 minutes,' Lisa added thoughtfully.

Fortunately for those who were its victims, there were appropriate, hardcore antibiotics in the truck's first aid store which would cure it – Metrinidiozon, apparently. Dave had taken his first dose but was still essentially disabled by the fever. Sitting under a dismantled tent, he swigged back the pill with gin, which evidently hadn't helped.

'Mind if I just shit here?' he asked. Nobody was unkind enough to object.

A convoy of a dozen or so ground to air missile launchers passed by. 'They're not loaded,' Rex called out wearily from onboard the stationary truck.

I lowered my hands again.

The drugs worked fast for Wayne. 'I feel like a new man,' he said, demonstrating that he had lost all trace of a beer gut and about three stone over the previous four days.

With nobody climbing until midday, the atmosphere was relaxed. Johnny was playing some old blues record on the truck. Rex emerged triumphantly to show off the two litre linen water pouch carrier bag he had made at a total cost of 30 pence. 'It's what this truck is for,' he said. 'Making dreams come true – righting all the wrongs.'

He began to tell me about the climbing. 'Here the rocks are sparse in quantity but the quality is so good – Heaven on Earth from a climber's perspective – and it's all virgin rock.' Despite my eyes rolling back in my head, he continued: 'And sparsely protected. Some good protection but you've got to find it. There's not a lot of tross so you can feel secure. Route I went yesterday, the rock face alone had 300 routes – a find in a million. This country has a lot to offer,' he said.

I pretended to listen until Tim returned to the camp looking revoltingly inspired.

'Where have you been?' I asked.

'Bouldering about 4C with God,' Tim said. 'Tricky start but then straight up over the overhang.' The more he spoke, the more confounded I became. He appeared exhilarated – for Tim, anyway.

He joined me in a multivitamin pill – his washed down with water, mine with beer. It turned out he was the only one to have been to Kassala and not picked up the runs. 'If the rest of me were as strong as my stomach I'd be Arnold f*cking Schwarzenegger,' he said.

A perfectly amiable chap, he seemed to find it harder than the others to reconcile himself to the fact that somebody like me should be on the trip. 'Talk about a fish out of water,' he said of me in disbelief on several occasions.

Meanwhile, Rex was bewildered by a small leaflet accompanying some climbing shoes he had purchased in Kassala. 'There are flamin' care instructions for these climbing boots. Are they thick? What's this – 'clean with a para rubber brush'? What's one of those when it's at home? Is it made for parachutists?'

Rex was preparing for the tea he'd been invited to. I pointed out that his T-shirt was a little too grubby for a visit to someone's house, and suggested it might be better if he make one from the cheesecloth material he had with him. He disagreed, instead going for a wash, shaving and putting on his clean spare pair of black jeans and his 'pulling shirt'.

With food on my mind, I tried to think of something I could eat that wouldn't be contaminated and hit upon the idea of eating a small, rusting yellow can of bull's balls in curry sauce. Rex offered me some bread. I took my first mouthful, only to realise afterwards he'd cut the slice of roll using the same knife he'd been using to cut the dry skin off his toes.

As I spat out the bread, it occurred to me why Rex was so excited about his impending visit. A 16-year-old Solomon had invited Rex for tea that afternoon and he was rather hoping Solomon might have an older sister or two.

'Haven't had a shag since two days after Christmas,' Rex winked. Wearing what might best be described as Scarborough nightclub-wear, he looked most out of place high in the remote mountains of Tigray, but I wished him the best of luck as he set off the five or so kilometres to the family's cottage.

There was filth and grime everywhere in the truck, much of it blown in by the high winds. I dropped my fork and didn't even bother cleaning it since the water was so contaminated.

Poor old Kate had a dodgy liver, which meant she could eat only certain types of food, and alcohol would kill her. She spent half her life having a dump, often while mountain climbing but, in the words of Mel, could talk authoritatively on everything from cystitis to diarrhoea. The food issue must have been a major problem for her. It's hard enough surviving on a restricted diet in England (as I once had to for some eight months after contracting something from a street vendor), so she must have been pretty hungry out there.

In Ethiopia, malnutrition among under five-year-olds is reportedly the worst in sub-Saharan Africa, at around 48 per cent. However, in all the mountainous regions we visited, few young children actually looked undernourished.

I glanced across the table and understood what was meant by the phrase 'general purpose' with respect to Rex's knife. Wayne was now using it to cut out a bee sting from the ball of his foot. Presumably I'd be using it again later to eat dinner. However, my stomach was finally calming down and continued to do so over the next couple of days. My hands weren't faring so well though, cut to pieces by insects, rocks, aloe vera and thistles.

The sky began to darken with what looked like rain clouds. Rain meant we had to undo all the bolts on the roof to close it. I suggested we leave it open and let the water clean the grimy floor, but I was bluntly told it would also damage the equipment.

Kate let rip at the other end of the truck. I had to stand up with my head above the open roof to avoid the noxious fumes. She had once cleared an entire pub in the Lake District with one of her farts, she told me by way of an apology.

My left hand had swollen to an even greater size than the right, which was still about one and a half times bigger than normal, despite having no new bite marks on it. It was also a lot darker than my right. I showed it to Lisa who looked puzzled. 'The high level of sunburn plus the high altitude are probably responsible,' she said. Still, it no longer hurt so I wasn't too bothered.

At 4:30 pm Rex returned looking sullen. 'I walked into his garden – about half an acre of it. The kid was at school according to his dad, and there was no sign of chicks, so I left. How embarrassed was I?'

I took this to be a rhetorical question. I pointed out that Amharic time was six hours ahead of our own, so they treat what we deem to be 6:00 am as midday. He scowled and asked why I hadn't mentioned that sooner.

Outside the local kids played with some highly impressive frisbees made with aloe vera. Inside, Pink Floyd played on the truck's stereo. Again.

By 7:00 pm, half an hour after darkness had fallen, there was still one climbing group that hadn't returned – Manne and Tom. They'd turned down the offer of a headlight from Adam earlier that afternoon. Dave left the campsite with a torch to look for them.

To pass the time until Dave's return, Gar suggested we find a Union Jack to place at the top of Mount Wehni (if we ever found it and if they ever managed to climb it). Jokingly, I suggested Rex make one, which he enthusiastically agreed to do.

Incidentally, I asked if he knew the reason behind the ridiculous claim that the Union Flag should not be referred to as a Union Jack – a term I'd been taught and used since an early age and which was widely used regardless of which Commonwealth country I'd been in.

Rex was furious. 'A Union Jack's a Union Jack and I'll deck anyone who says otherwise,' he said.

He proceeded to give me a history lesson which in the circumstances – atop a less-than-reassuring ledge in a scorching war zone – was entertaining. The Union Jack was first introduced in 1606, he said.

'From early in its life the Admiralty itself frequently referred to the flag as a Union Jack, whatever its use. In 1902, an Admiralty circular announced that their lordships had decided that either name could be used officially. Such use was given parliamentary approval in 1908 when it was stated that 'the Union Jack should be regarded as the national flag',' he said proudly. I suspect he had learnt it by rote.

That evening, despite the fact there was still no sign of Manne and Tom, the excitement at the prospect of finding Wehni reached fever pitch.

Dave prematurely said he had finally decided on the route we would take, one that followed the advice of our latest guide (or cattle herd).

The guide in question was totally blind. Waving a stick he'd pointed out the route wildly in the air. Of course, Dave believed him. It was as reassuringly unlikely we'd find the mountain as if we'd tried to follow one of Pakenham's crayon map drawings, created while the great man rode a donkey across roughly the same terrain.

By this time, everyone had at least flicked through the Pakenham book, studying the various pictures and trying to work out the best routes to take.

By 10:00 pm, most had drifted off to their tents. Despite the excitement, the altitude was making most of us tired. Well, except for Fi and Johnny, who sat at the front of the truck playing backgammon for the second night in a row.

And Manne and Tom, who were still lost.

Half an hour later I lay down beneath my jacket,

the sleeping bag serving as a pillow in the warm night. Fi finished the game victoriously and left Johnny on board the truck as my fellow guard.

Seconds later my bowels began to erupt. I hadn't eaten anything: this was pure fear. There was nothing I could do as I raced to try and prevent all but the first chunks of a great sludge from entering my underpants ('scoring a ten' in Rex's words). If I had removed my boots before going to bed then I would have had to have spent the next ten minutes trying to do up their ridiculous long laces. As it was, I simply grabbed a loo roll on the way out.

But someone had bolted the upper door, so I had to lean back and squeeze my way through the bottom door, thus eliminating any chance of the substance that had squeezed its way out of *my* bottom not staining the fabric I was wearing.

Manne and Tom chose that moment to re-emerge, and ignoring the laughter I finished my business and returned, a smelly mess, to the truck for another poor night's sleep.

I managed to sleep through the night and on waking was once again not quite fast enough to make it outside before letting rip.

It was the Thursday before we were to search for Wehni. I was resolutely not going to change my underpants. Although I hate sport I felt it my duty to carry them on like an Olympic torch.

'Are you sick?' asked Rex.

I told him I was, before demonstrating my symptoms by dashing off for another squirt. On my return I came face to face with Wayne. 'I hear you've got a new chapter!' he said.

'Yeah, it's inscribed on my underpants.'

Mel walked past. 'What's on your underpants?' she asked.

Wouldn't you like to know? I replied bravely.

Of course, she said she didn't.

Chapter Nineteen

Diesel don't explode. Much

Gar expressed (as he had done throughout the trip) genuine disappointment that I appeared to be enjoying myself too much. This impression was created because I felt the need to employ a degree of diplomacy whenever I was asked how I was finding the trip. An uninvited guest both in the country and on the expedition, I would explain that it was not as bad as it could have been.

Word spread of my condition. 'How're you?' Kate asked. Pretty shit, I wanted to reply.

Thankfully I had slept through a magnificent lightning storm early that morning, but now we were treated to the sound of gunfire coming from the other side of the nearby rocks.

'Artillery guns,' Gar helpfully explained, as he tucked into his roll containing the last of the eggs.

Hazel came to talk to me. In England she had been an IT contractor working on everything from government departments to telecoms.

'What are your feelings about the trip?' I asked, hoping for an ally.

'I'm really tired. If I wasn't I'd say awesome. It's one experience I'll probably never have again. This trip has changed me. It made me care less about things that used to bother me and forced me realise what's important.'

I resisted the urge to cut in and tell her I felt more bothered about snakes, rabies and disease than I had ever done before.

The lowest point had been in Wadi Rum, she said, because the weather was too cold. 'I couldn't stand it and when we reached Jordan, I left for a few nights in the Hilton. The others couldn't understand, but I needed time out. In an environment like this, people have to be direct with their feelings. Psychological changes are inevitable on a trip of this nature.'

I couldn't agree more.

She paused. 'I have since gone from being a holidaymaker to being a hardcore traveller,' she said. 'When I eventually get back to England I will look at using my resources much more carefully. I will be much more chilled out and less anal and miss not waking up in a tent to see the sun rise.'

I was itching to interrupt her and say if I was allowed to be direct I'd be screaming to be taken home.

She said it had taken her eight weeks to adjust to living in this fashion. Her friends back home had given her until the previous Christmas to give up and return to England. It was now March.

'I'm now completely used to getting little or no sleep and not washing. Now I prefer shitting in the open, where you can choose your own bathroom view.'

I wished I felt the same way. I had already taken some Imodium that morning, yet still had to rush off with no time for any concerns about the view. I didn't have eight weeks to spend with them and even if I did, I very much doubt I would have undergone such a change in attitude as Hazel.

The truck was about to take a few people to Axum to buy some bread, eggs, fruit and water. When I was sure I would have company, I volunteered to stay and help guard the tents.

The truth was, I didn't want to spend time unnecessarily driving along perilous mountain roads. As a result, I had a long day ahead of me in the glaring sun. In the surrounding area there was probably a total of about a square centimetre of shade.

I chatted to Kate. She was in a gap year between university and full-time work. She had graduated in ceramics, she told me.

Ceramics? 'Let me know which bar you're working in, won't you?' I said.

Kate was fond of Ethiopia which, like most visitors, she found to be a lot greener and prettier than she had expected. 'I will never go back to Egypt,' she told me, showing no wish to elaborate.

It was 8:30 am, around 30 degrees, and the clans of onlookers were gathering. My throat was sore and the sun was becoming more and more painful, yet I had no alternative but to sit in its direct path.

Adam warned me to drink plenty of water. 'Don't eat anything and don't drink beer. Drink gin.'

Who could argue with that? Besides, I never saw Adam particularly intoxicated apart from the first night in Gondar, despite the fact that he placed such great faith in the medicinal qualities of both gin and vodka. Then again, I might have been too intoxicated to tell.

The truck, and with it any shade, disappeared. I put on the mosquito net hat that Adam had lent me. He had bought the materials to make it when the expedition had passed through the Middle East, and had subsequently become the subject of envy in Sudan, where the flies were quite unbearable.

*

There were few distractions that day. A man walked across the camp site with a barrel twice the size of a beer keg balanced on his head. Quite why he didn't roll it along was beyond both me and Mark.

A long while later (during which time Mark had persuaded me to discard Adam's advice and open a bottle of beer), a group of ten or so angry-sounding, horned cattle wandered onto the site past the tents. They were being herded by a girl, not more than about four-years-old, with a crop, or cattle stick.

Solomon stopped by the campsite on his way to school. Like the friends of various ages who accompanied him, he carried a dusty cluster of books, desert-brown like scorpions.

I lit a cigarette and Solomon frowned, saying: 'Is unnecessary.' But then he saw what it was I was smoking. 'Rossmans,' he said, noting approvingly the brand I'd managed to buy. 'Is better than Nyala. Nyala burns you inside.'

He was absolutely correct.

Soloman left, Mark went for a wander and I was joined by Manne. He had decided to participate in the trip after learning about it in Thailand from Mel. His plan had originally been to travel on to Australia. 'I didn't know what to expect. I'd never done a group trip before. I'm liking it more and more,' he said.

Manne had an academic background as a university maths teacher and Internet programmer and was in the process of majoring in cybernetics. His plan was to stay with the trip through Africa as far as Zimbabwe. 'I'm not interested in South America,' he said, which was where the truck was headed after reaching Cape Town.

Tom, a plastics engineer by profession, was also staying as far as Cape Town. 'The trip's been good and it's only going to get better. Ethiopia rocks,' he chuckled. 'There's very good friction on these climbs and there's loads of potential for climbing around here, much like north-eastern Spain.'

He had been working in England for five years. I asked him why he had joined the trip.

The answer was very clear. 'I was living in Northampton.'

Say no more.

He was philosophical about the hardship they had endured in Sudan. 'We would have to dig the truck out of the sand two or three times a day. Definitely something you remember forever. Perhaps the worst time was in Kassala. The team had been stranded next to beautiful mountains that promised great climbs, only we didn't have the appropriate permit to do so.'

Sounded like a blessed event to me.

Tom was less keen on the Christian Ethiopians, (about the only ones we had encountered), feeling dragged down by their demands. 'Muslims give you stuff. Christians ask and take. In Muslim countries you can travel for free. Here they show you where the bakery is and ask for some bread. In Sudan they'd show you the bakery and buy you some bread.'

Becky emerged from under the tables to enjoy a few minutes in the blazing sun, but I warned her that because of the high altitude and fresh wind it was far more intense than it felt.

She was the only one of the participating climbers who had not climbed before and she liked the fact that Hot Rock accommodated climbers whose only qualification had to be enthusiasm.

My face was starting to burn to bone, so I decided to try and find some shade.

It was stiflingly hot in Gar's tent, my first resort. I wandered off to stand under a lone tree 100 metres away. It had just enough leaves on it – about six – to create a shadow across part of my face. A few minutes passed when suddenly there was a rustling sound above me. The tree turned out to be home to a well-camouflaged snake. Terrified, I edged away from my spot beneath it as slowly as I could, crouching down as I retreated lest it should try to lunge at me.

So much for the locals' claims. I wasn't going to hang around and exchange email addresses with it.

In order to avoid any charges of cowardice, I told the camp that I'd decided standing under the tree had been too tedious a way of avoiding sunburn. I sat on a deck chair and began to listen to views from people who actually had some kind of perspective on Africa (unlike myself who had never visited it before).

They insisted the Ethiopians were too pushy a people. While I agreed to an extent, I had to assert that my fascination for the Ethiopians stemmed from the fact that they will generally not go out of their way to rob you. Furthermore unless they are in a crowd they will usually take no for an answer.

But I had to agree that they did have their faults, as four children started to pelt a nearby donkey with stones.

No wonder it had tried to kick Mark earlier when hc had approached it.

What a miserable life these animals must have. Not unlike my own life, I thought as I returned to dreaming of shade: sunburn, swollen limbs, food poisoning and seemingly endless weeks of discomfort.

Despite the beauty of the landscape, it was one of the most inhospitable of places I'd ever seen (notwithstanding the men's loo at Paris Gare du Nord). With the sound of shelling in the distance I tried to imagine what it must be like, actually wanting to fight over land like this.

*

After seven long hours away the truck suddenly reappeared. Dave called out of the window that they had all had steak and chips for lunch. I chose to doubt that very much as I contemplated the cans of HP All Day Breakfast in my rucksack.

I was relieved not to have joined the trip that day, when I learned from Gar that he had been chased out of a church by a warden armed with a Kalashnikov assault rifle for refusing to pay 50 birr for the privilege of taking a photograph.

Becky offered me a slice of her Laughing Cow cheese, which I gratefully accepted. As I tucked into it along with a dry bread roll Gar came to try to tell me of his latest idea for the trip.

'What we can do when we get to Gondar is fly to Lalibela . . .'

'You fly where you like. The second I get the chance I'm getting on a plane to Addis Ababa, from where I intend to catch the first available flight to London,' I replied.

I was totally pissed off, having lost the motivation even to go and find food, and I went to sleep off a mild attack of heatstroke in the back of the truck.

I awoke at 5:30 pm to the sound of thunder. The

heavens opened and torrential rain began to pour onto the site, which was under water in a matter of seconds. While two members of the group pulled shut the roof of the truck, others began hurriedly bringing in camera equipment and various other select items, having ignored the warnings of the native onlookers just ten minutes earlier that heavy rain was imminent.

The wind was so ferocious it blew the parked truck wildly from side to side, knocking over half a dozen open water bottles. Then the tents began to blow away. Lightning began to strike as it had done when we had been in that overpriced hellhole of a state hotel in Gondar. The isolated, tall truck seemed to me to be an obvious target for the lightning, which was by now flashing like a strobe.

As I tried to hide from the elements, Tom assured me that the only dangerous place would be under the truck itself. 'Inside is safe,' he said. 'Diesel doesn't explode like petrol.'

In spite of the high winds and ridiculously heavy rain, Dave and a few others managed to light a fire by pouring a gallon or so of petrol onto some logs. The campsite meanwhile became a lake. The storm was directly above and ahead of us, its outline clear in the dark sky, and in the commotion Mel borrowed my jacket to step out of the truck and film it alongside Gar, who was talking pictures. Others were stripping off to stand in the rain and have their first wash in a week.

Some were hastily building walls of mud to

prevent their tents from becoming flooded. This redirected the flood directly onto Gar's tent, to my great delight. He promptly laid down his camera and, with Dave and Wayne, constructed an elaborate series of canals and ditches around the campsite, the fire and the kids that were sheltering – and clearly planning to sleep – under the truck.

The only thing not affected was the crowd of onlookers. The locals remained where they were, looks of puzzlement on their faces. Nevertheless, I guessed there would be more than just the two boys sleeping under the truck that night.

As the storm passed I could see clouds hanging over the tops of the mountains. They reminded me of those in Europe: low slung instead of being thousands of feet above as usual. An orange hue fell across the valley. The rain was still falling as the sun dropped behind the mountains. The scene was reminiscent of Australia's Ayers Rock (or whatever it is called these days) after a spot of rain, with reddish purple mountains reflected in the lakes of rainwater.

Streams of water came in and ran along the floor of the truck wherever there was a chance to do so. The conversations I could hear concerned logistics and were totally beyond me. I thought it was a disaster but to everyone else, it apparently provided the perfect excuse for high spirits. I'd never understand people like this. Oh yes, and to top it all, four of them decided it was an ideal opportunity to get in some exercise and began to hang with one arm from the grab rails that ran the length of the truck's ceiling, 'doing the sloth' as they called it. Until then, I had assumed the rails were for hanging on to for dear life when the vehicle was in motion.

Furthermore, some of the climbers returned and indulged in riveting conversations, which ran something like:

'Good climb, yes?'

'Too right, man.'

A total reorganisation of the inside of the truck was required once the rain finally stopped. I was glad that there were only 18 of us and that it was not up to its full capacity of 35.

I left for a pee. The rain had brought all kinds of insects whose breeds were new to me, including flying ants that were about the size of butterflies.

The fire having been brought back to life, dinner was cooked and as we stood around eating it, I approached Fi to ask why she was looking so pleased with things.

'I'm just smiling at the general situation,' she replied.

'Oddball,' I said walking away again.

There were still many upset stomachs and most of the vegetable pasta lovingly prepared by Kate was thrown away.

At 7:00 pm the storm returned, meaning the roads would be flooded the following morning for the long journey back to Gondar. Brilliant.

Dave noticed that, in the mayhem, the crowds of locals had disappeared, with the exception of the two boys of about 11, who had asked to sleep under the truck.

I settled in for the night, taking comfort in the fact any wildlife would feast on the native lads before coming for me, and moments later I was asleep.

Chapter Twenty

Things I will never do again
Part 20

There was not a cloud in the sky at dawn the next morning. Dave and Wayne – the latter of whom believed he had caught pneumonia – checked out the best route to take the truck back off the site without getting it stuck in waterlogged potholes. Dave was pleased that the torrential rain had cleaned the outside of the vehicle, which was now a blazing red once more.

Breakfast, which included feeding the two kids who had slept under the truck, was remarkably swift, and we were on the road by 6:30 am, with 12 hours driving ahead of us.

We dropped the kids off about 30 kilometres from the border at the town of Adwa. It was the site (Gar told me) of the famous battle of the same name, where the Italians were first defeated.

I was more interested in the welfare of the passengers we just let off. Neither spoke any English. They left saying what we took to mean 'thank you' when, of course, they could have been asking 'where the hell are we?'

On the approach to Adwa, we saw thousands more children (clad in faded blue uniforms like the good socialists their parents had been), walking to school. Adwa seemed to be a very large town – considerably larger than Yeha.

Rex had begun to sew the Union Jack that he planned to leave on the summit of Wehni and was already drawing blood. After a while he decided rather sensibly to settle for a St George's cross which was quite apt since, as we were later to discover, St George also happens to be the patron saint of Ethiopia.

We stopped at a Mobil garage to refuel and change another wheel. I checked out every truck in sight as a potential escape vehicle but I'd have had more scope for movement from kick starting an Austin Allegro at a British Leyland vintage car rally.

Before long we began the descent to the next plateau, which Dave estimated to be just another 1,750 metres. Searching for a fast, serviceable four-wheel drive to spirit me away I felt as helpless as a wasp in jam. We were once again back in the Middle Ages – bar the odd abandoned tank – with stone huts dotted around primitively-irrigated fields that were being ploughed by oxen.

The high number of tanks in some areas was alarming. Every so often we'd see one that had been seriously damaged by an explosion of some sort.

I was later to be told that the ground around each of these abandoned killing machines was littered with landmines. It was sobering to think that a little more inquisitiveness could have led to one of us becoming the first tourist to be blown up by a mine in that part of the world. Except, of course, that we were mentalists, not tourists.

At the next town, Ilhibret, one of the country's road-surfacing programmes was in full force and the truck had to take a diversion through its back streets – streets not designed for trucks with extraordinarily high clearances such as ours. It was unclear how we would manage to rejoin the main road at the other end. The truck had to reverse around corners several times, whenever it found streets impassable or with holes it had no way of avoiding. In one street, a power cable that ran the width of the street actually scraped along the roof. It probably had no electrical charge running through it, I told myself – none of them seemed to.

'Why doesn't he get out and ask directions for the way out?' I asked after a few more minutes passed by.

'That would be too easy,' Rex explained.

Eventually a child volunteered to direct the truck safely through to town's southern end to link up with the main road.

We had no choice but to go through a deep trench, and the base of the truck scraped along it before becoming jammed.

I closed my eyes tightly shut and prayed.

An hour or so later the prayer was answered as the truck rumbled on, relatively undamaged.

The roof was pulled up and, despite the heavy rain of the night before, the truck quickly filled up with dust. Fi was driving and we were bouncing down a mountainside at what must have been at least 20 kilometres per hour. Ahead of us loomed the staggeringly attractive but deeply perilous Simien Mountains.

Wayne sat recovering from pneumonia on the back seat, a cigarette in one hand, an inhaler in the other – the latter simply to deal with his smoker's cough. There was absolutely no chance of me writing any notes because the truck was rolling all over the place. I was in no mood to drink but Wayne and the others were tucking in to local gin mixed with tej, or mead – a kind of honey wine and the national drink of Ethiopia. They were soon laughing like children.

'I'm *not* having a good time,' I said pointedly, as we negotiated another hairpin bend.

'But you must be enjoying yourself – after all, you've got the stars as a bedroom ceiling,' said Rex. He just didn't get it and I was reduced to lying and agreeing with him.

Wayne intervened, unsure about the answer I had given. 'Seriously,' he said, with the first and only tone of mild anger I was to hear him express. 'Tell me whether you are enjoying it. You make a joke of everything and I want a straight answer.'

I gave him a straight answer. I told him I felt like a lobster that'd been thrown into a fresh water lake.

Calmly, he began a long and emotional account of how he believed me and of how he thought it might just make a worthy book. 'When I first met you and heard about the book, I was . . .' He paused.

'Sceptical?' I ventured.

'Ay, sceptical, lad. Now I can see what you're doing and I understand. Best of luck to you, mate.' Small comfort in the circumstances but comfort nonetheless, especially as most of the time I had no idea what the hell I was doing.

We finally stopped for the night and Becky staggered, more than a little drunk, from the truck and stumbled straight on to a rock. Without making a sound she lifted her foot, studied the flap of flesh dangling from her toe and said: 'Look at that! It'd hurt if I weren't so pissed.' Moments later she made a surprised noise. 'Ow!' she said. Possibly for the sake of symmetry she had done exactly the same thing to her other foot.

Dave and Fi examined one of the tyres whose surface was largely wire mesh. It was still fully inflated even though the rubber had been ripped all the way round. 'This is why Michelin tyres are worth the extra cost,' Fi explained.

Tyres were far cheaper in Ethiopia than in most other African states – just as well given the rate the truck was getting through them trying to navigate through the bloody mountains. Fi said she planned to buy the expensive steel radial variety to use when they got past Nairobi for the high-speed journey over the plains.

Dinner was simple but surprisingly refreshing: eggs and tomatoes. Kate wandered off in the dusk as Fi gave her assessment of what was to come the following day. 'It's less than an hour's drive to the top, then it'll be just undulating mountain-top all the way to Gondar.'

Kate suddenly reappeared looking somewhat shocked. 'Don't go that way if you need a crap. There are masses of huge spiders,' she said.

I warned my stomach to be on its best behaviour, lest I find myself in a spider orgy at 2:00 am.

A few swigs of kaolin & morphine later I asked Dave if I could try the satellite phone to call Liz. He set the device up for me and I dialled but she wasn't answering either the landline or her mobile. Perhaps she was still visiting her family in the US? I tried her friend Kim in Boston, who assured me she had made it home safely and wasn't it great we had received an offer on our flat for £193,000.

'I didn't know we were selling the flat,' I replied, but was cut off before Kim could answer.

What was going on? Was Liz already preparing for my almost certain demise?

That night, I worried about (in no particular order) my flat, spiders, snakes and Wehni.

Fi and Johnny played a backgammon rematch. Then Johnny, who had arrived at the campsite drunk and had continued to drink through the evening, dropped a bottle of red wine on the truck stairs he had lovingly built, slashing open his foot in the process.

Johnny would continue to experience remarkable, self-inflicted accidents even after the group went their separate ways.

I was later to hear more stories from Tim, who returned from Africa a couple of months after me to work for a year in London. For instance, when Hot Rock was in Nairobi, Johnny had broken his forearm when he fell off the truck's roof.

Still stressed about almost every aspect of my life, I spent the night mulling and coughing. I had a slight fever and was also sweating like a pig. God, did I have malaria? Had I missed a tablet? Would having malaria get me out of climbing that mountain?

However, as the night wore on, no further symptoms appeared and I considered the poverty of my mental state in being disappointed there was no hideous and potentially fatal disease.

The first people to board the truck at daylight were knocked back by the stench of my BO, so I decided it was time to wash, apply a little deodorant and change my T-shirt.

When I emerged I saw the site itself was still filled with locals. Nobody tried to fend them off because they were harmless enough. Dave handed them all the leftover food and they seemed most grateful, even if most of it was unidentifiable to them.

We packed up and headed off again.

Fi was a little concerned as the road was pretty rough; we were down to our last spare tyre; and Wayne was driving with an understandably major hangover. Although, like Fi, he was a safe and experienced driver, the long, final ascent to the peak of the mountain was scarier than its predecessors.

I reminded myself that the road had been built by the Italians following their invasion in 1936 and was therefore wide enough for a tank. Unfortunately, I couldn't envisage a tank being as wide as the Hot Rock truck and there were some more, ridiculously tight hairpin bends to negotiate.

A mile or so up the road we came head to head with a truck almost the size of our own.

I braced myself for a re-enactment of *Dual*.

Fortunately there were mountains protecting us on the right side, whilst on the left a sheer drop. I watched the driver of the other truck slowly manoeuvre his vehicle past and saw his tyres skim the very outer edge of the road, beneath which was a several-hundred-feet drop. Had the situation been reversed, the top-heavy nature of our truck might possibly have taken us over the edge.

'This is nothing, mate,' Johnny called out. 'You should see Sudanese roads. Bloody hair-raising.'

I vowed never to visit Sudan.

My fear, apparent to everyone else, wasn't duplicated in any team member. Not one seemed to display even remote discomfort themselves.

Grinning, Mark warned me not to read a book entitled *The World's Most Dangerous Places,* a copy of which was in the truck's rear-facing book case, until I was safely back home in London.

Oh God.

As we hit the top of the climb and the beginning of the plain that would lead all the way to Gondar, the smell of eucalyptus filled the truck. It made breathing quite awkward.

The truck stopped the other side of the next village, where two lads were standing with a large collection of firewood. Dave restocked the truck's store and offered them 10 birr.

There was more and more talk about what we would be doing after leaving Gondar for Wehni. Obviously I would be panicking, but Dave was to consult a blind, mute guide on the more likely route to the mountain. Then he was to procure a couple of four-wheel drives and some donkeys.

Donkeys?

I was dreading the next leg of the trip. If the Hot Rockers' calculations were correct, it would mean a 40-kilometre walk through mountains, followed by an 8-kilometre downhill trek into the so-called Happy Valley, where the mountain stood.

Happy Valley? 40 kilometres? I found it difficult to comprehend that distance, given I found walking the 200 metres to my local a challenge.

And there was still only a small chance we'd find the bloody hill. The very thought brought a rare smile to my face.

Chapter Twenty-one

Lies. Damned lies.

We returned to the Terara Hotel. I was determined to get a night's sleep on a bed rather than a dust-ridden truck, so I abandoned the tent-happy crew and wandered into the hotel reception, where I paid too much for my own half-a-star abode.

I took the keys, found 2B – which like all the rooms was on the ground floor – and settled down to enjoy myself. It was restful simply not to be within sight of people counting tent pegs, untying ropes or generally being excessively resourceful.

I lay back on the hard bed, placed my head on the two-ply pillow and began to doze.

Gar promptly appeared, took a look around and moved his own stuff into the room, settling himself down on the other bed and looking over at me – daring me to comment.

Speechless, I went to take a lukewarm shower. As I stepped into the cloud of thin mist that wafted from the showerhead I began to change hue. Weeks of dust had covered me from head to foot in red, grey and black grime. The water, relatively clear as it emerged from the showerhead, turned black as it disappeared down the plug hole.

I eventually emerged in clean clothes. Gar quite unreasonably complained about the appalling smell that permeated the room from the clothes I had been wearing before.

'There's not much I can do about that,' I said. Besides, I certainly felt no compulsion to address it.

Gar sat sulking on the other bed so I clapped my hands together energetically in the hope of annoying him into trotting back down to the truck.

'Time to dine!' I said.

Even Gar could not deny he was in need of food, so he followed me out to the hotel's restaurant.

Although we were both starving neither of us could confront the hazards of an Ethiopian meal just then. However, there was omelette on the menu so we put in our order and sat to watch the others finish setting up their tents in the hotel's grounds.

While the waiter searched for a chef who knew how to cook omelette, Dave beckoned us over.

There was excitement in the air. He had found yet another guide who claimed to have travelled with Thomas Pakenham, when the great man revisited Wehni in 1997.

'Who is it this time, an octogenarian with dementia?' I asked hopefully. But no. This time, the guide claimed to have been in the very helicopter Pakenham had taken to the mountain.

Plus, he had also asserted confidently that he knew how to reach Wehni by donkey.

Laughter exploded from Gar at that point, no doubt at the thought of me mounting a donkey.

Unfortunately, the guide also claimed to have landed on the mountain, a feat which Pakenham himself categorically stated in his book was too awkward a manoeuvre to achieve. Yet in the spirit of all insane adventurers, the Hot Rockers and Gar chose to ignore that particular piece of information.

Encouraged by the relatively positive news, Gar returned to the terrace for his omelette. I was despondent. We might finally be in sight of the ruddy thing and would soon perish in an extended goose chase in the wilds of a Third World country.

The omelette was barely distinguishable as such and halfway through I gave up and went back to join the others by the truck.

They all appeared downcast.

'Have you heard the news?' Dave asked me.

'No – is the guide a fake?'

'No. Worse than that. The BBC climbed and filmed the mountain two weeks ago,' he said.

I vowed never to curse the BBC again. This was definitely a blessing in disguise. Gar and the Hot Rockers would be wasting their time with the damned mountain if the Beeb had got there first.

And there'd certainly be no point in me going to document a non-event. I could legitimately pack up and head home pretending to have done my best (not to bolt).

'Says who?' I asked, keen on checking whether the information was true.

'An English teacher who was up here a couple of weeks ago. He said he met a BBC camera crew heading out there.' Dave didn't carry the same air of disappointment as Gar and the others, probably because he had almost another three years of global truck-climb lunacy ahead of him. The loss of one little mountain wasn't as keenly felt.

'We travelled all this way and now it appears to have been a waste of time.' Gar was indeed dumbfounded – a joyous sight to behold.

An air of total despondency descended on the entire group (with the exception of me, naturally).

Seeing my face, Gar said: 'There will be no story and therefore no book.'

As if I hadn't worked that out already.

'Why,' he moaned, 'Oh why, did the BBC waste licence-fees like this, copying us for the sake of a scoop?'

Meanwhile, I was composing a personal letter of congratulations in my head to whoever was head of the Beeb that month.

For ten or so minutes, Gar, Rex and other Wehni hopefuls sat in silence.

It was impossible to disguise my euphoria so I wandered out into the untidy grounds and through to the bar.

For the first time ever, I tried running around in slow-motion like a footballer who just scored the cup-winning goal. YEAH!

Hand raised, I stopped sharply when I saw Fi eyeing me curiously.

She was at the bar, chatting with an Englishman in his 20s who had bleached-blonde hair and who I assumed to be a fellow truck driver. I told them the happy news. Fi seemed devastated. The beers stopped flowing and silence descended until Becky walked in.

I gleefully told her as well.

'Is he the English teacher? A short guy with a goatee beard?'

'I think so,' I said.

Becky shook her head. 'I met him a few minutes ago outside. Told him what we were doing and got that BBC story too. I was gutted but then we got talking and he asked if it was my first time in Gondar. When I told him we arrived today but had been here before his face went red and he disappeared without saying goodbye.'

Noooooooooo I wanted to scream.

'Are you alright, Bill?'

I couldn't even say no.

It appeared that this enterprising 21-year-old had been swanning around telling this bogus story about the BBC to anyone who would listen, and as soon as he was rumbled he scarpered.

Apparently, he and a bunch of others from some British university were on a jolly in Ethiopia before embarking on careers in teaching.

'Ought to be reported. I wouldn't want someone like that teaching my kids,' said Becky.

Silly bugger, I thought. If he'd just had the good sense to restrict his lies to Dave. Reluctantly, I went to relay the news. Obviously the group was thrilled.

'Must be the guy I met last time we were here,' Rex said, 'I told him we had the press with us – that's you and Gar,' he stressed, helpfully. 'He obviously put the BBC spin on it.'

Oh, the bloody irony. Almost saved from Wehni by dud rumours about . . . ourselves.

Gar drew satisfyingly on an Ethiopian cigarette. 'It makes you understand what it was like for Scott when he reached the South Pole only to find Amundsen had left a flag there a month earlier.'

Red-carded, I didn't respond.

The so-called Team Wehni promptly resumed their quest for the best route via which to find the wretched mountain.

'We're so close, Billy-boy!' giggled Mel as she scampered into the map area of the truck.

'But I'm married and you're going out with Dave!' I called after her, but my words were lost.

Somewhat inevitably, Dave had met yet another guide who claimed to have been with Pakenham, but whose suggestion as to where we would find the mountain tallied with that of the previous guide.

Kinfemichael Adera, or Michael as we called him, seemed frighteningly credible.

Our new guide Michael soon put Dave in touch with another blind local, who claimed to know the exact whereabouts of the peak from a contact in a town located 100 kilometres southeast of Gondar.

'An unused road could get you 20 kilometres from the peak,' he said. 'But as the roads are so bad you will need a tank.'

Christ, I knew what that meant.

Donkeys.

Chapter Twenty-two

Beggars and beers

Wherever this mountain was, it was in a ridiculously remote part of the country. The last guide but four – our original authority, Tony Hickey – claimed it was around 70 kilometres from where the other guides and military maps suggested.

Deciding which direction to head now was like tossing a coin, yet Dave chose to go with the latest so-called guide, the one whose directions roughly concurred with the sketch drawn by Pakenham.

This irreversible decision suddenly and definitively made, Dave and Gar knelt down in the hotel lobby and studied maps.

Dave proceeded to plan the trip. A bus to take us to Wehni would cost 200 dollars. It'd drop us off to walk the 40 kilometres to Wehni.

I would be a virtual cripple after the first two. I sat watching them, thumbing my laminated note.

Given the quality of the guides, it was fairly certain none of us were in fact going to find the mountain, let alone climb it. To cheer myself up and distance myself from images of being stranded in the back of nowhere until I perished, my thoughts once again returned to reserving my flight back to London.

On my way to check out the fine-print on my ticket, I spied Fi in the bar, still chatting to the blond-haired Englishman, who was formally introduced as Al Humphreys.

Another nutter. He was cycling around the world, coincidentally following the same route as Hot Rock. Having met up with the expedition in Jordan, he arrived in Gondar that afternoon to stumble upon the truck once again.

His first impression of the vehicle was as lasting for him as for me. 'As I approached Wadi Rum their truck scared the living shit out of me.'

Although in my case I think there was actual shit.

Wandering from their enthusiasm, I headed for my room to sleep. I was approached by a man called Solomon, who offered his services as a guide.

At first I declined but as he spoke, I realised he might in fact be extremely useful.

Solomon would lend me his helicopter and a pilot for the day, which meant I could get to the mountain without having to do all that walking and climbing. A quick disembarkation atop Wehni (to gather up some gold for Liz) and then I could fly to Addis Ababa before picking up my flight to London.

I was terrifically excited.

'Job's a goodie!' said Rex to Gar as they burst into the hotel room.

I sat up with a start. 'Bastards. You woke me,' I said.

*

The next day I was almost moved by the appearance of a number group members: some of them actually looked subdued by the fact that they would not be fit enough to join the group climbing the sheer 300-metre walls of Wehni.

'We will be missing out on a great moment in history if it is ever reached,' said someone whom I was sure I had never seen before.

However, everyone but me cheered up as we headed out for the first restaurant dinner most had enjoyed since Luxor.

Over dinner, the last night before the group was to split in two, Adam produced a T-shirt he asked everyone to sign.

Maybe he envisaged not seeing the rest of us again. I certainly did.

Gar signed it 'Wehni. Widi? Wici?'

Wanker.

Before leaving the restaurant, Dave stood up to address the group. He made a few remarks about the progress made and the climb yet to come. Finally he gave us our orders: 'I work on the principle that if it ain't broke, don't fix it. I always pack for a trip either when I'm pissed the night before, or at the last minute hung over, and it's always worked. So, we're all going to the pub after this meal.'

Superfluous as far as I was concerned. I always pack drunk, and I was going to drink all night long, with or without the group.

Of course, we met up with the tanned cyclist, Al, who was immediately surrounded by Hot Rock women.

Gar hurried back to the hotel to find out whether the power had been switched back on, so he could recharge a lens or something, while the rest of us continued drinking.

Al, Fi, Becky, Rex and I sat at one end of a dimly-lit bar. Seeing Al was occupied, the barmaid made a beeline for Rex and kept him happy for the rest of the night.

The lock-in style of camaraderie was all very comforting: it took my mind off my looming death.

We learned Al was putting himself through years of hell for the purpose of raising capital for a charity.

'I am no expert,' he said. 'I have experienced a mere two weeks here and I deeply admire those who dedicate their time and effort to trying to help the extremely poor people of Ethiopia. But, from my superficial observations of life in this country, it seems that something somewhere has gone wrong with the provision of aid. Now I'm not claiming to have answers and don't want to criticise the work people are doing here, but in every village I have cycled through in Ethiopia, there are crowds of children and often adults running alongside me shouting, 'You! You! You! Money! Money! Give me money!' Passing people on the open road produces the same response, accompanied by outstretched palms. When money's not forthcoming stones are often thrown.'

'I've not actually had stones thrown at me,' I said. At least not by strangers.

'They're not isolated incidents,' he said, his voice getting louder.

The barmaid was distracted and looked up from Rex.

'Every village and almost every child is begging for money,' said Al. 'In all the countries I have ever ridden through I never experienced begging in rural areas. Rural poverty is very different from urban poverty; not so ugly and desperate, people generally have some food, some shelter, some support from fellow villagers and so on.' He paused. 'I found it very shocking to find kids knee high to an Oxfam grain sack screaming, 'Money!' at me.'

And this from a guy who was cycling around the world for charity. Making conversation and hoping to impress the Hot Rock girls, I suggested that foreign aid has undoubtedly saved lives in Ethiopia, but he said he did not think those who provided aid really considered the long-term consequences.

He took a long swig of his pint before saying with a light slur: 'The Japanese are currently building a good quality asphalt road north of Addis Ababa. But donating a road also means that poorly-trained drivers in poorly-maintained vehicles are able to drive far faster than ever before. Road casualties increase dramatically. With vehicles travelling faster, the multitudes of barefoot pedestrians and donkeys that share the road are also gravely at risk.'

Getting up to use the facilities, Al disappeared and a young lady came and collected our glasses. She took my hand. I smiled and shook my head as Al returned and continued moaning.

Not that there is anything wrong with moaning, mind you. I do it almost exclusively in place of regular speech.

'The huge input of aid by Western countries seems to have bred a culture where Ethiopians want to be rich, but don't want or perhaps feel the need to help themselves,' said Al. 'Why manage the village water supply carefully when white people will give you bags of grain for nothing? Why provide a service in a town when persistent pestering of white tourists will eventually lead them to giving you cash? White people are seen as bottomless, indiscriminate founts of cash.'

He paused to take a swig of Meta.

'If that's the problem,' I asked, becoming bored but scared to get up and move in case the waitress mistook the manoeuvre as a come-on, 'what do you think the answer is?'

'I have no idea,' he admitted. 'Ethiopia certainly has problems, but in many of the areas I rode through there seemed to be no excuse for being hungry: the land is fertile and green with plenty of space available for farming. Money's not the solution. Perhaps better education: how to make best use of the land, resources and time etc, and above all how people can help themselves.'

Al was interrupted again. Fi wanted the loo, and he stood gracefully to let her pass.

'I feel uneasy being a relatively affluent, white traveller surrounded by very poor beggars, but giving random handouts of cash to people will only increase the amount of begging and decrease the desire for the people to help themselves,' he said.

'I think you're right,' I said, 'but what if I were caught saying that in England?'

Al looked at me sharply. 'Why would you say that about England?'

Even full of Meta I understood the essence of his view. Something has gone terribly wrong with the world when no one says hello, instead screaming for money and hurling stones in disappointment when the free dosh is not forthcoming. To the locals in Ethiopia I was white and therefore not a person but a horribly-dressed, rather ugly, smelly, mobile cashpoint.

Fi bought a round and told how she'd been having a wash in a stream when a crowd of kids had come along to stare at her.

I didn't blame them.

'So I stared back at them. It works every time,' she said, demonstrating.

Wouldn't work with me. 'Were they saying 'I love you?'' I asked with a grin.

''You! You! You!' almost had me in tears at the end of a day's cycling just a couple of nights ago,' interrupted Al grimly. 'I sat down by the roadside and the shouting began and I felt like bawling my eyes out.

'I was then chased for two miles by these kids as I tried to get away from them.'

Given Ethiopia's reputation for athleticism, I wondered how he'd managed it.

Chapter Twenty-three

Back to bus-ness

The next morning I packed in the dark. The manager had steadfastly refused to put our power back on the previous evening (after Mel had dared to use a power point and blown a fuse), so I nicked a towel out of principle before checking out.

Gar once again missed his opportunity to photograph the legendary sunrise over Gondar, which elicited yet another wry smile from me.

It was the little things that made me carry on: vengeance in small doses against the sod responsible for putting me in this absurd situation.

In the driveway stood a bus that looked as if it had been teleported forward from the early 1930s.

Surrounding it like ants was the Hot Rock team.

Gradually, the bus was loaded with 30 kilos of oranges, 150 loaves of bread, 250 litres of water, 10 kilos of the smallest onions in the world, tents, the satellite phone and all the climbing kit they could stuff in.

The bus was a significantly older version of the vehicle that had driven us to Bahir Dar, but far more bearable without the crowds, vomit or diarrhoea.

It did, however, have the stock-in-trade cracked front windscreen.

'Have you all filled your water bottles?' Dave asked. Very organised was Dave.

'Yes,' we all chorused.

There were twelve of us in total: eleven very excited, me dreading having to sleep in a tent at the mercy of wild animals.

The bus drove around the cliff edges at twice the speed of the Hot Rock truck, and we were thrown around like clothes in a malfunctioning dryer. The driver had none of Fi or Wayne's caution. Every time we passed or overtook another vehicle there was no visibility ahead of us for the ensuing 30 seconds thanks to the dust. Still I don't recall the driver using the brakes or slowing down.

Gar, as usual, slept through the entire journey.

Unbelievably, the bus had even less suspension than the one we'd taken from Addis Ababa to Bahir Dar, although this time I had made sure we were not sitting over the back wheels.

The mountains to the southeast of Gondar were smoother and rounder than those to the north. The maps bore no resemblance to the landscape we were travelling through and all the research on Wehni's location was gradually proving to be useless. The climbers' dreams began to evaporate as my own spirits moved tentatively skyward.

Nevertheless, Dave and Gar had whittled the possible locations down to two, deciding that if any of the blind guides were wrong, the military map would be right.

In the event that the first guess was wrong we'd drive the 70 or so kilometres northwest to our second choice, although God only knew how, since the bus wouldn't be hanging around.

'Oh, we'll pick up another one in some town,' Dave said. His optimism was frightening.

Soon I was wondering if we would get there at all as the bus struggled up a long hill at the entrance to the dense Kulkual-Ber Protected Forest.

A small town at its peak illustrated how much poorer people were in this part of Ethiopia. People clamoured to sell us what looked like birdseed, and there was no Pepsi anywhere. Young men, some sporting nothing more than tattered rags, others wearing the most ill-fitting of shorts, eyed us suspiciously.

Not for the first time, I was reminded of Monty Python's *Holy Grail* and fully expected to hear a woman cry out, 'Dennis! There's some lovely filth down here!"

But no. All I heard was, 'You! You! You! You!'

Mel and Lisa climbed back on board complaining about having been kicked in the ankles 'for not giving those brats any money'.

Outside, Gar was being pummelled for haggling with the birdseed vendor.

Cue that wry smile of mine.

Adam was the last to board, bringing with him some good news for everyone (but me).

Someone called Solomon had approached him with a suggestion of where we would find the lost mountain. To my dismay, the location concurred exactly with the guides' plans.

A cheer went up, whilst a scowl pushed across my face.

As we headed further south-east, the north-eastern shore of the massive Lake Tana was visible in the distance. Gar and I had visited the southern end what seemed like fifty years earlier in Bahir Dar.

As before it was just like looking out to sea, for we could not see the lake's southern perimeter, despite being at a high altitude.

I chatted to our guide, Michael. 'Good news. I have just spoken to another guide who has been to the Wehni Amba in a helicopter and he tells me it is only a 32-kilometre walk,' he said.

32 kilometres instead of 40 was good news? This was still twice as bad as I feared, given that we were also apparently heading in the right direction.

'Every map of that region of Ethiopia that we've seen, with the exception of the sketch drawn by Thomas Pakenham, can be torn up,' I told Michael, who replied that he already knew that.

The driving became as erratic as a National Rail service timetable. Every time we stopped someone had to jump out and put blocks under the wheels to stop us sliding backwards. We raced round bends with sheer drops of hundreds of metres, just inches to our left or right. The driver seemed to repeatedly lose control of the vehicle, performing wild spins of the steering wheel to master the bends with little brake power at his disposal. Right at the foot of the long slope down which we'd raced was a roundabout onto which he spun anti-clockwise, narrowly missing a couple of donkeys and another bus.

My eyes were tightly closed when 500 metres further on our own bus broke down. I was almost delirious with gratitude, until I saw our guide Michael climb out with an armed guard and stand over the driver as he began to hit things under the bus with a spanner. The rest of us just sat in silence hoping for a quick fix and no gunfire.

It didn't look good. After my initial euphoria at the possibility of a delayed trip, I quickly realised this was an even worse scenario than the last – over 160 kilometres of walking back to Gondar instead of just the 32 we'd expected to get us to Wehni.

Outside the usual crowd gathered as the scale of the disaster became apparent. It appeared that the only way the bus could proceed was in reverse gear. The driver boarded again and attempted a three-point turn. One of the front tyres promptly burst.

Later we drove away backwards. I sat next to a guard Dave had procured while the wheel was being replaced and prayed. The man was armed with (according to Rex) an old German G3 rifle and was wearing a jacket bearing a large Adidas logo.

A short while after that, we parked in Addis Zemen, which was as far as the bus could travel in reverse. The town looked as if it had been torn apart by an earthquake. It was obviously one of the those places marked on the dodgy maps of Wehni as 'disused.'

Dave and Michael began serious bartering for donkeys. Despite the lack of habitable buildings there were donkeys and traders everywhere we looked. I had never seen such chaos, except for that time I drove straight through the stalls of a Welsh market town by mistake

Our donkey buying was big news and the whole district came to watch. One by one donkeys were considered, chosen, purchased and brought forward to be loaded with bags of equipment or 20 litre jerry cans of water.

The donkeys themselves had a tendency to wander off as they were being loaded up.

'Give us a hand, would ya?' called Dave, spying me doing nothing but staring open-mouthed in horror on the periphery.

So I found myself chasing donkeys around and herding them up – or at least trying to. I soon realised I was dealing with extremely weak, lazy donkeys, all of them too small for the job of hauling us and our belongings up towards Wehni.

Even though some of them had nothing more than two jerry cans either side of their haunches to carry, every single donkey collapsed, one by one, under the weight of their loads.

'I don't suppose they came with a guarantee?' I asked Dave, who told me to shut up and pick up the donkey closest to me.

There was little that could be done about the useless animals since the deals had already been struck and money had already changed hands.

'You! You!' cried a boy in front of me who proceeded to illustrate he had a reasonable command of the English language by asking me to come over.

I took it upon myself to explain to him that 'you!' and 'gimme!' as means of attracting someone's attention were hardly likely to win him any friends.

'What should I say?' he asked.

'Try saying, 'Excuse me, sir,' or 'excuse me, madam.''

'Excuse me, sir, your bottom is showing.'

Sure enough, a donkey had managed to muster up the energy to eat off my pocket and half the back of my trousers.

I glared at the boy, but gave him 2 birr for telling me before Gar could.

Chapter Twenty-four

Who's carrying who?

Eventually we set out on our trek to find the fabled mountain. Four minutes later my bag had fallen off the donkey. I was going to have to carry my rucksack, so I enquired how much it would cost to have one of the armed guards carry it for me.

'Bill!' said Gar, disgusted.

'5 birr,' said the guard happily.

I handed over the money before Gar could confiscate it and the guard promptly tied it onto the back of another overburdened donkey and gave me a wink.

'I tried to warn you,' mumbled Gar.

'Well, at least he can deal with it now,' I replied.

Truer words were never spoken, because that was the last I saw of the rucksack. The only consolation was that it contained one of Gar's cameras.

My stomach felt rough. I didn't want to embark on a one-centimetre walk, let alone a 32 kilometre trek – most of it across rugged, mountainous terrain. The first stretch was up Dry River Mountain, unsurprisingly so-named because at its foot there was once a settlement that had upped and left when the river had suddenly run dry some decades earlier.

Of course we were accompanied by the inevitably constant refrain from the young locals who had unfortunately taken it upon themselves to escort us on the journey. I discovered that the best way of shutting up the more persistent of them was to shout 'You!' directly back at them whilst holding one's ears. For some reason they backed off quickly.

The disused road came to an end and we began to climb. We ran around shepherding the stupid, idle donkeys – much to the amusement of the local onlookers.

An hour or so into the journey we sat down to devour some oranges – or rather greens – that had been bought in Gondar. They peeled easily and tasted fabulous. Ripe despite their colour, they were unexpectedly sweet and flavoursome.

Along with the 'You!' brigade were villagers still carrying their wares for sale. A couple of them carrying steel poles over their shoulders turned to survey the distance they had travelled only to find themselves knocked over by each other's poles.

Meanwhile the donkeys were still misbehaving, displaying the defining characteristic of donkeys: stubbornness. Several of them were stumbling with every step as the hill became steeper. Some sat down and refused to move. I knew the feeling.

I looked far ahead and saw a group of four or

five Hot Rockers (sans donkeys) becoming specks. I estimated they were moving at around five kilometres per hour. They had the guide with them and would be out of sight in a very short time. The donkeys and the rest of us, meanwhile, seemed to manage a top speed of half a kilometre per hour.

Fearing death beneath a particular lazy and stubborn beast, I lurched ahead for ten minutes until I was close to the guide and the front group. I called out on approach: 'The donkeys are falling all over the place. We are way behind. Stop and wait!'

They must have been able to hear me yet they continued to walk.

I tried again, desperate not to end up abandoned in that place, and equally desperate not to continue at the extremely unsuitable pace. 'You have the guide! Please! Stop!'

They slowed a little and I finally caught up with them. They stared at me as I wheezed and puffed. 'The donkeys are falling over?'

'You have to wait!' I repeated.

They carried on walking. Lisa, the Kiwi doctor, said: 'Maybe we should wait?'

Finally they stopped under a tree. I collapsed to the ground. Behind us half the donkeys had shed their loads and the rest of the group were slowly picking up and carrying what they could.

As they came up the mountain it was apparent that the 'You!' contingent and the wares' sellers had picked up the remaining bags.

'Give them some birr, Bill,' Gar instructed, telling

me we need to keep them sweet so they continue to help.

'Me? Why me?'

But Gar had nimbly busied himself toileting behind a rock and the Ethiopians were waiting for money so I handed out some notes.

It was then I noticed my own rucksack was missing from the guard's donkey. I ran back down the rocky mountainside until I saw the guard, who told me it was definitely somewhere, he just couldn't pinpoint its exact location.

Despite my heroic efforts to coordinate the expedition I received quite a few glances of annoyance. I suspected it was because I was carrying so little – a notebook and pen in fact.

'I've got a delicate back, and I need my hands to write with,' I insisted.

We carried on walking and walking, all of it uphill. Soon clouds began to gather. Rain was on the way. I prayed that wherever my rucksack had landed, it was sheltered from the elements.

All of a sudden the hilltop opened out onto a flat plateau. The leading group stopped in the shade of a tree to rest, letting the donkeys pass them by.

We didn't have far to go before we caught up with them again at the base of the next hill. The animals were steadfastly refusing to progress any further. Dave and a number of others began pushing them, a technique that worked for a while before the malnourished creatures simply lay down and pretended to be dead. I was certain one winked at me. Once again people (other than me) began to remove the loads and carry the jerry cans and food supplies themselves.

Just behind me, Rex was carrying two jerry cans and his own rucksack, as well as some satchels of food.

Gar caught me looking and suggested it might help if I carry one of his camera bags and his second rucksack.

'What about my back?' I said.

'It will be less painful than what I will do to you if you don't help out,' he replied.

Two hours had passed since Addis Zemen, much of it spent stationary. 'We will probably not get there before 10:00 pm at this rate,' said Adam.

There were Wehni-esque pinnacles, or volcanic plugs, as far as the eye could see. Apparently none of them was Wehni. I couldn't see how you'd tell, one way or the other.

The accompanying crowd of locals began to swell again to over 100 and eventually we all stopped.

One of the guides assured us we were almost halfway. Not welcome news as I had already asked Gar 'Are we there yet?' about 45 times.

Strangely, there was a church nearby and Gar dragged me in to explore it. It was a spooky, round building that didn't seem especially old. Like most Ethiopian churches it was colourfully painted. It had four doors leading in from the outside. Inside were square wattle and daub seats, and arched doors that led to the inner sanctum. Outside were a few shepherds' crooks, a cloth drape and a multicoloured umbrella.

'Props for the next Harry Potter?' I suggested to Gar, who promptly replied: 'Who?'

We could see no inscriptions inside or outside the church. Gar left to join the others and I stayed a few moments longer and prayed for mercy.

Panting, exhausted and thirsty, the entire expedition shuffled forwards. We reached an open plain, where Dave decided we should stop for the night.

'Just the one?' I asked, to no response.

Meanwhile the donkeys were still a long way behind us down the mountain. Only the fittest beasts were even in sight below.

Then Rex decided to walk on a couple of miles further to see if he could find Wehni.

I was about to wish him luck and sink into a pit and sleep when Gar called out the discovery of a nest of snakes.

'Hang on Rex, I'll come too,' I said, to the astonishment of everyone, including me. The fact that the sun would soon set and I had been climbing for almost six hours indicates the extent of my fear of snakes.

We rounded a corner onto a cliff which spread ahead for hundreds of yards and suddenly, in the far distance we could see Lake Tana again, the orange sun starting to set upon it.

Adam was still walking, way ahead of us, climbing the next peak. There was at best 40 minutes of daylight remaining. I walked with Rex to the eastern edge of the plain to confirm that Mount Wehni was definitely not in the valley up ahead. Job done.

I told Rex I'd return to find the others.

'I'll carry on to see if I can reach Adam. He obviously doesn't know we've stopped.'

I began the painful hike back to where we'd left the rest of the expedition. After about ten minutes of tiptoeing carefully to avoid disturbing snakes, I chanced upon Dave who was on a mission to find us. I told him Rex was around ten minutes ahead of him and that Adam was a further half hour beyond that.

I soon heard a cry of 'Mister! Mister!' Two boys 50 metres from the path I was following were pointing to tents which had been set up to my east, in a microscopic village called Garluski – a name of Polish origin and nothing to do with Gar.

I thanked them and wandered up to the newly-erected campsite where I found that the last of the donkeys had only just arrived. As the donkeys grazed, our Ethiopian entourage stood around watching us and the guides helped erect the last of the tents.

I sat on a ledge beside Gar's tent and stretched my legs (as Rex had suggested I should). I hardly had any energy left, a condition exacerbated by the fact that we were so high up. And my left leg had seized up completely.

Scowling, I muttered to myself as I recalled Gar's

words in persuading me to go on this godforsaken lark: 'The mountain's just a short walk from the new car park.'

Yeah right.

Adding to the joy, it was almost dark and the temperature was falling quickly. Dave returned with Adam in tow. 'I reached the top of the next mountain,' Adam announced. 'Another 40 minutes and I'd have seen it, I'm sure.'

He was being a little optimistic, given no one on this earth was completely sure where Wehni was.

In order to keep the hundred or so locals off the site, Dave ran a 60 metre climbing rope in the shape of a boxing ring around us and our tents. Not surprisingly, most of the locals just ignored it and mingled happily, begging amongst the climbers and the tents.

Engaging in another long chat with Michael, the guide, I was desperate to ingratiate myself with the one person who knew how to get me the hell out of there. It was slow going. He was a biology graduate, a subject he said came in useful when people were taken ill on his tours.

'I have taken many groups to Wehni,' he claimed.

'To climb it?' I asked.

Michael laughed. 'No one has ever attempted to climb it. That would be idiocy.'

I didn't disagree, just confirmed that his contacts didn't extend to an on-call helicopter available for immediate departure to Addis Ababa airport.

As the so-called dinner was prepared around 50 locals gathered, hoping for scraps. They, as I, would be disappointed: all there was on offer was powdered soup.

Before we tucked into the culinary delight, Dave announced that due to the high altitude we might find ourselves unable to eat or sleep.

Considering the soup and the snakes, that wouldn't be an altogether surprising outcome.

I asked Dave if I could attempt another call with the satellite phone to contact Liz. Her birthday was that very day and I knew she wouldn't deem being 4000 feet up a mountain in Ethiopia at the mercy of the elements an excuse not to call. He kindly agreed, and set the phone up in his tent, out of view of the crowds.

I got through. She sounded so pleased to hear from me that I momentarily forgot the discomfort of the expedition and emerged beaming from the tent. I stood beside it and just gazed at the moonlight view.

Lisa came up to me and said: 'Don't you try telling me it isn't amazing.'

I had to agree. 'I know. I can't believe she remembered to record EastEnders. What a woman.'

Looking for somewhere to relieve myself in safety, I had a long walk before discovering what seemed like the perfect spot – the far side of a large fallen tree trunk. As I sighed with relief, I noticed hundreds of pairs of yellow eyes focused on me.

'Argggghhhhhhhhhhhh!' I screamed, but

everyone was so used to me now that no one reacted, expect for Gar, who told me to 'shut it.'

We set off again at around eight the next morning, without a real clue as to whether we were heading in the direction of Wehni. There were snake pits wherever I looked so I made sure I trod as loudly as I could, and tried to walk directly behind Gar.

Ahead of me Dave carried his haul sack or 'pig' as the climbers called it. I was told it weighed over 65kg and was three times the size of a conventional rucksack. He seemed to love the challenge of it.

I walked dejectedly beside the armed guide I'd paid to carry Gar's bags. The others around me were filled with enormous optimism. Adam even bet me 50 birr that Wehni would be visible beyond the next ridge. An hour later it was not and, honourably, he paid up. I pocketed my winnings to spend on bag carriers.

Chapter Twenty-five

Are we there yet?

The hours passed. I was by now certain this whole expedition was nothing more than an exercise in futility and we would never find the lost and miserable mountain. I was hallucinating about the carpet pattern in the departure lounge.

Suddenly, as I staggered along the flat, rocky ground dreaming of home, Gar called out: 'Bill! Look up!'

I couldn't believe my eyes.

Just as Pakenham's book portrayed, in exactly the same dark colours, ahead of me over the edge of the plateau in the valley was the soaring, dark, sinister spectacle of the mountain itself.

Wehni Amba, unmistakable, according to Pakenham and Gar, by the presence of its smaller, vultur-shit-coated neighbouring spire.

In spite of my hatred for athleticism, I broke into a slow run, my face one of amazement at fate's cruelty.

The others were doing the same, for different reasons. Watching them, I decided that all the scene lacked was the theme tune to *Black Beauty*.

Dave approached Gar with a broad smile, reaching out to shake his hand. Everyone was silent for a few moments as they gazed at the sight.

I noticed our guide Michael had an expression of total relief.

The goalposts had changed: I now had to concentrate on making sure nobody made me climb the damned thing.

But first we had to reach it. Ahead was a sheer and spectacular drop of a thousand or so metres, down to Happy Valley, and we had no choice but to walk a few more miles around the surrounding cliffs to find a reasonably comfortable descent that the donkeys could manage.

I found myself thanking God for the donkeys.

We trundled past, of all things, a school. Its occupants immediately upped and joined us on our journey, led by the teachers.

As we marched down the steep hill to the foot of Wehni I looked through Adam's binoculars and could clearly see the monastery at the top of the mountain.

At the base of the rock was a village called Asta Mariam. Strangely, it was crowded: there must have been close to a thousand people spread out in tents across the hillside ahead of us in all directions.

How was it that Wehni was so difficult to find when so many people lived right next door?

Unfortunately, there was no time to rest because we had to keep an eye on our belongings, as well as the donkeys and guides. Throngs of people were filing down the hill before us like ants. Those in our immediate vicinity were a rowdy bunch. After setting foot at the base of the mountain forty years after his first visit, Pakenham wrote in 1997: *'Gone was the scrupulous politeness towards strangers. The grandchildren of the villagers, who had bowed low to me forty years before, now pushed and jostled like a football crowd.'*

Dave was arranging armed guards, necessary for us to clear the site of the throngs and enable us to set up an organised camp. Michael suggested hiring four guards from each of the three surrounding villages so that onlookers could be easily identified. In the space of a few minutes the boundaries of the site were set. If any locals tried to cross, they'd be threatened with guns.

The relief was short-lived. It did not take long for the spectators to realise that the guns, while a deterrent, were unlikely to be used. Soon they were back upon us like vultures on a dead mule. The smell of shit on their clothes was no more pleasant than my own. I tried wandering away 50 or so metres to the foot of the mountain peak, but a few hundred locals followed close behind me.

Dave was still negotiating the price we would pay for the guards when suddenly something magical occurred: the majority of the crowds filed back away from us onto the nearby hillside.

I had no idea how this was achieved, but expressed my relief only to receive a lecture from Adam on how I was a guest in their country; these people had never seen anything like us before and therefore that I should be more tolerant.

God, didn't he know me at all?

Dave began asking a guard some questions about the mountain and I went over to listen.

'So, has anyone ever reached the top?' he asked.

'Yes,' said the guard.

'How many?' asked Dave.

'Yes,' said the guard.

'How many have reached the top? Is it more than 500 people?'

'Yes,' said the guard again.

'When did they reach the top?'

'The top, yes.'

'But how many years ago did they climb?' he persisted.

'Years, yes.'

'When?'

'Yes,' replied the guard.

I left them and wandered back to where lunch was being served: oranges and water. My sunburnt neck was on fire.

A child of perhaps ten breached the climbing rope, which had been re-established as the boundary for the camp. One of the armed guards threw a rock that missed him, before addressing the crowd in Amharic to explain what 'boundary' meant.

The numbers began to shrink as another long

line marched off back up the hillside. It was like Glastonbury Festival after the penultimate act.

It was early afternoon. The crowd continued to thin for another hour until eventually there were just perhaps 150 people staring at us. This number halved again following another lecture from the guards.

We set up camp around an olive tree just a few yards from the foot of Wehni.

Its two-leaf shade was tremendously welcome. For something to do, I checked the walkie-talkies, which was foolish since anything unusual drew the crowds and these devices made a distinctive bleep-bleep sound when activated. Another large group of young onlookers suddenly appeared from nowhere on the ledge below the tree. One of the guards asked to see what I was holding. He took it and said 'hello!' per Michael's instruction. When I responded in kind by speaking into the other one his face took on the expression of someone who'd just stumbled upon the meaning of life.

I retired to the tent with the two-way radios and was soon satisfied we were remote enough not to be in danger of intercepting news of a military coup should we use them.

A few climbers wandered off on a half-hour tour of the base of Wehni while those that remained commissioned Michael to order a sheep for supper.

The guards soon gave up their duty of keeping the crowds at bay and the onlookers advanced and spilled across the site.

I asked Michael to tell them there was nothing to see.

Addressing them in Amharic he announced, 'There will be no climbing today,' or words to that effect. It didn't work.

Suddenly the clouds opened. I joined the others to pick up belongings, hurling them under the tarpaulin or into nearby tents, whilst our audience watched, amused.

As the rain eventually cleared we saw a farmer bringing four sheep down the hillside. At last! Supper!

Michael selected the tastiest-looking one and paid up what amounted to about a tenner. The other three sheep wandered back up the hillside from where they watched their friend struggle as she was carried away by her front legs to be slaughtered.

As it was Lent it turned out we heathens had to kill it ourselves. Wayne came over and asked to borrow a Swiss army knife because the guards were apparently opposed to shooting the beast in the head.

It made me wonder if they were really armed or maybe just didn't like wasting good ammunition. (Later Rex answered that one for me after asking to inspect the guns. He found 20 rounds in each magazine – each one of 7.62mm.)

Wayne was eager to join in the slaughter. 'I like it – it's a fighter,' he kept saying of the sheep.

I couldn't watch. I prefer not to see my food meet its maker, although a number of people including

Gar did catch every sequence of the slaughter on camera.

Tom came back to announce: 'The sheep is dead!'

'Long live the sheep,' I muttered under my breath.

'No Bill,' said Michael the guide. 'It's dead.'

'I kind of envy it,' I replied.

Dave and Manne returned from a three kilometre hike to fill some jerry cans, whose water supplies had diminished the night before. The guards had used their contents to bathe in while we slept.

'Saw a couple of dozen snakes,' Dave assured me.

Another storm approached and abruptly the heavens opened again, the rainwater helping to clean out the sheep's guts.

Soon the weather had whipped itself into such a frenzy that forked lightning was striking rocks and grass all around us. I did wonder whether the olive tree would be struck, but as it appeared to have survived at least one hundred years, I felt the odds were good it might survive another day or so.

I helped sling the remainder of the rucksacks into the largest tent to keep them dry as the rain pounded and thunder roared overhead.

Meanwhile the tree became a shelter for around 50 young locals.

An hour passed. The rain slowed and the wind dropped, but it was barely five minutes before another storm blew in – as ferocious as the last.

Sitting miserably under the olive tree, to me every Ethiopian voice came across as a shout, unbearable when there were fifty of them in close proximity. I pointed out to Adam that the previous night's racket would be a picnic compared to what we would be treated to next to Wehni. 'It won't be,' he assured me sternly before paying a guard 50 birr to get the locals to leave. I suggested he was wasting his money.

I went to our guide, Michael, with my own proposition: pay the guards to go to buy us a few drinks. Once I was pissed, the onlookers wouldn't worry me anymore.

'The nearest beer is 20 kilometres. They won't even have tella round here,' he said.

I put the kettle on instead.

The tempest finally abated. One of the spikes supporting the tarpaulin was taken down to use as a spit to roast the freshly slaughtered sheep. The process of pushing it through the animal then began, made harder as rigor mortis had set in.

A massive fire was started at the base of the tree. Wayne tied a length of string from a branch to hang the loose end of the spit. The other end wedged conveniently into a gap in nearby rocks.

The fire died down to a gentle crackle and I imagined we would be there all night before the animal was cooked well enough to be eaten. Liz made a damn good lamb, I thought longingly.

The voices of 200 or so onlookers on the campsite and the nearby hill echoed eerily against the mountain and were carried across Happy Valley.

Another storm could be heard coming towards us from across the valley, high winds preceding it.

'Will that bloody sheep ever be cooked?' I moaned, but no one heard because they were all looking at a huge black raven struggling to take off from high on the mountain. It was suddenly blown back into the side of the rock. We didn't see it after that.

The storm arrived a few minutes later. It was a dust storm at first.

I felt I had to hand it to the onlookers for their incredible staying power in the face of such weather – although I suppose many of them were so far from home that their journey back was hardly worth the trouble.

The rain beat down furiously once more. The storm was even more vicious than the one I'd witnessed from the hotel on the mountain overlooking Gondar. It was as though the gods were doing all they could to discourage us from ever reaching the peak.

Speaking of gods, I thanked a few for the huge tree that stopped the fire from going out.

In the face of all this, Manne and Becky sat preparing a pot of miniature onions and garlic. This, I feared, would be all we would be eating that night given the rate at which the meat was cooking.

The tarpaulin flapped violently in the wind, making an unbearable noise, and everyone was running around trying to protect whatever gear they could by dropping boulders on their tent pegs. The sound of the storm was deafening.

The high spirits of the expedition were drowned in a very short space of time as we battled for our very survival.

Or at least, the survival of our supper.

Chapter Twenty-six

Storming forwards and backwards

A guard with an AK47 approached and stood before me dramatically pointing the muzzle at my gut.

'Don't waste a bullet, the storm will probably kill me,' I told him, to no response.

The tarpaulin suddenly – inevitably – came down in the severe gale, and in the deafening thunder Gar climbed the tree to tie additional lengths of string to secure it. More and more birds of prey began to circle in the sky over the sheep and its makeshift oven.

Suddenly the wind turned exceptionally nasty and for the next 50 seconds blinded me with sand and dust no matter in which direction I turned. It was easily hurricane force by now. The tents were flattened. If it weren't for the boulders holding the pegs in place they would have blown away like tumbleweeds.

The more I wiped dust and sand from my eyes the more difficult it became to open them. I spat out a mouthful of dirt and phlegm. It was blown up, spun away in the air for a few metres before splashing into the side of Gar's tent. Result.

Michael passed me and I grabbed him to ask if it was always this bad up there. He nodded before struggling on through the gale to try and discuss something with the guards who were beckoning him. He returned and said they had suggested we should all sleep in one of the mountain's caves.

'What?' I said fearfully, 'Up there?'

Michael nodded.

The lowest cave was 10 metres off the ground. Gar had looked in it earlier and told me it was full of large animal droppings. 'Lots of wolves round here. It'd be where they sleep when the weather is bad,' he had remarked casually.

At that moment a rod supporting the tarpaulin was blown up and away through the air before hitting me. It knocked me straight over and I lay battling not to pass out. Finally struggling back to my feet, I saw a violent sunset with angry clouds closing in all around the peaks.

Then, miraculously, and contrary to all Michael's dire predictions, the storm itself soon began to abate. The winds dropped and we could once again smell the cooking mutton. Rex pulled the sheep's legs off and put them on the side to grill and people began to nibble the choice cut.

The sight was horrifying.

'Come on Bill, the skin tastes excellent,' called Adam, 'although the flesh looks too raw to eat.'

I was so hungry I couldn't resist and nibbled a bit of pink meat. It was too raw to chew and Rex assured me I'd get worms.

The wind died right down for ten minutes before predictably roaring back to life with a vengeance, coming in again from the west. Rain began pouring through the hastily re-erected tarpaulin. It was like a nightmare on rota.

The sheep was half an hour from being cooked when there was another lull in the weather. It was only 7:30 pm. That meant sleeping in intermittently savage weather. Or a wolf's cave.

Finally, the meat was brought forward on a large makeshift dish. Worms or no worms, I had to admit it was magnificent: succulent and tasty mutton ripped off the carcass to feed the starving group.

Lisa, a vegetarian, was not happy at all.

'Lacks one thing,' I told Gar, 'mint sauce.'

'Well next time you venture into the wilds of Ethiopia you can pack some, can't you?'

Barely ten minutes after eating dinner my stomach started to turn. Why on earth had I suddenly thrown caution to the winds and started eating half-cooked food with my hands? Heaven knows how much shit they had touched that day.

To my great relief the stomach pain abated and despite being anxious to get some sleep, I stayed up because Dave was promising to brew some ginger coffee he had purchased in Kassala.

Conversation in the camp continued along the lines of 'This is the life!'

What? As far as I could see *this* was an unpleasant obstacle course being tackled in absolute discomfort with the threat of baboons, hyenas and wolves turning up later to start on the leftover meat before starting on us. Admittedly the meat was okay, but I'd much prefer a lamb cooked with rosemary and garlic and served of course with mint sauce. In my own living room.

Fires peppered the outline of the distant mountainsides. I was cold, I was ill and my thoughts turned to escape.

Fi would have the truck in Addis Zemen on the Friday, which would mean getting to Bahir Dar just two days later . . . two days after the deadline for my pre-booked flight from Addis back to London.

Technically speaking I could re-book onto a later flight, but I was determined that wouldn't be necessary.

My thoughts were broken by the sound of hysterical laughter. 'What was the joke? I missed it,' I said.

'Nothing – we're just happy,' Gar said. They were all insane, or laughing at me.

I turned and walked off to find the tent. I tripped on someone's rope and fell to the ground, gashing my forehead again on a rock. I tried to pick myself up and crawled on in the rain for a further metre to the entrance of my tent. Then I spent ten minutes unzipping it to make my way in. I turned on my torch only to find the batteries were dead.

I had never felt so wretched.

Mud and other filth were everywhere inside the tent. Gar, who remained with the others by the campfire, had ordered me to leave my shoes outside. Why I couldn't just keep them on was beyond me, given the mess inside. I struggled to the back of the tent to find my sleeping bag, which I eventually decided to use as a pillow because I was unable to unfasten the zip.

I lay down and found I had about a square foot in which to move. My rucksack was at my feet – or at least it was when my legs were curled up. Lying on the ground was like lying on a bed of nails of different sizes, occasionally punctuated with the softer feel of the corner of a box of cigarettes or matches in my pockets. To make things worse my neck, shoulders and arms were severely sunburnt.

Gar came to the tent. The first thing he did was start complaining about the smell of my socks.

'You told me to take my shoes off and leave them outside the tent, you sod.'

'Maybe you could take your feet off and leave them there too?'

What a comedian.

For the next hour Gar did what every fanatical camper tends to do – opened and shut little zips in his camera bag and rucksack, neatly reorganising everything he had brought with him. Finally at about 1:00 am he put himself to bed and, after a final complaint about the smell, was snoring within 30 seconds.

Five minutes later his foot was against my cheek.

Christ, his own hoofers didn't exactly smell like roses.

I moved as far as I could into the corner. Both his feet followed, his big toe pressing itself into my ear. I snapped and slammed his feet across the tent, failing to interrupt his snoring in the process.

I turned over to face the thin, flapping wall. The ground against my hip was unutterably painful. The extreme discomfort was the catalyst I needed.

The ensuing dark hours were spent seriously planning a proper escape. It would not be easy. First I would have to avoid climbing. Next, all being well, and the story being complete with Gar up there on top of Wehni collecting gold and mapping out a survey of the top of the mountain, I would employ Michael to hire me a guide to carry me and my bags back to Addis Zemen. There I would spend a night in another flea pit hotel before catching a bus to Bahir Dar. Next, I would fly to Addis Ababa before finally catching the first flight home to London.

Job's a good'un, as Rex might have said.

Chapter Twenty-seven

Plotting and praying

The following morning I presented my plan to Michael. He frowned. 'Not good hotel in Addis Zemen,' he said.

'Has it got a bed?' I asked.

'Yes,' he replied.

'Then it's good.' I needed proper rest. I didn't ache as such; I just hurt all over.

'And you lot can f*ck off,' I said to the guards who had been talking to Michael about my plans and were now frowning at me. They appeared to be conspiring against me in their intermittent squealing castrato, but I had made up my mind.

I pulled out all the stops to ensure I didn't have to spend an extra second there. No wonder so few had ever got to climb Wehni. The place was completely inhospitable. Damn hard to figure out why the Hot Rockers and Gar were so taken with it.

Speaking of Gar, he seemed to have caught wind of my plans, because he voluntarily brought me a cup of coffee and sat too close while I drank it, speaking of 'our climb' to the top.

I felt wretched as I sought out a piece of ground where I might be able to sit without losing a limb to a snake. Eventually I found a rock at the edge of the camp and sat facing east, my feet resting on the ledge below. I began to feel vaguely human but shockingly the feeling didn't last as a posse of locals began to surround me. Where were the so-called guards? Asleep, no doubt.

Adam rose from his tent. 'Who was making the noise at 2:00 am this morning.'

'The guards,' I said, suspecting they were discussing me – the usual subject of their hilarity.

'Well tell the guards to shut the f*ck up,' he replied firmly.

God, he'd only been kept awake by people talking. I by contrast had got no sleep because Gar's feet had been kicking me in the face; because wild animals had been hanging around outside the tent; because of the sound of snakes scratching about; and because I had been suffering from claustrophobia. He had nothing to complain about.

I wandered off to take a leak and was taken aback by the sight of six huge red kites, helping themselves to what remained of the previous night's dinner.

Gar spent the first 30 minutes of the day once again undoing and then refastening the zips of his bags. All the hardware I needed to start my day in Ethiopia was my cigarettes, my lighter and my glasses. The rest of the campers apparently needed 105 things that were all in tightly stored (and zipped) compartments.

Crowds of jostling, noisy locals and not-so-locals were gathering for the day, and I was painfully aware that my three-day trek back to the Addis Ababa airport departure lounge would be accompanied by the phrase: 'Mister! Mister!'

I got Michael to write down two Amharic phrases for use as and when needed. First there was 'hédu', which meant go away. Should that not work, 'tébéda' meant f*ck off.

Knowing Michael, the first would turn out to mean 'I've got lots of money', the second 'stick around', so I decided I would try it out sooner rather than later.

'Tébéda,' I said to the first Ethiopian I saw, before noticing the AK47 beneath his cloak. About 100 birr later I was allowed to get up off the ground and leave; the close brush with death only serving to increase my determination to get the hell out of there.

The rest of the campsite was now up and about.

'I can't believe I've got 40 pictures of that sheep being killed,' said Wayne.

'Wayne, it's beyond a joke,' said vegetarian Lisa angrily.

I sniggered quietly to myself.

'Slaughtering animals is fascinating,' he corrected her.

No doubt.

I told Rex of the problems I had encountered with the walking shoes I was wearing. 'I can't stay upright on a steep surface if it's dusty, and most of these bloody slopes are dusty.'

'Heel down first, then foot,' he instructed me. 'That way you don't slip.'

Cautiously I tried it out, in case it was a joke and I ended up head first in the dust. But no, he was absolutely right. Why had that shopkeeper mate of Gar's not told me that in the first place? Presumably because he didn't really believe I'd actually be going anywhere that required their use.

The fact that I wore them everywhere – keeping them on for journeys in the truck for instance – was a source of quiet amusement to the rest of the expedition, who all went around in flip flops or bare feet whenever they weren't actually climbing.

Flip flops in a country largely populated by snakes.

It was then reported with much hilarity that, owing to the anti-malarial Larium he had taken, Manne had been singing Pink Floyd in his sleep but had not known the words – 'Der der der der der der der der – welcome toooo the machine'.

'You lot know how to have a good time,' I commented, trying to keep a battalion of flies off me. My hands were black and the perch I had found was becoming intensely uncomfortable.

'Alright lad?' asked Rex.

'No,' I said.

'We're all the same – we're all f*cked!' he laughed. In fact, everyone laughed except me.

I reserved the right to believe no one was more f*cked than me.

While waiting for Michael to confirm my travel

arrangements, I guessed my journey back to Addis Zemen would be mostly downhill.

I calculated that what had taken two days with donkeys could presumably be done in just one on the back of a sturdy Ethiopian.

As Dave joined the others in preparation for the assault on Wehni, he announced there would be considerably less weight to carry back, given that all the jerry cans would be empty.

Someone said something about teamwork. Bollocks to that, I thought. If I were still there by that time, I'd be paying a local guide to carry my stuff. No way would I be guilt-tripped into carrying back tents or climbing gear.

Gar tried a new tack: he told me he wished he could leave sooner too, because he wanted to see his wife. I told him I had the same sentiment.

At that moment a stone thrown by someone in the crowd hit me hard on my already injured head. I was seething. The sun was already burning my neck wherever I stood and now my forehead was bleeding again.

The climbing team was in great spirits, however, laughing and joking. They seemed to be missing something. Dave walk passed. 'Morning, Bill!' he said.

'It is the morning, yes,' I replied coldly.

Word of that day's attempt to climb the rock must have spread because clans were gathering in their thousands. Did none of them have anything better to do with their time?

I sat with my back to the mountain, my frustration boiling over. I wrote 'hédu' and 'tébéda' on the back of my right hand, pushing off the crawling insects.

Michael obviously had no idea that you could sue for breach of confidentiality because Adam had heard of my plan to return. 'What about the climb?' he asked, with an expression that suggested he took it as a personal affront.

'I want to return to civilisation,' I replied coldly.

He rounded on me angrily. 'This *is* civilisation. The cradle of it, in fact.'

'Not in my book.' I said.

Chapter Twenty-eight

And there I stay

I wandered over to the drinking tank at the foot of the tree and filled my hip flask with some reassuringly sanitised water. I took a long swig, replaced the cap and then chose a large, green-hued orange from the sack alongside the tank.

Oranges and bananas were about the only things safe enough to eat: protected by skin they'd be less likely to give me the kind of morbid illness that kept Ethiopia's life expectancy at 33 years. I was bored senseless and with no sign of Michael and my people-carrier in sight, I went back to see what the death-mission mountaineers were doing.

A group of them sat in a circle to discuss new climbing strategy. Two principal routes were planned, four in total. The first followed the line of the original stairway, which had long-since crumbled away and led to a lengthy, diagonal traverse up to the gatehouse. The second was a steeper, more direct route to the top and by-passed the gatehouse itself. Adam began a serious lecture on what he saw as the hazards of each. I tried to keep a straight face.

They didn't seem to believe it yet but they wouldn't catch me going any higher above sea level than I already was.

Discussions moved on to whether they should stay on top of Wehni for the night. It would involve excess baggage on the climb but they reasoned that it would be unlikely that they could make it down again on the same day.

They were taking it all a bit too seriously for my liking. I stood up and took a walk to the very foot of the rock to look up at the route. My eyes followed the crack which led to the gatehouse two-thirds of the way up and I wondered whether the last of the princes to descend had pulled them down to prevent anyone else suffering a similar fate.

Everyone but me had the runs – small comfort but comfort nonetheless; something of which I felt badly in need that morning, as I still had to avoid being forcibly pushed up that damned mountain.

The climbers began to divide up into teams, which I took as my cue to disappear. I slowly edged backwards until I reached a large rock strewn with onlookers.

'Mister, mister!' they yelled.

'Don't worry, Bill's there behind that rock,' I heard Wayne say, followed by the sound of laughter.

Dave called order. 'Right. We'll approach from three locations, A, B and C.'

He obviously had some chart or other. I didn't care enough to raise my head and look over the edge of the rock.

'Gar, you come with me, Mel and the camera. Adam, you go route B with Lisa. The rest of you can go the less hazardous route C.' Route C began out of sight from where we were, on the other side of the mountain. Plenty of opportunities to give them the slip.

I saw Mel getting prepared for the climb. 'I thought you were only here to film,' I said.

She smiled broadly. 'I'm going up with Gar and Dave. I'm made up about that!'

Route A. I'd have been shocked and horrified.

Suddenly, there came a manic cry from the hill overlooking our campsite. A man had stripped naked and was running down towards us. He reached a spot about 20 metres away, stopped and began whipping himself whilst dancing in a style of what I can best describe as a religious stomp.

It's what I imagined happening to me when I was eventually sent mad by Gar.

'Holy shit!' cried Mel.

Michael translated the man's cries. He was upset, he told us.

No kidding. He was also mental.

'You are threatening to steal the Ark of the Covenant that he says is on top of the peak,' he explained.

We were? 'Well if he wants it why doesn't he get it himself?' I asked.

Michael ignored me. 'The local priests take seriously the suggestion that you are on a mission to steal. They say every bag you take with you will have to be checked before and after each ascent to satisfy them that you are not bringing anything down from the summit.'

'There goes your gold,' I said loudly to Gar, in the hope that he might be arrested and jailed and I would have to fly quickly back to London to begin negotiations for his release.

However the commotion and checking just gave Dave and Gar a buzz, as it illustrated that even those living at the foot of the rock really had no idea of what was really up there.

Just as well they were having their belongings checked. I could just see a priest nodding and saying, in Amharic, 'That climbing chain belonged to the Princes'.

From a position safely out of view over the crest of a nearby hill I watched the climbing teams gather at the foot of the rock, carrying their ropes, chains and other clobber. As they set off I stood in the shade of an olive tree and let out a long sigh of relief.

'Let's go, Bill,' called Rex, coming back for me.

'I forgot the walkie-talkies!' Thinking quickly, I pointed to our tent.

'You do realise it's illegal to swear on the airwaves?' grinned Rex. 'Hurry up or you'll miss out. Your group's over there. You'd better get a move on. They're allocating ropes.'

Ropes. I think not.

'Sure, just a second,' I said, buying time. I looked across again to see the group I was supposed to join tossing a coin to see who was going to be taking the more dangerous position. Not me, that was for sure.

The wind was picking up. If it got as strong as it had been the previous night, they'd all be blown off the side of the rock. And me too, if I joined them.

Finally, my group set off without me. Given that they didn't care whether I was there to document the first sight of the summit in two centuries, they weren't perturbed when I said I might join the other group.

Feeling elated at my escape, I sat around waiting for Michael to arrange transportation back to civilisation. At 75 dollars, the flight from Bahir Dar seemed a bargain, even though I'd been living on less than a quid a day for the last few weeks.

Gar, blissfully unaware that I had not obediently joined my group, contacted me on the walkie-talkie to suggest I use a 6-iron or something.

It still felt too soon to let on that I wasn't joining the climb.

Looking around, I saw a man with calves the same breadth as his thighs and massively swollen feet. He approached one of the guards and they began an animated conversation. He waved his stick at the mountain. Maybe he was trying to say: 'Stop them. This is what happens when you climb up there!'

More likely he wanted the doctor, Lisa. The day before she had given some advice to a man who had a bad case of glaucoma. Her advice had been to go and see a doctor. That will probably not have been much use since there is just one doctor for every 100,000 Ethiopians, according to the World Health Organization.

Apart from the thousands of onlookers, I was left alone, the others climbing and Michael some metres away chatting to the guards. I noticed my lip was bleeding. The locals and not-so-locals began to migrate towards me, but I decided to be more tolerant towards them. After all, I was leaving soon.

Besides, a good few of them were armed, and they were a suspicious lot. Every native man, woman and child was indulging in something I'd not witnessed from them before: functional spectatorship. They were all watching in awe as the climbers painstakingly snaked their way slowly up the near-vertical rock face.

I asked Michael if it might be possible to get moving before the climbers returned.

'I thought you changed your mind,' he said, chuckling.

He meant that Gar had told him I changed my mind. Bastard. I could kill Gar, but looking up at the speck of him on Wehni, my job might be done for me fairly shortly. Loose rocks were falling like rain.

The walkie-talkie burst into life. 'That crowd below is staring in disbelief!' Gar said. 'Look at them! It's incredible! Can you see them?'

'Very clearly,' I told him, pushing off two onlookers who were leaning on me.

After an hour or two in the blazing heat, I asked Michael if, for 10 birr, the guards would guide me at least part of the way around the rock, as far away from the onlookers as possible.

Not surprisingly, they agreed. An unarmed guard then walked me across the crumbly terrain of the rock face in his bare feet, breaking branches to clear the way for me, saying 'whoa!' whenever I went too fast and was about to poke out my eye on an acacia branch. He held my arm through the more unprotected reaches, and not unnecessarily so. He clearly recognised incapability when he saw it.

When we reached a stretch of flatland he began to throw stones at the grazing cattle. I made gestures that said this was unnecessary. He gestured back at me as though to suggest these things would attack. What kind of place was this? In England the bloody cows weren't out to get you. Then he stuck his arms over his ears and sure enough I did see a certain similarity between them and the length of the creatures' horns.

We were a quarter of the way around the mountain and, I suppose, two thirds of the way we needed to travel in order to get a glimpse of the other side of the mountain, when we came across some of the climbers.

Shit.

Some were still at ground level, their companions at about 5 metres up a bit of awkward-leaning rock. They hadn't seen me.

And ahead of us was a drop of perhaps 50 metres.

'Great. That'll do,' I said to the guide.

He made a gesture as if to suggest that I should sit and rest instead. I declined the offer.

He shrugged as though to suggest it was the easiest 10 birr he had ever earned in his life.

Money well spent for me too. I hadn't climbed Wehni but at least I could tell Liz I had clambered around it.

Once back at the camp I was applauded – somewhat sarcastically, I thought – by Michael and a few thousand onlookers, who had no idea why they were clapping.

Stomping off to my tent, I broke open a can of All Day Breakfast. Naturally I couldn't get the stove to light, so I ate it as it was. Cold comfort.

The walkie-talkie burst into life. 'We're at 120 metres and have just found our first piece of pottery!' Gar informed me from above. This was shortly followed by desperate shouts of 'Drop the coil!' and 'Gimme some slack!' so I responded by announcing to the walkie-talkie that I was just going to settle down with a nice warm mug of coffee as Michael had filled the stove with petrol.

There was silence from on high, then: 'What did you say? Coffee with Michael?'

Shit, had I pressed the 'talk' button by mistake? I garbled something about rocks falling and him hearing me incorrectly.

Gar, who by this time was a third of the way up the rock, activated the walkie-talkie again.

'It's absolutely amazing up here. I can see everything.'

Clearly not everything, seeing as I was giving him a special sort of salute from down at camp.

A few seconds went by and the two-way radio beeped again. 'What about you?' Gar asked. 'How far have you got?'

I decided to give up the pretence: they'd all got so far there'd be no chance of anyone coming back to force me up that mountain.

'Behind you!' I said. He turned and from base camp I waved to him.

A string of expletives came through the device in my hand (although he was so loud he could be heard without it).

I remained mercifully undisturbed by any further radio calls from Gar for a couple of hours while he calmed down.

From down by the tent it was possible to see Dave climbing about 50 metres of sheer vertical rock face with no visible protection. Insane. Totally insane.

As they reached the more lush part of the mountain, I warned them helpfully via the walkie-talkie to look out for snakes.

Gar didn't answer.

They still had a long way to go but yet another storm was approaching from the West.

Michael told me it would reach us in a couple of hours.

How was I going to protect the tents without the others?

Chapter Twenty-nine

What lies above

Suddenly there was a huge roar of approval from the crowds of onlookers. I looked up and saw Dave had made it to the man-made entrance near the top of the amba. Moments later Gar called jubilantly on the radio: 'I've just reached the ledge before the gatehouse. The stonework is very polished here – it's as though lots of people walked over here many times.'

Little did he know how true those words would end up being.

'How are you doing with the wind?' I asked.

'No wind up here,' he replied. This was unbelievable. A couple of hundred metres below him, I was having to rush around all the tents reinforcing the weights that were holding in the pegs.

In a state of panic I contacted Gar again to ask him how to secure them, as they all looked as if they might blow away. As the tarpaulin's penultimate rope snapped, causing it to flap violently in the wind, Gar began shouting instructions through the radio. I couldn't hear him because of the high winds. At that moment a rock fell on my hand from which blood then began to pour.

'Sodding typical,' I cursed. But at least this would be where my investment in a deluxe Boots first aid kit would pay off. Or would have if someone hadn't pinched my rucksack.

Then I remembered, Gar had one too.

I unzipped his tent, deliberately smearing the entry-way fabric with blood. Just as I tore open Gar's multi-zippered rucksack to find the first-aid kit, the walkie-talkie sprang to life again with its distinctive treble bleep. 'I'm on the highest point!' Gar announced.

I was at about my lowest so I simply turned it off as I dug around for his first aid kit and swiftly learned what we had got for the extra ten quid we'd been conned into investing: a bunch of unlabelled syringes.

For a while I could find nothing functional in the kit – nothing I either recognised or that was labelled using words that the average citizen would understand. I did finally manage to disinfect and dress the cut but by this time had ripped open most of the sealed contents of the first aid kit.

It was tempting to stay in the tent, uncomfortable and cramped as it was, since it provided excellent protection from the brutal storm outside.

After an hour or so of severe gale and hurricane force winds, I suddenly heard what sounded like cries for help from a woman up the mountain. This was impossible. In that wind I couldn't have heard anyone speaking if they were two feet away.

I turned the two-way radio back on.

'We're in the church,' said Gar, I think.

'Speak up – I can't hear you in this wind!' I shouted.

'There's absolutely no wind up here at all,' he repeated, before giving me an architectural monologue. 'There's a vaulted ceiling and some inscriptions. Set into the walls of the church are one-and-a-half-foot high red stone windows with a cross above them.'

As I listened I drew an outline in my notebook of what I interpreted as him telling me, in case I needed to convince a publisher I had actually climbed the rock.

The onlookers, standing a few millimetres from the tent, poked their heads in, interested, fascinated by the walkie-talkie – and that someone on top of the mountain was telling me what to draw.

And possibly amazed that I *could* draw.

'One part of the inscription has been covered up by plaster,' Gar continued. 'It's hard to tell why.'

He paused.

'It appears as though perhaps a later generation didn't agree with the sentiment of the original inscription,' he said.

'Speak up. I can barely hear you in this gale.'

'It's not at all windy up here,' he repeated. 'The church has a vaulted roof which has collapsed in places.' There followed a long silence, then: 'The church is six by eighteen metres, divided into two sections with an arch eight to ten metres high between them.'

Yeah, yeah. 'What about the rest: the gold, the bones, the other buildings, the prison?' I asked.

'It's just a mass of walls and corridors, most of which have collapsed,' he said. 'There's a building with three of its walls still standing and covered in trees. Thick grass everywhere. It's a huge area, the top.'

There was a long pause before he announced that he had found some pots. 'Any gold?' I asked eagerly.

'No, I can't find any gold at all. Not even an ark. We're all a bit disappointed.' He paused. 'These pots are two feet high with a globe as their base, a cylindrical spout and a little hook so they can be suspended.'

I drew as he described them and the guards pointed at the images on the page, gesturing excitedly to each other. I nodded proudly at them, proud of my innate talent. I felt as a senior Apollo space programme technician might have done, enabling people to see the first live images of the moon from their living rooms.

As I drew the cross beneath the church's vaulted roof just in the way Gar described it, the locals remarked to each other in excited, whispered astonishment, 'Christian!'

For a few seconds it was as though I wasn't there

at all, with all eyes and attention being focused on my notebook.

There was another long pause. 'Around the walls of the church is a circled cloister, the remains of a couple of circular pillars, which have been covered in plaster to give them a nice round finish.'

A few minutes minute later he was back on the air again. 'I've found something that looks like a well but clearly isn't,' he said.

'Why not?' I asked.

'You can't draw water from a 300 metre high rock,' he retorted. He was probably right. 'There's really nothing else up here.' The radio fell silent again.

The second group was now approaching the summit, much less noticed by the locals below than the all-important first lot. Michael came over with some news for me, gleaned from a guard who lived on the hill overlooking the base of Wehni.

'The local name for Wehni is Amba Eger,' he said.

'Really?' That explained a lot. No wonder hardly anyone had ever found it.

'It means *ye'wizorowoch*, or house of the ladies who the imperials took up there with them.'

Rex reappeared at the camp site all of a sudden.

'I thought you were climbing?' I said,

He stared at me. 'I thought you were?'

A moment's pause. Then he said: 'I got pissed off with one or two of the other climbers.'

Just one or two?

To distract himself from whatever was on his mind, he told me yet another Pakenham tale.

'On his first visit to the mountain in the 1950s Thomas Pakenham had been introduced to a tall, old man. This man insisted that 30 years earlier, he and four others had made it up to the summit at a time when there were wooden steps up the rock.'

'Sounds like our mountain,' I replied.

'Apart from the steps, which have apparently vanished, the old man's description of the top does tally uncannily with Gar's in at least one respect. Although the old man himself had not made it past the gatehouse to the top, because he was scared of devils that were said to live there, one member of the group apparently had done so.'

Riveting. 'And?'

'And Pakenham asked: 'Did he find any treasure?''

'And?' I was becoming interested now.

Rex grinned. 'The answer was 'No.''

Chapter Thirty

A toast, almost...

Before going to sleep, Gar announced over the radio that he and Dave were sharing a miniature bottle of vodka to toast their success.

How had he kept that hidden from me? Meanwhile there was confusion among those of us on the ground as to Adam and Lisa's whereabouts. They could not be seen on the mountainside even through binoculars. Rex prepared himself to go and look for them. It felt reassuring that someone from the armed forces with mountain rescue experience was able to take control in a situation like this. I quickly handed over my walkie-talkie.

For a few worrying minutes I had wondered if the haunting woman's screams earlier had been those of Lisa crying for help. I kept reasoning that I couldn't have heard her in that wind and from that distance.

From lower down in the valley Rex finally made contact with them by shouting, and he promptly radioed this news to Dave.

I walked down from the col into the valley itself and heard Rex shouting. Then I saw Adam and Lisa – 100 metres up on a ledge.

They had reached a juncture from which the others knew would take at least two or three hours to reach the top.

The relief at finding them was temporary. They had no equipment with them and on the advice of Rex decided not to proceed. They also only had a little over an hour of daylight ahead of them and hours of climbing left.

Lisa shouted they would stay on the ledge for the night – which basically meant the next 13 hours until sunrise.

'Lisa, can you traverse back to that tree?' asked Rex.

'No!' she shouted back.

'Are you in any kind of shelter?'

'No,' she replied again.

There was absolutely nothing to be done but hope they would survive the night. My own extremely important problems faded from my consciousness – briefly.

'Any problems, just shine your torch at the campsite,' Rex said. The former bomb disposal expert then turned to me and said: 'I'm sick of saving people's lives. That's why I came out here.'

I suggested he should have chosen a nice half-board deal in Spain instead.

Rex instructed the guards to take it in turns to look out for any light coming from the rock face.

'Are those two going to be safe up there all night?' I pointed at the ledge.

'They won't sleep and it'll be a hell of a long and terrifying night. As long as they use their heads they should be alright,' he said, adding: 'I'm just glad I'm not with them.'

Goes without saying what my position was.

The situation seemed to me to be desperate, yet everyone else remained perfectly calm.

Rex and I settled down with Michael to prepare the dinner I'd watch them eat.

I went to find Michael to negotiate a rate for hiring a guard to get me home. Seeing I was serious, he said it would be about 150 birr. I said I'd go no higher than 100, knowing full well that any one of the armed guards milling around the mountain would be happy to do the work for half that amount. Michael left to discuss the proposition with the guards and returned a minute later and told me yes. I said I'd like to leave by 9:00 am the next day.

A couple of hours later, I suddenly heard the sound of falling rock. I looked up to see if there was any flashlight before the sudden need to secure my own survival took over: from the far side of the tree came the sound of several howling wolves.

My few hairs stood on end.

'Wolves?' I asked Michael.

'Oh yes,' he said, but his smile was so huge I couldn't work out if he was joking.

All of a sudden two large silhouettes with pointed ears appeared on the far side of the tree and performed a howling duet. Michael's jaw dropped and he clicked his fingers urgently. Three guards came running up from the other side of the camp, guns poised.

The sight of an AK47 in Ethiopia was evidently enough to send wolves packing. However, I was not going to hang around simply to put this theory to the test and I hurried away to secure myself in the tent (because there was no way a wolf could gnaw through canvas, was there?)

I still had no torch and found it hard to sleep with the noises of a million hard-core animals filling the air.

I consoled myself with the fact that at last I had enough of a story and could set off home the next morning.

While I slept without Gar's feet in my face, the rest of the campsite became an incident control centre.

Rex was up at the crack of dawn. I greeted him as he headed off into the valley again to stand directly below Adam and Lisa's ledge. I accompanied him because, according to Michael, the damn guard wouldn't be ready for at least an hour.

'I'm feeling shit,' Rex told me. 'The only climbing I'm going to do is to fetch them two down. I'll take you up route C tomorrow,' he added generously.

Silently I handed him the two-way radio. Why shatter his illusions.

Moments later Rex began to shout up to the two climbers. 'Are – you – both – okay?' he yelled.

'Yes!' shouted Lisa in a croaky voice.

'Are you going up or down?'

'Up. Can they drop a line?' called an exhausted-sounding Adam.

Rex cupped his hands. 'You are too low! Go two pitches up and then they can drop a line!'

Rex then summoned Dave on the two-way. 'Abseil down on a 60-metre static secured line. Bring two ascending devices, some high energy food and if possible some warm clothing. Over and out.'

Rex turned to me and said, 'Job's a goodie. Dave's coming down. And we've got the water on the boil for a cup of tea.'

'Rex, I'm climbing up!' shouted Adam.

'No. Both stay together safely on a ledge!' Rex ordered. 'If you can get Lisa to your location and get anchored in then I will direct Dave to you.'

'I can get five metres higher,' Adam replied. The panic in his voice was audible even from that distance.

'Okay. Go vertical up the chimney. Dave is there,' Rex shouted.

'There is not enough rope,' Adam responded.

'Secure yourself!' shouted Rex.

'There is not enough rope!' Adam said again.

'Secure yourself!'

The suspense was incredible and I couldn't bear to watch so I went into Gar's tent to clean out the mud and litter. A second later a huge hornet flew in. It was almost the size of me and I certainly wasn't going to hang around to see whether it was a stinger.

I was on my knees so I didn't have the space to turn around and simply fell backward out of the open end of the tent.

I returned to the rescue event.

Dave had by now abseiled down and was ready to make contact. There was then a certain amount of belaying and other climbing procedures and then suddenly they were all safely on top of the second pitch. The voices over the radio carried the same euphoria they felt.

Then Gar came on the radio and asked to speak to me.

'Yes?'

'Don't say anything to the others, but I found something just before I reached the summit.'

'Gold?' I asked excitedly.

'No, Bill. Not gold. A small shoebox with some stuff in it.'

'Valuable stuff?'

'No. Military stuff.'

'Two hundred years old?'

There was a pause, then: 'No, it looks modern.'

*

It was approaching 9:00 am and I had nothing more to stay for – except, perhaps, to see the look on the faces of the others when they discovered someone had probably managed to get to the peak before them (no doubt snaffling the gold and the ark in the process).

Still, I had witnessed the successful assault on the peak, and I knew that Adam and Lisa were safe.

Gar would stay for a couple more days, nursing his disappointment and undertaking a survey of the prison and surrounds and trying a few more routes to the summit.

I needed to make an exit before he insisted I help.

Too much of a coward to dare tell Dave and the others via the walkie-talkie that I was leaving, I shook hands and said farewell to an astonished Rex. He clearly hadn't believed it when he'd heard rumours that I'd planned to leave. That was the thing about these outdoor-type people: they wouldn't – or couldn't – possibly believe that others didn't enjoy their way of life.

I headed off with my armed guard, Gahtu Woobooh, and an unarmed one named Tarrquin Terfsi, who carried my rucksack and backpack.

Sadly, he refused to carry me.

I turned for a last look at Mount Wehni.

There must be a story in here somewhere, I thought. If not for the mountaineers, then at least for me.

Epilogue

IN ORDER TO AVOID disappointing the locals, Dave had mentioned he had heard a woman crying on the summit of Wehni. Maybe this was the same sound I myself had heard when I was in the tent during the gale? It was eerie.

I'm no believer in the supernatural, but when I returned to the UK I learned that Barbara Toy had died just a few weeks earlier. She was the explorer who landed on the summit and spent a terrifying night up there before being airlifted miraculously back onto the helicopter.

Maybe, Gar suggested, maybe, we heard her cries.

Or maybe it was just Gar moaning about how I had left him behind?

However, there still remained the question of precisely what had been achieved. Was Hot Rock the first to climb the mountain in 200 years, or not?

'We should do some more research,' insisted Gar, when he had finally arrived home and tracked me down in my local.

'We?' I said worriedly. I had hoped the whole awful episode was behind me.

But guilt overcame me and Gar and I set about trying to solve the mystery. It proved difficult. Any information on Mount Wehni (beyond the handful of books we'd already studied) was sparse.

Gar began with the Alpine Club. Perhaps somewhere in its extensive library of climbing and mountaineering expeditions since 1857 would be buried reports confirming other successful assaults on the lost mountain.

The library was exactly what most would expect of such a venerable institution: musty shelves of books, reports and annuals, and a middle-aged librarian – with both an encyclopaedic knowledge of every page in her charge and a remarkable ability to ferret out relevant information, however remotely associated with the search in question.

We found a review of Thomas Pakenham's book from a 1959 edition of the *Geographical Journal*, the Royal Geographic Society Magazine of the time; a handful of articles relating to other expeditions to Ethiopia; a complete absence of anything in the relevant issues of Army Mountaineering Association newsletters – and one interesting footnote unearthed by the librarian.

From *The Alpine Journal* Volume 24 (February 1908 to November 1909) – an extract from *About Abyssinian Alps* by George Wherry which read: 'There was a famous phrase by Disraeli after the brilliant campaign of Magdala that *'we planted the banner of St. George on the mountains of Rasselas'*.'

Rex had brought the very flag down on his return,

although since St George was also the patron saint of Ethiopia there should have been no reason why he couldn't have left it up there.

Somewhat cheered at having found absolutely nothing indicating previous ascents of Wehni, Gar contacted the Royal Geographic Society itself.

This proved to be a terrible mistake.

Expedition : ROYAL MILITARY ACADEMY SANDHURST

FIRST ASCENT TO THE ROYAL PRISON, ETHIOPIA 1972

Country :	Ethiopia
Organisation:	Royal Military Academy Sandhurst
Year:	1972
Start:	1/8/72
End	1/9/72

Summary: Royal Military Academy Sandhurst expedition to Mount Wehni, a 700ft extinct volcano core near Lake Tana on which stands a royal prison dating from 17th and 18th centuries.

This seemed to prove that Gar and Hot Rockers had not been the first Europeans to climb the wretched mountain. To be sure, Gar called up the librarian at the Royal Geographic Society.

Not only did she know of the expedition, but she also happened to keep in touch with one of its members (who was still around despite having been seriously injured in 1974, when a volcano erupted around him, killing his climbing partner and removing a significant portion of his skull).

The librarian put us in touch with Dr Richard

Snailham, who had been on one of two expeditions to Wehni. On contacting him, it turned out that he had taken part but had chosen to go to the Rift Valley with a separate group.

The man we needed, he assured Gar, was Andrew Baines, a Captain instructor at Sandhurst at the time who joined the Wehni leg with some of his officer cadets and . . . a civilian film crew.

Gar finally got through to Andrew Baines, who confirmed that he had indeed climbed Wehni, although as a non-climber he had waited for others to set up fixed ropes (for filming and to remove some of the earthenware pots), so hadn't been one of the first to the top.

Strangely, he had no recollection of the second spire, which seemed to us to be such a defining feature of the location.

We were therefore still unclear whether we were talking about the same mountain. It seemed perfectly possible that they may have conquered a different peak of the same name. There were plenty of mountains around.

Andrew Baines promised to meet with us soon to provide his notes of the expedition.

Meanwhile I made a discovery.

Hidden in a paragraph early in Pakenham's account of his plans to find the mountain was this – Colonel Shifferaw of Gondar, the expert on the area who was to help them find the mountain, claimed at the time that there were in fact two Mount Wehnis.

'One is near the motor-road so you could do it in a day

from Gondar . . . The other Wehni must be about three days' journey by mule into the mountains of Belesa.'

There were definitely other peaks used for imprisonment in the Gondar region. I asked the guide Michael via email if he knew the names of any others, and (after asking if I knew anyone who could help a friend with a visa), he had come up with Amba Gishen, southeast of Dessie in a place called Ambassel.

Suddenly it all began to make sense. Both Pakenham's map and those drawn by the army were accurate representations of what each was illustrating. Each showed the respective site of Mount Wehni. It seemed as if there were indeed two of the buggers, in which case the Marines' map for its aborted 1999 expedition was accurate in pinpointing a Wehni; just not the Wehni we had found.

In other words, it was 70 kilometres or so northwest of our own mountain and just 3 kilometres from the road.

For a few days Gar was elated, choosing to hope we were right – that the 1972 Sandhurst expedition in fact went to the more northern Wehni.

We studied the Sandhurst press release. It described a two-day march with donkeys and the climb itself to a plateau *'about the size of two tennis courts, though uneven and densely over-grown. Dilapidated living quarters, two gatehouses and a church were all that remained of the old prison-palace.'*

This description encouraged both of us.

Firstly, the top of the mountain Gar had climbed was considerably larger than two tennis courts and secondly there had only been one gatehouse. According to Gar's survey, the top of the Wehni he had climbed was eight times the size of the summit described by the Sandhurst team, give or take a tennis court.

The 1972 expedition reported finding three wine jars of the sort discovered by Barbara Toy (the only person known to have reached the top before by helicopter), but as Gar pointed out: 'the report makes no mention of the large jugs we found in the church.'

I then recalled what Michael had told me about the route from Addis Zemen to Wehni, when I had been anxiously trying to arrange my escape from the foot of the mountain.

He had said something about having made the trip himself before. At the time I had dismissed it as typical of Ethiopian guides and their tendency to talk up their experience. I'd asked him whether he'd made the trip to take people who had wanted to trace the steps of Thomas Pakenham, and he'd nodded. This had been enough to convince me it was untrue: Pakenham had approached Wehni from the northwest and had not gone any closer to Addis Zemen than Wehni itself.

However, the more I thought about it the more it seemed plausible that Michael was right.

I took a call from an old friend who was curious to hear whether I'd made it back alive. He asked how the latest book was going and what it was about.

'It's about the lost mountain of Ethiopia,' I said.

He responded in disbelief: 'How the hell can you lose a mountain?'

While we waited for Gar's slides to be processed in the hope that the inscription found in the church on Wehni might provide further insight, I checked my inbox.

I had received emails from every one of the Ethiopians to whom I had given one of my business cards. Each one claimed that its respective author was having to spend all his money on hospital fees and requested I send money immediately.

It seemed strange that they should all have gone down with a kidney infection in the days or weeks since I'd met them.

Gar's slides arrived. He quickly scanned the picture of the inscription and sent it by email to Dr David Appleyard at the London School of Oriental and African Studies.

The very prompt reply came within hours.

It was Ge'ez. The left hand text could be something like *Those who erected [this] are Adara Krestos, Takla Haymanot and ... - nos.*

As for the rest, apart from a couple of phrases it was undecipherable, at least to us.

No clues there.

Ge'ez, by the way, is the liturgical language of the Ethiopian Orthodox Church – the Latin of Ethiopia, if you like. It ceased to be a spoken vernacular some time towards the end of the first millennium but has remained the language of the Church ever since.

We met Andrew Baines for lunch at the Institute of Directors on Pall Mall, where he lent us the notes he had made during the 1972 expedition.

For Gar, the tension was incredible. It was the moment of truth, when we would establish whether indeed the Sandhurst expedition had conquered the same peak we did or simply another rock of the same name.

A few minutes into our meeting, a clue. Baines told us how the trip had come about.

'In those days, cadets did two years at Sandhurst as opposed to just one now. In the long summer break, between the first and second years, they were more or less compelled to do some form of expedition or adventurous training and it was in that context that this happened,' he said.

'And the inspiration for the trip?' I asked.

'Thomas Pakenham's book.'

'Have you seen the 1997 edition?' Gar asked.

'With the colour photos? Yes,' he replied.

Suddenly there was no doubt he had climbed the same mountain. He had used the same photo we had to find Wehni. He lent us his notebook, which we studied at length later. Sure enough, every detail of the scenery matched what we had seen on our own trip.

Rather than describing it as thumb-shaped, the Sandhurst team refer to Wehni Amba as a rock that 'rears up like a canine tooth'.

According to the 1972 account the pinnacle

had remained unclimbed because *'it is in almost inaccessibly remote highland country and is jealously guarded by the priests of the village which nestles at its foot'.*

Sounds about right.

They had found buildings containing jars of the kind Gar and the others had discovered in the church.

The Sandhurst team also reported herds of hundreds of zebra. I had seen just two, pulling the gharry as we had travelled by bus to Bahir Dar.

However if, as our climbers had found, there were so many good climbing routes up Wehni, then why had only one team ever made it to the top before us (okay, them) in 200 years?

The former presence of baboons may provide a possible solution. The Sandhurst expedition reported that it had to avoid the easiest route – the one followed by the steps – because a family of angry baboons had taken to throwing rocks at them as they approached.

Furthermore, vultures that once had nests up there would dive-bomb any climbers. But (luckily) Hot Rock hadn't encountered any such problems.

By way of closure we tracked down Thomas Pakenham.

A charming man, he congratulated us (well, Gar) on climbing the mountain and confirmed that he had been equally confounded by the maps of the area.

*

Hot Rock and Gar were therefore to go down in history merely as the first European *civilians* to climb Wehni.

They were also the first people known to have climbed the rock in 30 years, and the first ever to produce a survey of the summit since the church and prison were first built.

And, of course, the only group to have endured a journey of such length and time with me.

That's got to be worth a pint.

THE END